Assessment for Teaching

Assessment for Teaching is a comprehensive and highly practical introduction to assessment and learning in primary and secondary school settings.

Grounded in contemporary, evidence-based research, this book treats assessment as a source of data that informs teaching strategies. It replaces a deficit model of assessment with a development model: a framework which recognises the importance of identifying what the student is ready to learn, rather than 'teaching to the test'. The book also promotes collaboration between teachers in professional learning teams – encouraging the sharing of assessment data and team-based interpretation – to improve student outcomes and to plan goals for students based on a development scale.

Each chapter contains:

- an exercise for applying the course content to classroom practice
- a response template for the exercise
- guidelines on assessing the value of the exercise in a professional learning team
- a short test for participants to cross-check their understanding of the course content.

Further examples of test questions are also available on the companion website at www.cambridge.edu.au/academic/arcots.

Written by a team of experts from the Assessment Research Centre at the University of Melbourne, this is an essential resource for both pre-service and in-service teachers.

Patrick Griffin holds the Chair of Education (Assessment) at the University of Melbourne and is Associate Dean of the Graduate School of Education. He is the Director of the Assessment Research Centre and Executive Director of the Assessment and Teaching of 21st Century Skills project.

Assessment
for Teaching

Edited by
Patrick Griffin

CAMBRIDGE
UNIVERSITY PRESS

CAMBRIDGE
UNIVERSITY PRESS

477 Williamstown Road, Port Melbourne, VIC 3207, Australia

Published in the United States of America by Cambridge University Press, New York

Cambridge University Press is part of the University of Cambridge.

It furthers the University's mission by disseminating knowledge in the pursuit of education, learning and research at the highest international levels of excellence.

www.cambridge.org
Information on this title: www.cambridge.org/9781107636095

© Cambridge University Press 2014

First published 2014

Cover designed by Marianna Berek-Lewis
Typeset by Newgen Publishing and Data Services
Printed in Singapore by C.O.S. Printers Pte Ltd

A catalogue record for this publication is available from the British Library

A Cataloguing-in-Publication entry is available from the catalogue
of the National Library of Australia at www.nla.gov.au

ISBN 978-1-107-63609-5 Paperback

Additional resources for this publication at www.cambridge.edu.au/academic/arcots

Contents

Contents

Abbreviations

ALP	Assessment and Learning Partnerships
ARC	Assessment Research Centre
ARCOTS	Assessment Research Centre Online Testing System
ATAR	Australian Tertiary Admission Rank
CARL	curriculum, assessment and reporting leader
CAT	common assessment task
IRT	item response theory
LOTE	languages other than English
MIP	Managed Individual Pathway
NAPLAN	National Assessment Program – Literacy and Numeracy
OECD	Organization for Economic Co-operation and Development
PISA	Program for International Student Assessment
PLT	professional learning team
SOLO	Structure of the Observed Learning Outcome [taxonomy]
SOSE	Study of Society and the Environment
SWANs	students with additional needs
TIMSS	Trends in International Mathematics and Science Study
UNESCO	United Nations Educational, Scientific and Cultural Organization
ZAD	zone of actual development
ZPD	zone of proximal development

Contributors

Nafisa Awwal has a Bachelor of Computer Science (MIS) and completed her Master of Information Management and Systems at Monash University. In her present role at the Assessment Research Centre, University of Melbourne, she is involved in the design and development of web-based educational assessment and reporting tools. She has also worked on projects that have included data management and analysis, item writing, and test and scale development.

Esther Care is an Associate Professor in the Graduate School of Education, University of Melbourne. She specialises in assessment and is the Deputy Director of the Assessment Research Centre. She is a Fellow of the Australian Psychological Society and coordinates the educational psychology programs at the university. Her doctoral work focused on measurement of vocational interests and aptitudes, and since that time she has extended her psychometric interests in the areas of educational assessment, assessment of early literacy and collaborative problem-solving.

Michael Francis is Coordinator of Assessment, Learning and Teaching (Secondary) and a Teaching Specialist at the Assessment Research Centre, University of Melbourne. In a career in education spanning 44 years, he has been Director of International Schools (P–12) in Cambodia, Denmark and Botswana, worked as Principal Consultant (Ministerial) in Victoria and been employed in the Aga Khan Education Service in Kenya. He has also worked as Academic Director of RMIT University's pre-university program in Indonesia, and as a teaching volunteer in Tonga. He was the principal of several Victorian government secondary schools before taking his career overseas. In 1994, Michael was awarded the Commonwealth Relations Trust Fellowship in Education at the Institute of Education, University of London.

Patrick Griffin holds the Chair of Education (Assessment) at the University of Melbourne and is Associate Dean of the Graduate School of Education. He is the Director of the Assessment Research Centre and Executive Director of the Assessment and Teaching of 21st Century Skills Project. He has published widely on assessment and evaluation topics that include competency, language proficiency, industrial literacy, school literacy, numeracy profile development, portfolio assessment, and online assessment and calibration.

Danielle Hutchinson coordinates teaching for the Assessment Research Centre, University of Melbourne. She has designed and implemented teaching programs in the Master of Teaching and Master of Instructional Leadership within the Melbourne Graduate School of Education. Danielle also coordinates the delivery of the Assessment and Learning Partnerships (ALP) professional development program.

She has designed and implemented professional development courses for the Bastow Institute, which is the leadership institute for the Department of Education and Early Childhood Development in Victoria. Prior to working at the University of Melbourne, Danielle taught in the independent and Catholic school sectors in New South Wales.

Roz Mountain is a Research Fellow at the Assessment Research Centre, University of Melbourne, with research interests in assessment of students with additional learning needs, assessment of early numeracy skills and support for teachers in inclusive settings. She has a Bachelor of Science (Hons) (Applied Mathematics) from the University of the Witwatersrand and a Graduate Diploma in Psychology from Monash University. She has worked on projects involving assessment for teaching, running teaching strategy workshops, evaluating school improvement policy and developing professional learning modules for assessment of students with additional needs.

Masa Pavlovic has worked in the fields of educational assessment, test development, data management and analysis, neurosciences and software development for the past 10 years. Her primary role within the Assessment Research Centre, University of Melbourne involves working on test development, including item writing and banking for a number of projects requiring assessments in numeracy, literacy and problem-solving. She has also undertaken work on a variety of projects that have included research design, data management and analysis of large-scale studies, as well as test and scale development. Masa has been working on the Assessment and Learning Partnerships research program since 2009.

Pam Robertson worked for many years as a secondary teacher of mathematics and science. In her current role at the Assessment Research Centre, University of Melbourne, she has worked on projects relating to developmental learning and the use of assessment data to inform teaching. For her Master's degree thesis, Pam developed an instrument to measure the functioning of professional learning teams and a developmental progression of team functioning. She also provides professional development for teachers in the areas of assessment use and professional learning teams.

Kerry Woods is a Research Fellow and Lecturer at the Assessment Research Centre, University of Melbourne, where she has specialised in the design and use of surveys and achievement testing materials for large-scale programs of evaluation. She has conducted evaluation studies of the deployment of native-speaking English teachers in Hong Kong and of the impact of new technologies on learning outcomes for students in primary, secondary and special education schools. Since 2006, her research interests have centred on the design and validation of measures of communication and literacy to support teachers' decisions about the instruction of their students with learning difficulties. Her work has led to the development of an integrated program of advice and support for teachers of students with additional learning needs.

Figures

Tables

Tables

Preface: A collaborative approach to assessment for teaching

Patrick Griffin

About this book

This is not just another book on assessment. Many of you will have read generalised books on assessment, and some of you will even have written them. I published one myself in the 1990s. This book is different: it takes a clinical approach to assessment and the use of data in the classroom. It is about changing the culture of schools based on the use of assessment data and developing skills among teachers to enable them to use assessment information to make decisions about targeted teaching intervention. The book introduces a new kind of thinking, though some of the content is not new – note the case study written in 1970 that concludes the Introduction.

The approach described here is simple, but it is not simplistic; rather, it demands conceptual reasoning and higher-order thinking. In the six years during which a program based on this approach has been taught at the University of Melbourne, it has developed and matured. We now know that pre-service teachers can cope with this use of assessment and that in-service teachers can also change their practices in the light of it. Over 1500 teachers have participated in the program through online and face-to-face delivery. Over 3000 student teachers have studied the program and many have told us that they were able to secure employment because of their knowledge of this approach to assessment. Many of the 1500 practising teachers who have participated in the online program have testified that it has changed their way of thinking about the use of assessment data and the ways in which they can help teachers to organise classrooms. Of course, some did not change.

There is no point in adding to the assessment literature based on translating psychometric theory and multiple-choice test design. This is not a book that regurgitates the old ideas about assessment wrapped up in the language of psychometrics. Instead, it takes a new approach. The old ways of teaching principles of measurement, specifications and item analysis for multiple-choice test design have had many consequences. Teachers have become alienated from testing because of the complexity of the process and the lack of meaning for their teaching practice. Despite the fact that the deficit method has been in schools for more than 100 years and it continues to fail, teachers persist in identifying deficits and trying to fix them without a scaffolding approach to intervention. Parents have been asked – even encouraged – to endorse a deficit model of teaching and learning. Teachers are afraid to take a new approach in case that doesn't work either. So instead, they continue with a system that we (and they) know is not effective.

Systems of education reinforce these old approaches by ranking students and schools using statistical comparisons to goad schools into action by focusing only on improving scores. In such a context, where the emphasis is on methods of objective test development, teachers are expected to have an advanced knowledge of statistics and quantitative methods. Consultants feed on this expectation by offering programs and in-service courses on how to interpret test and statistical data. Quite often, they provide well-meaning but misleading advice, and teachers become even more alienated from assessment. They focus on low scores and the dangers of failure when they should be focusing on all students and the celebration of every individual student's successes. The problem is exacerbated by teachers working in isolation rather than in collaborative teams such as those we discuss in this book. In general, their assessment literacy is not profound, and the current assessment literature adds to and reinforces the confusion around the use of assessment data to improve teaching. So the teaching profession seeks comfort in rhetoric. It offers the rhetoric of assessment *of*, *as* and *for* learning. There is a rhetorical thrust towards what is called authentic assessment. I often wonder what is meant by this, and what inauthentic assessment might be.

Under these conditions, assessment and teaching regress into a sea of folk wisdom about the use of assessment data. Most of the common ideas of best practice in authentic assessment are, in fact, no more than folk tales spread by discussion groups through which people are looking for answers that don't involve an ocean of statistics. In this book, some recognition is given to the old style of approach to assessment (see Chapter 8) without taking it to the same lengths as other textbooks.

For years now, the areas of assessment and curriculum have been combined in education administration and teacher training. Curriculum specialists have been the major providers of information about assessment. If assessment specialists were to provide information about curriculum and teaching, there would be an outcry, but because everybody has been assessed – everybody has sat tests and suffered under the weight of oppressive assessment – we all regard ourselves as experts and we are all looking for different ways and means of getting information about learning. But our knowledge of assessment in general is often not a result of experiential learning. Instead, it is a result of experiencing failure – either to understand the process of assessment or to link the concept of assessment to the ideas of success and the lack of it.

This book eschews the concept of failure and takes a developmental approach involving targeted intervention under the rhetoric of readiness to learn. It assumes that everybody can succeed, and that all we need to do is find out what they are ready to learn and able to learn when encouraged by teachers who draw on professional knowledge of background factors to guide their interventions.

Jay McTighe and Grant Wiggins (2004) developed the idea of a process called backward mapping. They recommend the following steps:

- Review the assessment task to identify prerequisite knowledge and skills.
- Develop driving questions (to organise the learning unit), revisit the essential teaching questions and break them down.
- Outline major teaching points for each question.
- Identify formative assessment procedures.

This is not the focus of the approach presented in this book. The basic difference is a shift away from assessment questions to an emphasis on a level of development and a zone of proximal development. The intervention at that zone is the major emphasis. Hence ours is more of a forward mapping than a backward mapping approach.

A developmental approach makes no assumptions about the effects of background factors on teaching and learning. In a deficit model, student demographics such as age, gender, race, socio-economic status, language background, intellectual capacity and other factors are treated as explanations for why people have failed to learn. A developmental method views that approach as a search for excuses. This book encourages teachers to identify, within a developmental paradigm, the point where students are ready to learn, and to intervene appropriately at that point. Then the factors listed above – age, gender, race, socio-economic status, language background, intellectual capacity and so on – determine how the intervention takes place, not why the student is struggling. We assume that if these factors are taken into account in the professional judgement of teachers to select the appropriate intervention strategy, then every student will learn. Under this approach, the ideas of remediation and deficit make no sense at all. We also strongly advocate that teachers work in collaborative teams, removing the isolation of individual teachers making decisions without the support of their peers.

It is important that a consistent stance is taken into account in reading each chapter of this book. The focus is on teachers working in teams – which does not mean team teaching – in order to collaborate on evidence-based decision-making that can improve student learning markedly. Our published papers on the research underpinning this program, some of which are provided on a website that accompanies this book, present almost irrefutable evidence of the impact of peer-group collaboration on teachers and targeted intervention. The evidence shows that collaboration among teachers yields significant and important gains among students. But it requires a cultural change in schools, and this cultural change is an integral part of the success that schools can enjoy if a collaborative, evidence-based approach to the use of assessment data is implemented on a whole-school basis.

We make no apologies for what at times can be a confronting approach that challenges the ways in which teachers use assessment data and how assessment is

reported. We regard the teacher as a facilitator, not an expert who passes all necessary information to the students. In the digital age, students can quite readily gain
information via the internet and other sources. Our role as teachers needs to change
to that of facilitators, as outlined in the case study in the Introduction to this book,
which demonstrates the effectiveness of our approach in the 1970s. It is even more
important now. Students need to be taught how to critically appraise information as
well as to access it. Teachers need to show students how to access information, but
also give them the problem-solving and critical appraisal skills that are necessary in
the digital age. Education – both teaching and curriculum – needs to change. And if
this is to happen, assessment *must* change.

How to use this book

This book is about the necessary change in assessment. It links the new ideas to
teaching and learning, assessment and reporting, and curriculum resources. All
three areas or domains need to be rethought and redeveloped. We hope this book is
a beginning. With this in mind, a set of Learning Objectives is provided at the beginning of each chapter, identifying what we hope you will gain by reading the chapter.
We invite you to explore the ideas presented in each chapter and, together with your
fellow students or colleagues, exercise your right to challenge the concepts, ideas and
instructions that are included. We encourage you not to simply accept the written
word but to challenge and discuss the content. In order to encourage this discussion,
we ask you to apply the ideas in practice. For those in pre-service programs, the
opportunity to apply them will be limited, although tutorial groups and placements
in schools may provide opportunities for discussion and challenge. For in-service
programs, we ask teachers to apply the ideas in the classroom and evaluate their
effectiveness for both student learning and teaching practice. Our premise is that if
these practices do not change or improve student learning, they are not worth implementing. The whole point is to help promote, accelerate and support student growth
along a developmental continuum. The application in practice is important because
the observation of student engagement and learning is a critical indicator of success,
no matter which approach is being used. Finally, at the end of every chapter there
is a series of Check Your Progress questions to help you assess your understanding.
Throughout the chapters, we also ask you to engage in other exercises that will help
you and your fellow learners or colleagues check whether you have understood, or
even agreed with, the approach suggested.

The book has a particular structure to help deal with its dual purpose: while it
is written primarily for pre-service education, it is also written to meet the needs
of in-service teachers. It would be folly to change the approach of only pre-service
programs if the new approach were unwelcome in the schools where graduates
seek work.

The Introduction illustrates a mathematics approach in a secondary school. Each has led to the ideas embedded in this book.

Chapter 1 outlines the book's major concepts and ideas, and provides a rationale for each of these.

Chapter 2 discusses our approach to developmental teaching and assessment. It is critical of the deficit model and encourages the reader to take a developmental approach using a series of developmental paradigms and frameworks. It shows how assessment data can be used to identify the zone of proximal development.

Chapter 3 describes the procedure for conducting assessments, and explains why it is important that these assessment administration instructions are followed closely. An example is provided of an online assessment system that gives immediate and detailed feedback to teachers and students.

Chapter 4 shows how these successful approaches to team-based learning can help teachers develop collaborative practices based on the professional use of data. This is the first stage in what we describe as a cultural change in schools, which extends to staffrooms, professional meetings and classroom teaching. It emphasises the need to focus on teaching decisions that are informed by evidence rather than inference.

Chapter 5 describes the role of the school and team leadership in both enhancing and reinforcing the cultural change that is needed. While the book is targeted at pre-service and in-service teachers, it is critical that everyone understands the important role that leadership and cultural change play in improving the use of assessment data in teaching decisions.

Chapter 6 explores subjective assessment, otherwise known as judgement-based assessment, and provides a method that our research has shown produces reliable and valid data on which inferences about learning and intervention can be based.

Chapter 7 shows how judgement-based assessment can be interpreted within a developmental paradigm, and provides a systematic approach to the writing of assessment rubrics and the interpretation of data linked directly to teaching intervention.

Chapter 8 acknowledges the notion of test design for more objective assessment. It is perhaps the only part of this book that gives recognition to the old forms of measurement-oriented assessment. Those who wish to study more of this form of assessment can consult the plethora of books and articles available on test design and multiple-choice testing.

Chapter 9 suggests that it does not matter whether the assessment approach is subjective or objective. The important things are that assessment data be interpreted within a developmental paradigm and that the developmental paradigm be defined by a 'construct' or over-arching concept. This chapter empowers teachers to design assessments that can be used to identify an underlying developmental progression that can be linked directly to teaching.

Chapter 10 takes this exercise a little further. It illustrates how a relatively simple method of item analysis can be used to identify zones of proximal development. Early in the chapter, the emphasis is on dichotomous data (derived from assessments that allow only two responses – yes/no, true/false and so on). In an extension of this idea, the item analysis is applied to rating scales and rubrics such as those discussed in Chapters 6 and 7.

Chapter 11 brings all of this together in reports that are designed for individual students (the learning readiness report), for teachers (the class report) and for parents (the profile report). The use of these reports is then linked directly to teaching intervention rather than taking a summative approach that addresses what has been learned and whether this is acceptable or unacceptable. The reports are formative, and we take the view that they should be helping students to learn, teachers to teach and parents to understand the overall performance of the student and the growth that has taken place regardless of age, gender, race, socio-economic status, language background or intellectual capacity. Development is about growth and the impact of teaching on student learning.

Chapter 12 illustrates the application of these ideas to the teaching of students with additional needs. It summarises the approach described in the preceding chapters with a focus on students who have disabilities and special educational requirements.

Chapter 13 provides a case study of a secondary school where the approach described in this book has been implemented. It illustrates how this approach to assessment requires not only a cultural change among teachers, but an administrative and organisational change in the school, demonstrating a whole-school approach to assessment for teaching.

Appendix A describes how to use the online tests and reports that are available via a link provided with this book, which offers short-term access to the ARCOTS system to provide some practice with online testing and reporting.

Appendix B deals with some of the common issues that have arisen over the past few years in the research that informs this book. These are covered in the form of frequently asked questions for professional learning teams.

Finally, Appendix C provides a condensed version of the overall approach for school leaders.

Pre-service teachers should focus on the Introduction and Chapters 1–3, followed by Chapters 6–11. They would also benefit from reading the implementation chapters, Chapters 12 and 13. In-service practising teachers should read all the chapters, including Chapters 4 and 5 on cultural change. School leaders and principals should focus on the Introduction, Chapters 1–5 and 12–13, and Appendix C. We hope the book offers something for everyone in your course or school, and that we are educating student teachers to take their place in a supportive and informed professional environment when they start teaching. We encourage all participants in education to read the relevant sections of the book.

We hope you enjoy this book but, more than that, we hope it helps you to improve evidence-based decisions and teaching interventions, and that students ultimately are the beneficiaries.

Introduction

Assessment is for teaching

Patrick Griffin and Esther Care

It is common to hear assessment described as being *for* learning, *of* learning or simply *as* learning. Our stance in this book is that assessment is for *teaching*. This view underpins a successful research project called the Assessment and Learning Partnerships (ALP) project, which provides much of the evidence for the theory developed in the chapters of this book. The project is run by the Assessment Research Centre at the University of Melbourne, and is ongoing. It has had demonstrated success in raising levels of student literacy, numeracy and problem-solving, and has been implemented in over 400 schools.

The message of this book is that if assessment information is used appropriately, students will learn, teachers will be able to monitor learning and students will have the chance to engage with relevant learning opportunities. To reach this point, several key conditions must be in place.

Criterion-referenced frameworks

There is no best way to assess learning. Perhaps the most powerful approach is the continuous observation of student activities, and interpretation within a relevant frame of reference. For example, the frame of reference for young children's acquisition of reading comprehension skill would reside in understanding the skill's developmental sequence, and the contribution of phonological awareness and phonics, fluency and vocabulary to skill development. Our view is that the framework must be criterion-referenced (that is, referred to a defined progression of developmental outcomes) so that the growth and development of the student can be monitored through successive levels of increasing competence.

Our approach thus rests on criterion-referenced frameworks, which are used to develop profiles of student development. These frameworks are achievement based rather than curriculum based. They are not standards – they emphasise what a student is ready to learn and not what an external body argues they should be learning. Curriculum standards indicate what should be taught and expected at specific grades; achievement frameworks indicate what has been learned and what the student is ready to learn. There are no year-level expectations in a series of criterion-referenced frameworks. No one is at, on, above or below expectations. Every student is simply at a level of development defined by what learning is developmentally appropriate. This approach enables and requires differentiated and targeted teaching.

Teacher knowledge and pedagogical skills

It is essential that teachers understand the discipline they are teaching. Understanding implies knowledge of both the content area and developmental progression, or the hierarchical nature of learning, in the area. For example, in the cases of literacy and numeracy, it is necessary that the expert teacher be literate and numerate as well as understanding the components of literacy and numeracy, and how they aggregate and combine to generate expertise.

Different subjects and levels of development call for different pedagogical approaches. The teacher needs to be flexible to ensure that teaching method and resource allocation match individual students' learning needs. Therefore, the teacher must have a large repertoire of skills known to be linked to specific learning needs in the targeted subject area. For this reason, specific professional development is often needed to maintain and enhance developing teachers' skills in discipline-specific teaching.

Student learning

An essential component of our approach is that assessment data are not used to identify problems as they would be in a deficit model; instead, we use a developmental model, in which assessment is used to identify the zone of proximal development (ZPD) (Vygotsky 1986). This is the point at which the student is most ready to learn, and where intervention will have the greatest impact on them.

If the point of intervention for each student is identified, then it is not necessary to fix problems, deficits or misconceptions. Instead, the teacher builds bridges, or scaffolds, to those things the student is ready to learn. The student will learn at this point; however, if there is intervention or help based around the ZPD, then it is possible that the student will learn faster than they would on their own.

Collaborative teams

Our approach depends upon teachers working collaboratively. Collaboration is not synonymous with sharing, acknowledging and supporting; it requires challenge, and confirmation should occur only when supported by evidence of success. Challenge need not be offensive – teachers need the language of challenge, based on evidence, not inference. Those who learn to focus on what students do, say, make or write find it easier to challenge ideas and suggested strategies.

Teachers need to observe and encourage each other to use mutually agreed solutions and strategies. This means that teachers work in teams and do not isolate themselves within closed rooms. The fact that the team owns the ideas, strategies, applications and solutions means that all members need to share in interventions and to observe the effects. Procedures that do not work need to be investigated as much as those that do work. This builds experience.

If a teacher is advised, encouraged and supported by team members to take a particular approach and use specific resources, and if team members do not have the opportunity to observe outcomes directly, it is natural and appropriate that they ask what happens when these measures are implemented. This is accountability – but it is accountability without threat, fear of exposure or the heavy hand of a top-down model.

Evidence

One of the most important elements of this approach to assessment is the use of evidence. Evidence is directly observable: it is not evidence if you cannot see it, touch it or hear it. Evidence is what people do, say, make or write. There are no other forms of observable evidence that we can use in the classroom.

Discussion among the team members must focus on this evidence, which in turn drives observation and teaching in the classroom. Teachers teach explicitly at the level of evidence so that they can identify change. Where there is change in what students do, say, make or write, we can infer change in what they understand, know, feel or think. These latent processes cannot be measured directly, nor can they be influenced directly. To achieve these changes, we must work with the observables. Hence we focus on the operation of team members at the level of evidence rather than inference.

Evidence is the basis of challenge, and teachers need to replace the culture of sharing with one of challenge. A culture of sharing is a culture of endorsement in which ideas are accepted unquestioningly. This is not a healthy or productive professional dialogue, which depends upon professional discussion and challenge of ideas. The challenge focuses on the inference but there must always be a call for supporting evidence. Teachers should challenge the inference and call for the evidence of what students do, say, make or write.

Identifying the point of intervention

Every student has a ZPD, and every student can and will learn if teachers can scaffold at and around that zone. So the importance of identifying the zone of proximal development – and therefore the focus of interventions – cannot be over-stated.

To identify the ZPD using a test requires that the test be constructed properly and targeted at the correct range of student ability. Each student will be able to complete the items that are below their ability level successfully, but not the items that are above their ability level (harder items). In between the items the student finds easy and those they find too difficult are a small number of items where the student struggles, and is able to succeed on some but not others. This series of items between the easy and difficult ones, where there will be a mixture of correct and incorrect responses, defines the zone of proximal development.

Analysis of the items in the ZPD and identification of the skills required to get the correct answer help teachers to appropriately interpret those skills that the students can demonstrate and those that they cannot. Teachers then use this information to scaffold student learning. It is pointless to teach skills that underpin items beyond a student's ability.

Teachers need assistance and professional development in order to help them identify this zone for students across particular disciplines. The zone is difficult to identify without a developmental continuum, and impossible to identify in a deficit model.

The importance of having both a systematic method of collecting the information and a way of interpreting it cannot be over-stated. The skill of teachers in interpreting these data is important. Teachers also need additional professional development to help them implement action plans to make the best use of the evidence they collect.

Leadership and professional development

Changing the culture of a professional team of teachers to endorse a developmental model – where it is absolutely believed that all students can and will learn if the zone of proximal development can be identified – requires a change of language. This change is not only from the language of sharing to that of challenge, but also in the language of assessment. Test scores must be seen as starting points for learning rather than end-points of instruction. The role of the professional learning team (PLT) in guiding this change in perspective and process is critical.

PLT need to have someone in charge who can provide instructional and assessment leadership. Team leaders need to be identified and offered the opportunity to develop their skills in several critical areas:

- They must become highly skilled in team leadership.
- They need advanced skills in assessment and reporting that will enable them to help their team members to change their language, culture and involvement.
- They require additional skills in the target disciplines – for example, literacy and numeracy.
- They should have an intense and unwavering belief that all students can and will learn if the zone of proximal development can be identified.
- They need a deep understanding of how data can be used to make decisions.
- They should understand the difference between evidence and inference.

- They have to be able to identify among their colleagues those team members who need additional professional development in each of these areas.
- They need to be able to explain assessment data and assessment results to their colleagues, and embed their explanation in developmental, criterion-referenced interpretation frameworks.

Sustainability and infrastructure

Like every change that is introduced into schools, this approach to assessment provides an element of novelty. The novelty itself begins to lead to changes in behaviour. But once the novelty wears off, so too may the advantages and even the results in student learning. A strong and sustainable platform for permanent change is needed. Once again, the leadership of the team is critical: training in leadership and change management will help to sustain change in the culture of teaching and learning.

School leadership, and in particular the involvement of the school principal, is a critical component in implementation of this assessment approach. The principal who is supportive of the approach, who understands the difference between evidence and opinion, and who understands how evidence is gathered and used in decision-making is more likely to provide the necessary infrastructure: time must be allocated to meetings; the teaching teams often need support staff; when the team identifies a critical resource that is required, funding needs to be found; the location for team meetings must be identified and made available; and professional development must be guaranteed where it is needed.

Where teachers can clearly demonstrate with evidence that resources can and will lead to improved student performance, the support of the principal should be there.

Case Study

Differentiated and developmental teaching in mathematics at Sea Lake High School

Patrick Griffin

This historical case study describes an early practical application of some of the key ideas of this book. It shows what dramatic results can be obtained by the practical use of assessment for teaching. A more recent case study is provided in Chapter 13 to illustrate the application of the approach as it is now practised.

Teachers often avoid ability-based grouping because of both the classroom organisation required and the belief that there is a stigma attached to lower-ability group formation. This case study illustrates an approach used by Patrick Griffin, the lead author of this book. It is a description of the method of teaching mathematics put into practice by him as a new teacher at Sea Lake High School in Victoria. Using this method, the mathematics teachers of the school succeeded in overcoming problems of student apathy and poor performance.

The program

The program was developed over four years of secondary mathematics and focused on three levels of competence. Failure in mathematics was eradicated. A primary goal was to target instruction at a level where students would be challenged but where they could experience success. The three levels were:

1 fundamentals
2 practice involving use of these fundamentals and some theoretical work
3 advanced work for better students involving some research.

The students advanced at their own rate, depending on sub-test results for each section of the work. Testing was carried out at three levels targeted at the student ability level.

Initially, the students were apathetic towards the discipline, and their abilities varied enormously; there were no Year 12 mathematics students in the school, and only correspondence classes at Year 11. The teaching team decided to set down overall aims for mathematics in this school, and the method grew from the following aims.

Aims of the program

1 To offer a common course for all, but to cater for different levels of ability within it, regarding no level as closed to higher studies.
2 To enable the students to be independent, so that they might be able to read and learn from a text and not rely solely on 'spoon feeding'.
3 To form an attitude that mathematics is an enjoyable subject and is meaningful, and by doing so to stimulate interest in the subject.
4 To give all students experience of success in the subject, as a lack of success traditionally accounts for many chronic failures.
5 To enable the low achievers to work more slowly and to grasp the necessary skills, rather than be relegated to a remedial class where time does not permit them to learn with their peers.
6 To enable the high achievers to:
   • study each topic in depth
   • advance to a higher level than their year indicates (the goal: to have the higher achievers studying Year 11 mathematics by the time they finished Year 10).

Lesson structure

In each class, each student had a textbook and an assignment slip or worksheet for a particular chapter. The assignment sheets were printed on coloured paper: pink, yellow and blue. The pink assignment sheet directed the lower-ability students to learn the fundamentals of each section of their text. The yellow sheets directed the middle-ability students to learn fundamentals and perform standard application tasks included in the text. The blue sheets directed the high-achieving students to:

- learn the fundamentals of numeracy
- perform standard applications
- study each topic in depth and carry out research assignments relevant to the topic.

The assignment sheets contained:

- exercises to be done
- aids to use
- references from the library
- difficult sections of work and programmed instructions for these sections
- pronunciations of words
- directions for each student, depending on the level at which they were working.

The students were required to find the solutions to their own difficulties in the following manner:

- Read the relevant instruction in the textbook and, if this is not understood, read again and again.
- If this is unsuccessful, discuss quietly with neighbouring students, or other students who are more advanced in their work.
- If both the above strategies are unsuccessful, resort to the teacher, who can then determine why the student is having difficulty with the particular section, and take appropriate action.

As can be inferred from the above, the classes employing these methods could be rather noisy and, for effective work to be done, the cooperation of all students was required. Students were free to wander around the class discussing their work with others, and at times small-group instruction was carried out by the teacher if more than one student was unable to make progress on the same section of the work. As students advanced at their own rate, the teacher often needed to help individual students or small groups at different levels, with a possibility of up to six or seven different topics being taught within one 50-minute period. Some work was initiated by the students, who were given the opportunity to pursue their own ideas.

The facilitating role of the teacher in this class structure was to:

- guide each student at their own rate of learning (the essential thing was the learning of the pupil, not the teaching of the teacher)
- become a guide showing the student what to do, rather than solving the problem for the student
- ensure that all students were working at their best rate (which may *not* be their fastest rate, or their own chosen rate)
- ensure that cooperation between students existed at all times, so that the maximum could be achieved by all students
- give individual instruction to those students who had tried all means at their disposal and failed to discover solutions for themselves
- discover by testing (which will be explained later) whether a student had progressed to an understanding of sufficient depth (depending on the student's level) to proceed to the next section of the course
- ensure that all materials were provided for the spectrum of work being covered by the class at any one time
- instil enthusiasm and appropriate aspirations in each student, and give each student confidence that mathematics is something that can be learned by everyone.

Correction of work

Because students were left largely to themselves, they were taught the habits of correcting their own work and deciding for themselves whether or not they had understood a particular section of an exercise. No student was allowed to proceed from one exercise to another until each exercise was corrected, so that students could see for themselves whether or not they had understood the materials. If a student chose to continue and take a test when the work was not understood, there had to be an understanding that the unit or exercise would be repeated after the test result was known. It did not take long for all students to realise this. It was part of the process of developing their skills in learning how to learn and taking responsibility for their own learning.

Homework

Because students were spread over a wide range of ability groupings and worked on different topics, it was not possible to set any particular homework for the entire class. However, this did not mean that none should be done. On the contrary, all students were encouraged to study at home for the following reasons (reinforced in the students' understanding of the process):

- If students fell behind, then they needed to use homework to catch up.
- If students were up to date, then home study was a means of getting ahead and achieving promotion before the year ended.

Organising the program

Students were allocated to one of three instructional groups in each class. These were identified as Levels A, B and C. Allocation to groups was determined by test results in basic mathematics. Students in the lower level (Level A) developed basic numeracy skills in the first two years (Years 7 and 8), then proceeded in their third and fourth years to basic arithmetic and commercial skills. The official curriculum was not followed for these students because the foundation skills had not been developed. It was regarded as inappropriate to try teaching skills to these students that they were not ready to learn. Instead, the emphasis was placed on the four operations within whole numbers, fractions and decimals. It was more important that these students developed foundation numeracy skills.

The middle group, Level B, had to cope with the basics (as for Level A students) as well as undertaking fundamental algebra, geometry, solid geometry and trigonometry from Years 7 to 10. The highest group, Level C, had to cope with the basics and the standard Level B program as well as directed research from references. These students were also expected to cover the work at a faster pace than those working at lower levels, and to move ahead of the rest while also working on higher-order development. Their advanced program followed the official curriculum in preparation for external examinations in Year 12. While this could be argued to be undesirable, we could not reasonably argue that the program was a success if, at the end of six years, the students were unsuccessful at Year 12. This was the evidence of success expected by the local community.

The middle-ability group (Level B) was divided into two sub-groups. One group followed the formal curriculum and the work of these students differed from the advanced students' work only in its depth and the time taken to cover it. The other sub-group followed a commercial or terminal mathematics course, which was designed to finish at the end of Year 10. These students identified themselves during Year 9. The decision was essentially theirs, though it was made in consultation with their teacher and their parents during the parent–teacher interview. By Year 9, the students were considered capable of deciding whether they should continue to study mathematics at the senior levels of high school or attempt other courses.

The lowest ability group (Level A) was different in nature. The students entered Year 7 at levels ranging from Year 2 upwards, and had to be developed to a basic level before they could begin to cope with a full Year 7 course of mathematics. As a rule, they began at below Year 7 standard and concentrated on developing basic numeracy skills. Their progress was closely linked to their reading ability, so close liaison was maintained between the English and mathematics teaching teams. Level A material contained more explanation and more worked examples, and the students were encouraged to seek as much help from their classmates as they could muster. The work in their text was linked to a programmed unit of work cards in the areas of addition, subtraction, multiplication and division for positive whole numbers, fractions, decimals and percentages. These were obtained from a commercial series (SRA). Added to these were a unit on measurement and some work on number facts.

These topics were given only an introductory treatment in the students' first year, and followed in some depth in their second year. The students were assessed at the end of their second year to determine whether they were capable of coping with work similar to that undertaken by the Level B students in the commercially oriented course. Their mathematics program then became a preparation for a non-mathematics-based program, but it was designed to ensure that on leaving school they had sufficient numeracy skills to cope as citizens.

Mobility

No student was permanently placed within any specific level. If students coped adequately with the work for Level A, for example, they were given the opportunity to try Level B, and likewise for Levels B and C. On the other hand, if a student was continually struggling, a lower level could be attempted. In this way, the ability groupings were dynamic and there was considerable mobility in the early stages – especially in Years 7 and 8.

There was no stigma attached to Level A. The students were pleased to be working at a level at which they could cope and experience success. If a Level B student experienced difficulty with the work and was regularly submitting poor work, morale was affected and the work rate decreased further. If the work was reduced in difficulty so that there was success at a lower level, confidence was restored through the experience of success and the work improved correspondingly. As is now evident, the whole scheme was based on giving the students experience of success and adjusting their work difficulty by allowing mobility between levels. No level was closed to higher-order skills, although it was unlikely that many students working on Level A would achieve higher-order skills in mathematics.

Testing

Where possible, Level C tests assessed students for application of the skills they learned in a particular area. The emphasis in their tests was on application, analysis and synthesis, as well as on lower-order skills in recall and understanding. The Level B tests emphasised learning of mathematics skills, and the ability to demonstrate skills in problems similar to those in the set textbook. These students were also expected to demonstrate that they could recall words and ideas learned in their work and apply these to authentic contexts. The Level A tests were not rigid mathematical tests. These students were the low achievers, and the tests were designed to find out only what had been learned by them. The problems were objective and simple, and focused on their ability to demonstrate the basic skills listed above.

A test was set for every topic for every student at the relevant level. Consequently, some students in Level C who had worked faster than others could complete over 20 tests, while others in Level A may have covered only seven topics and completed only seven tests for the year.

Feedback

The teacher marked the test as follows:

- 'C' – Continue to the next section. If the teacher was satisfied that the student had understood a section of the work sufficiently to answer correctly the majority of the questions at that level, 'C' was used to indicate that the student was ready to continue to the next section.

- 'R' – Repeat the section. If the teacher was not satisfied that the student had grasped all or some of the more important sections of the work, then the student was required to repeat those sections. At times this decision was reached by discussion between the teacher and student, particularly if the problem was due to a lack of understanding. Initially, the teachers had difficulty in explaining that 'R' did *not* mean fail. The students had been conditioned to regard every grade as a pass or fail, and some time elapsed before the students would believe that nobody could fail mathematics in their first four years of high school.

Students who successfully completed a year's work before the end of the school year were immediately given the next in the series of texts, along with the appropriate assignment sheets, and allowed to continue. As a consequence, all grade structure – that is, Year 7, Year 8 and so on – was broken down, but teachers had to be wary of the students' enthusiasm for this improved rate of progress, so that the slower students were not embarrassed and the better students were not progressing before comprehending the subject-matter. As soon as one student finished a year's work and started on the next book, a snowball effect emerged. Everyone wanted to do the same. This made the real meaning of individual work clear to the students, and the amount of work done almost had to be seen to be believed. The prize of early promotion was there for all who wanted to work.

In marking a student's work, no percentages were used but instead a series of letters and dates applied, giving the teacher an idea of the rate and depth at which the student had worked.

Progress and reports

A student's progress was not assessed by tests alone, but from the following process. Both objective and subjective judgements were used, taking into account the amount of work covered and the ability of the pupil.

Mobility

Mobility between levels was taken into account. A good student on Level B was invariably slowed when upgraded, as there was more work to be done.

Workbook

Workbooks were collected from time to time and records kept on:

- the setting out of the work
- the correction of the work
- homework (frequency or lack of it)
- improvement – changes from A to B to C (the classes steadied after some time and an objective judgement was possible after early fluctuations ceased)
- class cooperation – class behaviour and the amount of help sought and given between members of the class.

At the end of the program's first year of implementation, an attempt was made to evaluate the scheme. The Year 7 students were re-tested with the same intake test and statistical methods were employed to establish the significance of the results.

Findings

It was found that:

- significant learning had taken place overall
- boys improved more than girls
- low achievers showed a far greater percentage improvement than high achievers.

This last result was gratifying, but the positive effects of the scheme were also clear among the high achievers. It was found that the Level C group had finished Year 11 by the end of four years. After five years, all students who enrolled in Year 12 mathematics (85 per cent of the year cohort) were successful. There was no failure.

Source: Adapted from Griffin (1970).

Acknowledgement

An earlier version of this chapter was published in *Independence*, vol. 34, no. 2 (2009).

Chapter 1

Professional learning teams and decision-making

Patrick Griffin and Pam Robertson

This chapter introduces the notion of professional learning teams (PLT), and discusses the ways in which these teams can focus on the use of assessment data to provide collaborative approaches to teaching. The chapter is designed to help teachers identify the key components of assessment. It discusses how these components can be implemented in the classroom, and emphasises the importance of shared decision-making and the substantiation of decisions taken by teachers on the basis of assessment data.

Learning objectives

In this chapter you will:

- develop an understanding of the use of assessment data to inform teaching
- identify the features of a developmental model of teaching and learning
- differentiate between evidence of learning and inferences made about learning
- develop an understanding of the role of collaboration in teachers' use of assessment data.

The approach taken to assessment and teaching in this book is evidence based: it relies on observable and measurable behaviour to inform effective teaching. Yet the approach is also collaborative, stressing the importance of teachers working in professional learning teams (PLT). You may wonder how these two strands of good teaching relate to each other. A teacher working alone can use evidence, basing their instruction only on those things that are observable or measurable. So what does membership of a team contribute to this approach?

A brief analysis of a case study may help to answer this question. In a study of evidence-based literacy teaching conducted over a 10-year period by the Catholic Education Office, Melbourne (the Literacy Assessment Project), outstanding early results were observed in some schools. The study examined the effectiveness of using evidence to identify the point on a criterion-referenced developmental progression at which the students were most ready to learn, so that reading comprehension instruction could be targeted to that point. The purpose of the project was to build teachers' assessment knowledge and skills so they could use assessment data to inform their teaching. Students were tested at the beginning of the school year to identify their position on a criterion-referenced developmental progression and then explicitly taught the necessary skills to move along the progression to the next level. This approach at times represented a reversal of standard teaching practice, in which assessment occurs only after instruction is complete. In the standard approach, assessment is for or of learning. In this approach, *assessment is for teaching*.

All students can learn

In the Literacy Assessment Project, a second testing period later in the school year showed that students could improve beyond the levels that would be expected from maturation or from normal teaching. However, the rate of improvement among students at some schools was higher than at others. At schools where the greatest gains were made, teaching strategies were shared and discussed by teams of teachers who challenged each other to support their teaching practices with evidence. The teachers in these teams brought a range of observations and experiences to their discussions, but they also ensured that their colleagues did not persist with comfortable or familiar practices that were proving to be ineffective. The view that some students were simply unresponsive to even the best forms of teaching was challenged with evidence that, if teaching is targeted to the level of development demonstrated by students, *all students can learn.*

Development, not deficit

The use of assessment to inform teaching has major consequences for classroom practice, requiring teachers to recognise a range of abilities in their classes and to teach accordingly. Rather than teaching all students as though they are working at the same level, teachers are encouraged to use targeted instruction, in which students at different levels are taught different skills and knowledge, depending on what they are ready to learn. The ultimate form of targeted instruction would be to teach each student individually. However, we argue that this is not necessary, since students in most classes can be grouped into three, four or five readiness groups for teaching purposes. It is rare for more groups to be needed.

The more significant change occurs in the minds of teachers and school leaders, where the long-standing practice of assuming a particular standard for a particular year level is abandoned. That assumption encourages the view that students who do not meet the standard are operating below the expected level, so attention focuses on what they cannot do. The developmental approach does not establish a standard or expectation that some students may not meet. Instead, it recognises the developmental level at which students are actually operating, and targets instruction to focus on the skills and knowledge the student needs to develop in order to move to the next level. The focus is on *development, not deficit.*

Skills, not scores

A part of this change in attitude towards assessment is the recognition that scores such as percentages, and grades such as As and Bs, are not helpful or informative representations of assessment. Standardised scores and grades tell us only where a student appears on a scale relative to other students. They do not tell us what the student is ready to learn – what actual skills or knowledge they have learned – or what they are ready to be taught next. If students are given tests to assess their progress through different stages of development, the important comparison is between their current skill level and the result of their previous skills assessment, not between their results and those of other students. Moreover, for reasons that will be explained later, in this approach students are tested at a level where they are likely to answer approximately 50 per cent of questions correctly. This is the level at which they are likely to learn most, but this change can be difficult to accept for students who are accustomed to receiving a grade (for example, 'A') or a high percentage score. Teachers, too, can struggle to accept that a high score for a student is not helpful. Nevertheless, as the chapters to come will make clear, greater progress in learning can be achieved by this approach – one that emphasises *skills, not scores.*

Reflective question

Shifting from a deficit approach to a developmental one has widespread implications. What could be the impact on the ways students see themselves as learners? And what could be the impact on what teachers and students see as successful?

Evidence, not inference

Teachers bring many skills and strengths to the classroom, including knowledge of their discipline, understanding of student learning styles, resource and teaching strategies, ability to select suitable activities for students, classroom-management skills, and their home background and its influence on learning. They may also bring intuitions regarding the strengths and weaknesses of their students. These intuitions can encourage teachers to make inferences about the intellectual ability, or academic potential, of individual students. An evidence-based approach ensures that teachers' inferences are founded on observable and recordable behaviour. Because these behaviours provide evidence of skills that can be located on a developmental progression, they form a useful indicator of a student's progress. However, when teachers discuss their students, unsupported inferences or intuitions can sometimes begin to replace these pieces of evidence. One of the advantages of working in a team is that intuitions and inferences can be tested or challenged by colleagues. In many cases, teachers' intuitions are tested and confirmed, and this can provide great benefit in terms of building their confidence. The members of teacher teams can help each other to stay on track by reminding each other to rely on *evidence, not inference*. This can be done quite simply – it is only necessary to focus on how an idea or suggestion will change what students do, say, make or write and ask how this will enable more accurate (valid) inferences.

More than tests

It should never be assumed that tests provide the only acceptable evidence of learning. Additional data, in the form of classroom observations, are required to provide evidence of student progress to complement test results. Teachers often feel that a test result does not match their view of a student's ability. Inevitably, factors other than the student's ability will interfere with test results. But this will not happen with every student in the class. Teachers can sometimes be distressed by two or three student results that are inconsistent with their expectations. Other evidence of student ability should always be sought to complement test results. Written assignments can provide additional evidence of literacy skills, including knowledge of vocabulary, grammar and logic. Work on a maths problem can provide evidence of method or strategy that is not mere trial and error. A class presentation by a student can provide evidence of planning and organisation as well as verbal ability and knowledge. An alert teacher can make many observations that provide evidence of how each student is progressing, and all these observations can help to inform teaching, giving teachers a more complete picture of what their students are ready to learn. It is certainly acceptable – in fact, necessary – for teachers to *use more than tests* as a source of assessment data to inform teaching.

Do, say, make, write

The evidence that can be gathered from the classroom, for all its richness, falls into only four categories. The only things admissible as evidence of student learning are those that students *do, say, make* or *write*. These can be directly observed, measured and recorded. Assertions regarding their existence do not rely on inference, intuition, imagination or guesswork. The formation of judgements based on this evidence is a more complex matter that will be discussed in Chapter 6, but teachers gathering evidence can rely on this rule, and their colleagues can help to ensure that they do so by being on the lookout for anything in their conversation that is presented as evidence but is not something that a student can do, say, make or write.

Teaching to the 'construct'

In recent years, large-scale tests such as the National Assessment Program – Literacy and Numeracy (NAPLAN) in Australia and the Program for International Student Assessment (PISA) internationally have increasingly been relied upon as measures of performance for schools and education systems. The importance placed on these tests by education administrators has led to the phenomenon known as 'teaching to the test', or test-based 'washback', whereby students are taught a limited range of skills and knowledge that are known to feature on the tests, along with some test-taking strategies. Essentially, what is taught under these circumstances is how to succeed in the test. Deep understanding, broad knowledge and skills that might be identified through the use of the test may be sacrificed for the sake of success, defined in terms of high scores in the test. In any subject area where higher test scores become the main goal, greater knowledge of the discipline or *construct* being taught may be compromised. Pressure on teachers to teach to the test is strong, but teachers who work in teams can give each other the necessary encouragement and support to *teach to the construct, not to the test.*

What is a construct? The answer is simple: a construct is something we construct (or build) to help make sense of observations – what people do, say, make or write. A construct does not exist on its own. We invent it to help us understand data. The most famous is 'intelligence'. This construct helps us to understand differences between different people in terms of their reasoning, verbal and numerical skills, and general knowledge. In the areas of curriculum-based learning, we now invent developmental progressions as an approximation of an underlying construct of learning. And we interpret as development the progress of students towards higher levels on the empirically constructed progression. So a series of developmental progressions is at the heart of our developmental assessment and teaching approach. These are like a road map designed to help the teacher steer the learning progress of the student. Constructs are discussed further in Chapters 2 and 6.

Targeted teaching

Under a developmental model, a crucial part of teaching any discipline is the recognition that different students will be at different levels on a criterion-referenced (or developmental) progression. It is also important to recognise that even those students at the same level will learn at different rates. The chapters to come will introduce an assessment system and a range of reports to help teachers identify where their students have reached on a criterion-referenced progression. Those chapters will also explain how assessment data can be used to find a student's zone of proximal development (ZPD). This is the zone between the level at which a student can do things without assistance and the level that is beyond their current capacity. Between these two levels is the zone in which the student can succeed with the help of an adult or a more capable peer. For teaching to be effective in helping students move to the next level on a progression, instruction needs to be *targeted* at this zone. It still offers students challenges they could not meet on their own, but ones that are not beyond their current capacity to learn. It almost guarantees experiences of success and intrinsic rewards for effort.

A focus on students

When teachers meet as a PLT, they may share stories of their pedagogical methods – classroom strategies or teaching techniques. These may be 'success' stories, telling how a teaching method or approach has succeeded in engaging a class or communicating a new concept; or they may be stories of 'failure', telling how a lot of hard work in planning, preparation and execution led to a disappointing outcome. Whether positive or negative, what these stories have in common is that they are focused more on the teacher than on the students. They emphasise what the teacher does, but not what the student must do in order to learn what is being 'taught'. They illustrate the old joke about the teacher who says, 'I taught him; he just didn't learn.' By directing teachers to use assessment data to shape classroom practice, the approach described in this book shifts the focus from the teachers to the students. The more effective PLT groups focus on what students do, say, make or write, and on how teaching strategies and student activities improve the quality of students' performance. Effective pedagogical techniques are crucial, and student learning will not be achieved without them, but successful teaching begins with the accurate assessment of the students' readiness to learn, and when teachers gather to share their experiences, it is crucial that they *talk about students, not about teachers*. Meeting in a PLT is, after all, about student learning, not teacher performance.

In a successful PLT, this strong focus on the learning readiness of students leads to a further shift in thinking among the team members. Their level of involvement in understanding and assisting each other's work includes engagement with the specific intervention points of one another's students. The result is that the team effectively takes joint ownership of, or responsibility for, all the students taught by the PLT. Through helping each other, the team members find collaborative ways to fulfil their primary responsibility – the welfare and progress of the students. As this shift in thinking embeds itself, it broadens so that whenever teachers meet, their focus is on the students. Ultimately, this attitude finds expression through the habit of talking about 'our' students, rather than 'my' students.

A culture of challenge

In a study of professional learning communities conducted by Platt and Tripp (2008), professional learning communities were divided into categories of greater and lesser effectiveness. The characteristics of the various teams were investigated, and the worst of them labelled 'toxic'. These were marked by many kinds of negativity, but tended to be united in their view that new initiatives would not succeed and should not be attempted. 'Laissez-faire' communities, by contrast, were not united, but instead characterised by the desire of individual members to be left to 'do their own thing'. Their members rejected shared goals in favour of arrangements that suited their individual needs or desires. The next category was somewhat surprising. Described as 'congenial', these communities were willingly collaborative and viewed by their members as supportive and nurturing, but their focus on harmony meant that they did not discuss performances in a direct or confronting way. The team members' desire for empathy and understanding allowed mediocrity to go unchallenged. The most effective communities differed from these in this crucial respect. They were described by Platt and Tripp as 'accountable'. They did not give reassuring messages to members whose students had not learned what they needed to learn. They were characterised by a culture of challenge, in which the choices of teachers were always open to examination and revision. This form of challenge was found to be effective when it was focused on the effects of teaching on student learning, rather than on the teachers themselves. These groups took shared responsibility for supporting their members to teach effectively, but when the data did not support the teaching strategies in use, these teams made it their business to *challenge, not share*.

Reflective questions

Think about a successful team experience you have had outside of education.

- What made this experience so successful?
- What parallels can be drawn between this experience and those of teacher teams?

Leadership and professional learning teams

Strong and skilful PLT leadership is needed to embed the practices discussed in this book. New teachers in particular need support from experienced team leaders. They also need to understand the leadership framework within which they are working. It is the PLT leader who models the desired behaviours and helps scaffold the learning of individual team members so they can become more effective members of the team and, as a result, more effective teachers. The PLT leader is often the link between the team and the school's leadership, and is therefore in a position to lobby for the interests of the team. It may be necessary for the PLT leader to negotiate more time for meetings, access to particular resources or specific professional development opportunities. As a champion for the PLT, the leader must also ensure that the PLT has a place in policy formation within the school. Without adept team leadership, it is impossible to develop a PLT that makes a substantial difference to the learning of its students.

Behind the approach of successful learning teams is an ongoing willingness to *question practice*. Members of PLT can best serve each other by questioning their own teaching practices and those of their fellow team members. This is the first part of the collaborative process of improving outcomes for students. The next part is the joint development of better targeted or more effective teaching strategies. The PLT supports its members not just through constructive criticism but also through the development of creative solutions to the challenges they face together. The questioning of practice continues into the further stage of testing and reporting on any solutions. The effectiveness of teaching practice must be supported by evidence before it can be adopted in a more permanent way or recommended to others. The ongoing tasks of the PLT are to *collaborate, challenge* and *check*. That is how teams help improve teaching practice and ensure the best outcomes for students.

Resourcing teaching

Beyond developing and evaluating classroom strategies, PLT can play a role in supporting teachers by identifying effective resources and lobbying for them. Targeted teaching informed by developmental assessment can require resources beyond those normally employed in the classroom. Regular assessment and analysis are needed to establish student ZPD, and differentiated teaching requires simultaneous instruction at different learning levels. Individual students with a ZPD significantly higher or lower than those of their classmates may require individual instruction, for which a teacher aide may be needed. A PLT can help identify its members' professional learning needs and, when new resources are required, can form an effective lobby group to acquire them. Membership of PLT by school leaders can further facilitate the acquisition of resources.

Assessment and school policy

In a similar way, PLT can play a constructive role in the development of school policy and even broader education policy. School leaders who join PLT can gain first-hand understanding of the collaborative processes that lead to the strategies which support developmental assessment and teaching. When these ideas result in improved outcomes, PLT leaders can build strong cases for changes in policy. With the support of school leaders, new policies can be formulated as part of school improvement plans that focus on evidence of student development. The process from classroom measurement to policy development has five steps, as outlined in Figure 1.1.

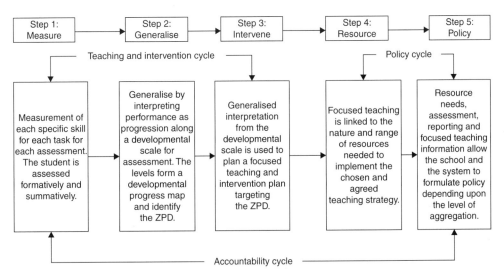

Figure 1.1 *Five steps from measurement to policy*
Source: Adapted from Griffin (2007).

The five steps from measurement to policy constitute the framework within which the use of developmental assessment for teaching is conducted. The first step is to measure learning using any form of assessment. From the measurement, it is necessary to identify the level of the student in the domain of learning that the assessment addresses. This is the second step, requiring a generalisation from a specific assessment to a judgement about the student's overall level of ability. It requires an interpretation of the assessment within a framework defined by a developmental progression. Different levels of performance point to different levels on the progression, and different levels on the progression suggest the use of different teaching strategies or interventions. This is the third step, in which the teacher, with the support of the PLT, devises strategies or interventions specifically tailored to the level at which the student is ready to learn. The fourth step involves the recognition that different teaching interventions may require different resources. If sufficient resources are already available, the first three steps of the process can be repeated. The success of teaching interventions will be tested by reassessments that check student progress, at which point new interventions, if appropriate, can be introduced. This is indicated in Figure 1.1 by the arrow connecting Step 3 (Intervene) and Step 1 (Measure), indicating the teaching and intervention cycle. In cases where new resources are required, the effectiveness of the additional resources can be evaluated only when sufficient resources have been secured.

The fifth step involves moving beyond the classroom to the development of policy for the school. When this affects assessment and teaching practice in the classroom, the change can be evaluated only when new policy has been implemented. This repetition of the five steps is shown in Figure 1.1 by the arrow connecting Step 5 (Policy) to Step 1 (Measure), indicating the accountability cycle. The third arrow, on the other hand, indicates the policy cycle – a common error that must be avoided, in which policy decisions lead to the allocation of resources without adequate assessment or trial of teaching interventions. In such cases, where the first three steps of the process are bypassed or not sufficiently implemented, resourcing can be driven by other motives, such as political expediency.

This five-step process shifts the emphasis of assessment on to targeted intervention, and illustrates how assessment data can be used to inform school policy directly. This approach to the use of assessment for teaching represents a strong contrast to the way in which assessment traditionally is used in schools. Most testing programs stop at the first step – measurement – and report total scores. The appropriate point of intervention is rarely identified, and subsequent teaching tends to focus on what the students cannot do (the deficit approach). This results in resources not being matched appropriately and then, at the wider policy level, critics of testing programs charge that testing does not improve learning. This is justified when teachers do not know how to use the information that tests or other forms of assessment can provide, and do not use them to improve their teaching – mainly because of the unhelpful ways in which assessment information is presented to them. However, if a developmental progression or criterion-referenced framework is used to its maximum advantage in a developmental approach based on skills rather than scores, it can and should change teaching and learning. This potential to improve teaching and learning is what the five-step approach represents.

The PLT cycle

The five-step process leads to a set of questions that aid the practical application of the framework. The resulting PLT cycle, shown in Figure 1.2, focuses on the practical task of implementing policy in the classroom. It is designed for the implementation of teaching strategies and the assessment of their effectiveness. The cycle renews whenever a review of progress is conducted. The detailed implementation of this cycle is discussed in Chapter 4.

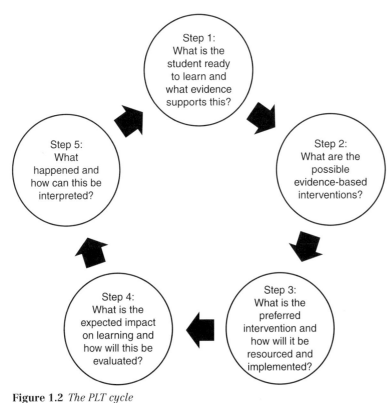

Figure 1.2 *The PLT cycle*

Each step of the PLT cycle is enhanced by collaboration, which brings additional viewpoints, experiences and ideas to bear on any step in the cycle. High-functioning collaborations do more than this: they challenge thinking, use shared decision-making and encourage peer accountability. A collaborative approach maximises the benefits to both students and teachers.

Professional learning teams already exist in many schools. Their aim – which is to build teacher capacity and, in doing so, improve the learning of their students – is directly aligned with the purpose of the cycle. Many different arrangements for PLT exist, and some lend themselves more readily than others to the use of assessment data to improve teaching and learning. Some focus only on administrative matters. Whatever the arrangement and team membership, PLT implementing the cycle move through stages of implementation. Not only do these stages relate to the proficiency with which the team is able to use the cycle; they also relate to the extent to which shared responsibility, peer accountability and the use of challenge are established within the team. The implementation has two distinct aspects: the activities the PLT undertakes and the commitment of the teachers to these activities. Chapter 4 details the activities undertaken by PLT using the cycle, while Chapter 5 discusses the culture of engagement or commitment within PLT. Each chapter describes the typical order of development observed in PLT.

Summary

This chapter introduced the principles on which this book and the approach to assessment and teaching are based. It outlined a new way of thinking about assessment for teaching, and linked the ideas of assessment data being used by collaborative teacher teams. It also set out a way by which a team leader can work with school leadership in the development of school policy that is firmly based on the assessment of student outcomes.

Our research has shown that improvements in student outcomes can be achieved by collaborative teams of teachers working with an evidence-based approach. The principles outlined in this chapter are keys to the successful use of assessment data to improve teaching. Keeping these principles in mind – both in reading this book and in your teaching practice – will help you fulfil the fundamental goal of improving student learning.

Apply to practice

For this task, consider a school or PLT setting with which you are familiar.

1 Consider the ways you and your colleagues or fellow students make use of assessment data. How do your assessment practices compare with the principles of assessment for teaching as outlined in the Introduction and this chapter?

2 How do you interpret observable evidence of student achievement? Are inferences challenged? If so, how does this happen and who does it?

3   Consider your collaborative practices. How do the practices compare with the principles outlined in the Introduction and this chapter?

Check your progress

Below is a set of rubrics to help you reflect on your answers to the Apply to Practice questions and assess your understanding of this chapter. These can be used to help scaffold learning.

1.1   Your description of the use of assessment data in your school or classroom:

    a   was general in nature

    b   identified similarities and differences in the practices

    c   evaluated the extent to which the principles outlined in this book are used.

1.2   Your reflection on the use of observable evidence of student achievement in your school or classroom:

    a   was general in nature

    b   described how the observable evidence is interpreted

    c   critiqued the ways in which observable evidence is interpreted.

1.3   Your comparison between your collaborative practices and the principles outlined in the Introduction and this chapter:

    a   was general in nature

    b   identified similarities and differences in the practices

    c   evaluated your practice on the basis of this comparison.

Chapter 2

Developmental teaching and assessment

Danielle Hutchinson, Michael Francis and Patrick Griffin

This chapter promotes the understanding of developmental learning, introducing hierarchies and taxonomies developed by Bloom, Biggs and Collis, Dreyfus and Krathwohl. It consolidates the distinction between the deficit and developmental approaches to teaching and addresses the implications of data use in these two models. The chapter shows teachers how to identify the zone of proximal development, following Vygotsky, and uses examples of student work to illustrate this concept. The implications of correct identification and the importance of differentiated instruction are also discussed. The establishment of a strong link between teaching and assessment data provides the reader with a framework within which to operate as a teacher.

Learning objectives

In this chapter you will learn to:

- understand the developmental model of learning
- understand developmental frameworks, including taxonomies, hypothetical progressions, curriculum progressions and derived progressions
- identify the zone of actual development (ZAD) and the zone of proximal development (ZPD) using examples of student work against progressions of reading comprehension, numeracy and problem-solving.

The developmental learning framework

Students accumulate skills and knowledge through a process of maturation and via engagement in learning activities. A teacher's role is to identify how best to promote this growth. It is common to hear the description of the teacher's role linked to diagnosis. Although this word typically and traditionally has been used to indicate that something is wrong and needs to be fixed, increasingly it is being used to identify individual needs in the educational context. This is exactly what teachers need to do, but it is important that we do not confuse student needs with student weaknesses or inadequacies. Students do not go to school to be fixed – they are not sick or in need of prescribed remedies; they go to school to grow socially and cognitively. In order to facilitate and support this, teachers need assessments and observations that enable them to monitor student growth and ascertain how their teaching has an impact on accelerating or promoting growth. Teachers plan interventions that will promote students' intellectual growth and social well-being. Teachers build on what the student already knows by having an idea of where the student is headed and intervening to ensure that the student progresses. In order to do this, teachers must identify the place – the zone – where the student is developing information, concepts and skills.

This chapter focuses on how to map inferences from assessment on to a developmental continuum, thereby identifying what the student is ready to learn. It illustrates the second of the five steps from measurement to policy introduced in Chapter 1 (see Figure 1.1). Step 2 – generalise – involves mapping inferences from assessment on to a developmental continuum. It is intended to identify what the student is ready to learn. This step is important, as without it teaching is more likely to be targeted towards the test or the 'next topic' in the curriculum, rather than provided in response to what the student is ready to learn. Appreciating this distinction requires an understanding of constructs, the developmental model of learning and developmental frameworks.

Constructs

The first step in creating a situation in which students will generate evidence of their understanding in a particular skill area is to define the construct of interest. A construct is a concept or entity that we cannot see – that is, it is not tangible and we cannot access it directly. As pointed out in Chapter 1, a construct is something we invent to explain observations. Anxiety is an example of a construct. We cannot see it so we do not have direct evidence that it exists. We infer its presence from the fact that we have come across multiple examples of the concurrence of different observations. For example, we see a person sweating, flushing red and/or speaking with tremors in their voice in a situation that we can imagine is uncomfortable. We infer the presence of an underlying cause for this set of signs – something that accounts for the manifestations. Over a period of time and many experiences, we come to an understanding of the broad array of signs that typically are manifested by many people in similar situations, and on this basis start to assemble a description of the concept. This is a construct. Constructs used in education include written communication, mathematical problem-solving, skill in science inquiry and ability in creating art. Thus a construct is something we create or invent to make sense of what we observe. Constructs are discussed further in Chapter 6.

The developmental model of learning

The developmental model of learning brings together the work of Glaser (1981), Vygotsky (1978) and Rasch (1960), each of whom has made a significant contribution to education in his own right. This chapter extends the initial synthesis of these three theories by Griffin (2007). The synthesis elaborates on a paradigm within which the aim of education becomes the movement of student learning along a path of increasingly complex knowledge, skills and abilities. Under this model, the teacher's attention is focused on a student's readiness to learn so that instruction can be designed to build upon the current level of learning. This developmental model sits in contrast to the deficit approach, which instead focuses on diagnosing and then remediating the things a student cannot do.

Robert Glaser

Robert Glaser (1921–2012) developed a theoretical framework of assessment interpretation known as a criterion-referenced interpretation (Glaser 1981). The cornerstone of his framework is that knowledge acquisition can be conceptualised as a continuum, ranging from low to high proficiency. Points on the continuum are identified by behavioural criteria that indicate a particular level of proficiency has been reached. Thus the aim of criterion-referenced interpretation is to 'encourage the development of procedures whereby assessments of proficiency could be referred to stages along progressions of increasing competence' (1981, p. 935). In this definition, the phrase 'stages along progressions of increasing competence' is very important. First, it requires distinct levels of competence. Second, it implies that there is an increasing order of sophistication among these levels of competence. Finally, it prompts us to monitor student progress through the stages or levels of increasing competence. Thus the following sequence for conducting assessment is suggested:

1 Identify the construct.

2 Articulate the construct in terms of observable evidence (criteria).

3 Validate the progression levels that are to be used for interpretation of the evidence.

4 Devise ways of assessing a person so that their performance can be placed at a level or stage on the progression of increasing competence.

5 Monitor progress by assessing at more than one point in time. Do this by collecting evidence of proficiency, interpreting it as representative of a stage or level on the progression of increasing competence and repeating these actions after a teaching intervention or learning period.

A crucial feature of Glaser's approach is that the student's level of competence is described in terms of the tasks performed or competence displayed. This is illustrated in Figure 2.1. When considered as a whole, the levels of competence describe the observable behaviours that allow us to make inferences about the student's capacity in relation to the underlying construct.

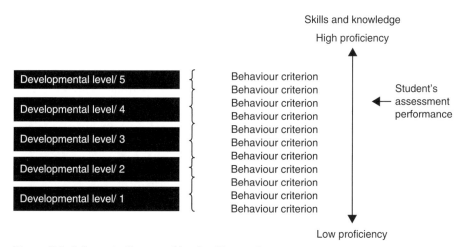

Figure 2.1 *Schematic diagram of levels of increasing competence*

This type of assessment interpretation contrasts with a norm-referenced assessment interpretation, in which a student's performance is compared against the performance of other students instead of being considered in relation to the task itself. A common example of a norm-referenced assessment is the interpretation of a person's performance on an IQ test. When the results of an IQ test are reported, a person is given a score that indicates a position above or below the average person of the same age. The person who is statistically average in relation to their peers is given a score of 100. Every score is then compared with (referenced to) this norm. A person who performs at a level below the average will be ranked and given a score below 100. Similarly, a person who performs above the statistical average will be given a score above 100. How far above or below the norm any individual is ranked will depend on where they sit in comparison to others on either side of the norm.

In criterion-referenced interpretation, a student's results indicate their position on a continuum of developing competence in relation to an area of learning, not in relation to their peers. In this kind of assessment interpretation, it is possible for an entire cohort to do well, or for an entire cohort to do poorly, because their results depend only on the level of skill they display, not on their rank compared with their peers. There are no adjustments to align results with statistical norms. Nor does the interpretation take into account the age or other characteristics of the students. It is simply a record of how well a task is performed.

A common example of a criterion-based scale is a driving test. In its simplest form, it has two levels of achievement: either you are competent to receive a licence or you are not; and it makes no difference what level of competency is displayed by other drivers. Further, apart from having a requirement that a driver must be a particular age to apply for a licence, your age is not taken into consideration when determining your level of competency, which is measured solely upon the performance demonstrated.

Standards-referenced interpretation combines elements of criterion referencing and norm referencing. In this kind of interpretation, as in criterion referencing, an assessment score is referred to sets of multiple criteria, creating levels or stages of competence, but in this case the levels are set as standards or expectations for students, depending on the age or grade level they have reached. So standards referencing uses performance criteria but it also uses grade or age to set an expectation within the criterion-referenced framework – as a standard – and student performances are referred (referenced) to that standard of expected performance.

Due to an increasing emphasis on functionality and performance quality (Woods 2010), there have been international educational shifts towards standards- and criterion-referenced assessment. Table 2.1 uses examples of Australian assessments to summarise the three types of referencing frameworks.

Table 2.1 *Summary of referencing frameworks*

NORM-REFERENCED	STANDARDS-REFERENCED	CRITERION-REFERENCED
e.g. Australian Tertiary Admissions Rank (ATAR)	e.g. The Australian Curriculum	e.g. AusVELS
The ATAR is calculated as a percentile, but is a rank rather than a mark. It provides an indication of each student's position relative to other students across a state. An ATAR of 80.00 indicates that the student sits in the top 20 per cent of the cohort.	The Australian Curriculum is organised according to year levels ranging from F (Foundation or Prep) to 10. The levels serve to provide information about learning contexts considered to be appropriate at each year level. They also exemplify the types of content and levels of complexity with which students are expected to be working at a particular year level or year grouping.	AusVELS is structured according to levels F–10. Unlike the Australian Curriculum, levels are not associated with particular year levels or year groupings; instead, the levels are intended to indicate increasingly sophisticated levels of performance along an 11-point continuum of learning.

Sources: http://www.uac.edu.au/documents/atar/All-About-Your-ATAR.pdf; http://ausvels.vcaa.vic.edu.au/Overview/AusVELS-Structure.

Reflective question

What are the differences in the types of decisions teachers can make using norm-referenced, standards-referenced and criterion-referenced assessment data?

Lev Vygotsky

Lev Vygotsky (1896–1934) was a Russian psychologist who wrote extensively on learning and child development (see Vygotsky 1993). He suggested that education was most effective when it emphasised teaching targeted towards a student's emerging skills. He argued that the aim of instruction should be to elicit, stretch or extend the knowledge, skills and attitudes that are in the process of developing (Miller 2011, p. 121).

To provide a conceptual framework around which teachers can plan to maximise student learning, the developmental model draws upon Vygotsky's zone of proximal development (ZPD). Vygotsky (1978, p. 86) described the ZPD as 'the distance between the actual developmental level as determined by independent problem solving and the level of potential development as determined through problem solving under adult guidance, or in collaboration with more capable peers'.

This zone therefore sits between two thresholds. The lower threshold is the student's actual developmental level, or zone of actual development (ZAD), which includes all previous learning. The upper threshold is the student's potential developmental level. The ZPD captures the skills that have not yet come to fruition but are in the process of maturing (Figure 2.2). A simple way of dealing with this concept is to look for the range of skills between the things the student can do and the things they cannot do. It is often characterised by inconsistency of performance: sometimes the students can perform the task and sometimes they cannot. This inconsistency or struggle is symptomatic of emerging development and characterises the ZPD.

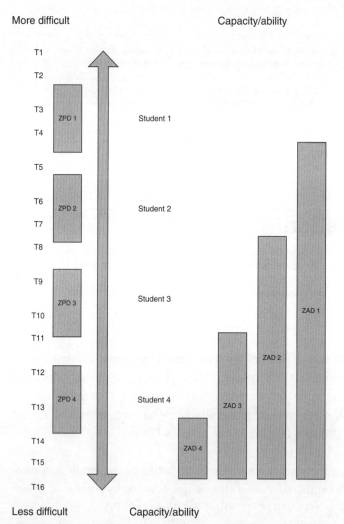

Figure 2.2 *Schematic diagram of student development showing ZAD and ZPD*

On a practical level, a student's ZPD can be described as 'a state of readiness in which a student will be able to make certain kinds of conceptual connections, but not others; anything too simple for the student will quickly become boring; anything too difficult will quickly become demoralising' (Burbules 1993, p. 122). In this way, the ZPD is analogous to the Goldilocks principle, in which the task is to find something that is neither too hot nor too cold, but just right. When teachers are able to teach skills that are neither too easy nor too hard, they are more likely to facilitate opportunities for their students to enter a state of 'flow' (Csikzentmihalyi 1990), or optimal learning experience. This is characterised by a state of complete engagement with a task, and is most likely to occur when the skill of the student is matched to the challenge of the task.

As a consequence of this shift in focus to the student's ZPD, teachers must gather information about what the student can do, what they struggle to do and what they cannot do. Armed with this information, teachers are able to target their interventions at the point at which Vygotsky asserts they will have the greatest impact. This approach to planning interventions is now commonly associated with the term *scaffolding*, which has been described as '"controlling" those elements of the task that are initially beyond the learner's capacity, thus permitting him [sic] to concentrate upon and complete only those elements that are within his range of competence' (Wood, Bruner & Ross 1976, p. 90).

To scaffold students effectively to the next level of competence, teachers need to be proficient in two areas. First, they need to be able to locate the actual and potential levels of development within which the student is operating – this will allow the teacher to identify a student's ZPD. Second, they need to be able to articulate and/or validate the continuum of knowledge or skill against which each student's performance is to be measured.

Reflective questions

In Figure 2.2, four zones of proximal development (ZPDs) are shown – one for each of Students 1 to 4. Sixteen tasks (T1 to T16) are also shown, as well as four zones of actual development (ZAD).

1   Which student is the most able? Which task is the most difficult?

2   Which student is the least able? Which task is the least difficult?

3   Which student has the most advanced ZPD? Which tasks is this student ready to learn?

4   Which student has the least advanced ZPD? Which tasks is this student ready to learn?

5   Discuss with your peers each of the four students in terms of the tasks that each:

   •   can do

   •   cannot do

   •   is ready to learn.

6   For T1 to T16, substitute skills in your teaching area. Make sure they are ordered according to increasing difficulty with T1 the hardest and T16 the easiest. Then discuss with your colleagues the type of intervention you would use for each of the four ZPDs. Use your interpretation/description of each ZAD to plan scaffolding and discuss how this scaffolding would be done. How would you extend – that is, stretch – each of the four students?

Georg Rasch

There is a natural association between student ability and task difficulty – students with greater ability may succeed at tasks with greater difficulty. Georg Rasch (1901–80) was a mathematician who developed a method of measuring the location of student ability and task difficulty on the same scale. This yields a mathematical model that can be used within a criterion-referenced framework. In Rasch's (1980) model, the probability of a correct response to a task is a function of the distance between the ability of the person and the difficulty of the task. If the person is more able than the task is difficult, then success can be expected. If the task is more difficult than the person is able, then failure can be expected. The interesting result, for our purposes, occurs when the task difficulty is exactly equal to the ability of the person: 'Odds of success are a function of the difference between the ability of the student and the difficulty of the task. When these are equal the odds of success are 50:50.' (1980, p. 107)

If we are monitoring growth along a pathway from simple to complex, from easy to difficult, from naive to sophisticated, from simplistic to elegant, from novice to expert and so on, we look for that level on the progression where student ability is roughly equal to the difficulty of the tasks, because that is the level at which the student is ready to learn. This can be done empirically, but few teachers have the time, the software or the training to undertake such an analysis. In most cases, a professional judgement on the part of the teacher replaces the empirical calculation.

To form such a judgement, the teacher needs to have in mind a developmental progression – for example, from simple to complex. In addition, the teacher needs to have an idea of the student's ability and where the student might fit on that developmental progression. Matching the student's development to the difficulty level of tasks on a progression is central to developmental teaching and learning. The levels on the progression help us to understand Glaser's criterion-referenced framework for interpreting performance. Matching the student ability to the level of difficulty is an application of Rasch logic. Identifying how to move the student from one level to the other using scaffolding is an application of Vygotsky's approach. Matching the ability of the student to the difficulty of the task is a professional judgement-based activity. In this activity, what teachers are looking for are the things that students can do sometimes but cannot do at other times. They lie in the region where the student's behaviour and performance are inconsistent.

In theory, the 50:50 chance of success can be exemplified in the following way. If there were 10 students of equal ability attempting a task that was equal in difficulty to their ability, five of the students would succeed and five would not. The identity of those who succeeded would be random. Alternatively, if there was one student and 10 tasks all equal in difficulty and equal to the ability of the student, the student could be expected to do five of the tasks successfully and not the other five. The identity of the five tasks would be random. If this seems theoretical and implausible, it is easier to think of the tasks in the ZPD as being at that level where the student performance is inconsistent.

Combining the three theories

The combination of the three theories allows assessment results to be interpreted in terms of Glaser's levels of increasing competence and, when interpreted in a Rasch-like manner, to provide an indicator of the point of intervention where learning can be scaffolded. It is then possible to link the relative positions of a student and an assessment task on the developmental continuum to an interpretation of what a student can learn when the odds of success are 50:50.

In finding the zone of proximal development, it is necessary to order the tasks that the student is expected to perform in terms of their relative difficulty. The easiest task can be placed at the bottom of a progression and the hardest at the top. It is then possible to see how far up this 'ladder of difficulty' a student can go. This is like ordering test questions from the easiest at the beginning to the hardest at the end, which allows a teacher or examiner to see how far through the test a student can progress before becoming unable to provide consistently correct answers. If such a test is developed using the logic of the Rasch model, this is easy to do. The score obtained by the student on the test is simply a count of the number of questions for which they had the right answer. At the beginning of the test, among the easy questions, the student would be expected to get mostly correct answers. Then, as the questions became more difficult, the student would be expected to answer some correctly and some incorrectly. Beyond this range of test questions, as the difference between the difficulty of the task and the ability of the student increases, the student would be expected to answer most questions incorrectly. Hence the score on the test is a pointer to where a teacher might intervene. If the test questions are analysed and the skills embedded within them are identified, a description can be developed of the kinds of things that the student is ready to learn. If this is scaffolded using the skills below that level to build a foundation, and if the skills above that level are controlled and introduced gradually, the student's learning is scaffolded.

The challenge for teachers is to identify students' emerging skills and provide the right support at the right time at the right level. Teachers need to be able to identify the ZPD, or the 'state of readiness' in the domain of learning. This has implications for teaching and learning practice. Traditionally, teachers are not trained to use test score data to identify the ZPD for students. Identifying the ZPD is difficult without developmental continua and impossible if working within a deficit model.

The combination of the theories of Glaser, Rasch and Vygotsky provides a mechanism for assessment practices to move away from the interpretation of summative test scores of past student achievement. Instead, interpretation of test scores becomes the starting point for instruction, indicating where a student's ZPD is located and where they are 'ready to learn'.

Many examples exist of generalisable developmental progressions. These can help teachers to formulate the idea of a pathway of increasing sophistication and complexity of learning within which they can monitor student progress and identify specific signs of the ZPD.

Developmental frameworks

Four types of developmental frameworks can be used to underpin developmental learning. They are developmental taxonomies, hypothetical progressions, curriculum progressions and derived progressions.

- A *developmental taxonomy* is one born from experience and a theoretical basis of learning. A taxonomy is a classification framework, and a developmental taxonomy lists generic levels of complexity or sophistication that can be used to classify and interpret both student task requirements and student task responses. These taxonomies are often hierarchical. Examples of these include Bloom's Revised Taxonomy and Dreyfus's model of skill acquisition (see below).

- A *hypothetical progression* is developed from knowledge of a construct or an adaptation of a developmental taxonomy to a specific learning area or task. It imposes an order or sequence on to the classifications. It is a hypothesis that teachers formulate about the order of learning. Hypothetical progressions are discussed further in Chapter 7.

- A *curriculum progression* typically is grounded in curriculum standards, government policy, education experience and perhaps research literature. It might be expressed in terms of developmental progressions aligned to age levels or grades. Curriculum progressions are discussed further in Chapter 7.

- A *derived progression* is one that is derived from expert comparative analysis or large-scale data collection and calibration using an item response model approach. Such progressions usually are derived from standardised testing procedures. Derived progressions are discussed further in Chapter 9. The examples in Table 2.2 are discussed in more detail in later chapters.

Table 2.2 *Comparison of examples of developmental frameworks*

	TAXONOMIES	HYPOTHETICAL PROGRESSIONS	CURRICULUM PROGRESSIONS	DERIVED PROGRESSIONS
Examples	Bloom Krathwohl Dreyfus SOLO	Examples of simple hypothetical progressions based on developmental taxonomies are included in Tables 2.4, 2.6, 2.8 and 2.10. Examples of expanded hypothetical progressions are included in Chapter 9.	AusVELS Australian Curriculum	ARCOTS numeracy, reading comprehension and problem-solving progressions NAPLAN E5 C21 collaborative problem-solving progressions SWANs progressions
Advantages	Can be applied to many different situations	Easily adapted to current teaching Make use of an established knowledge or research base	Can be used when empirical data is not available Readily available for teacher use	Derived from data (evidence) Readily available for teacher use
Disadvantages	May be used in developmentally inappropriate ways	Require expertise in relation to the construct or some level of familiarity with the developmental taxonomies	May not represent reality May be used in developmentally inappropriate ways	Require expert input or large data set May be used in developmentally inappropriate ways

Developmental taxonomies

Bloom's Revised Taxonomy

Developmental taxonomies are general in nature and can be applied to many situations. They use the concept of 'stages of development' to develop progressions of increasing competence. Bloom's Taxonomy is familiar to many teachers. It is summarised in Table 2.3. Although research has indicated that Bloom's Taxonomy is not a monotonic progression (one that monotonously increases) or a hierarchy, it is often used as a means of classifying learning outcomes. In this chapter, it is regarded as a continuum, although it may not be linear. The version described below was revised by Anderson and colleagues in 2001.

Table 2.3 *Bloom's Revised Taxonomy*

6.0 Create	Putting elements together to form a novel, coherent whole or make an original product	6.1 Generate 6.2 Plan 6.3 Produce
5.0 Evaluate	Making judgments based on criteria and standards	5.1 Check 5.2 Critique
4.0 Analyse	Breaking material into its constituent parts and detecting how the parts relate to one another and to an overall structure or purpose	4.1 Differentiate 4.2 Organise 4.3 Attribute
3.0 Apply	Carrying out or using a procedure in a given situation.	3.1 Execute 3.2 Implement
2.0 Understand	Determining the meaning of instructional messages, including oral, written and graphic communication	2.1 Interpret 2.2 Exemplify 2.3 Classify 2.4 Summarise 2.5 Infer 2.6 Compare 2.7 Explain
1.0 Remember	Retrieving relevant knowledge from long-term memory	1.1 Recognise 1.2 Recall 1.3 List

Source: Adapted from Anderson et al. (2001).

The taxonomy describes six levels of increasing competence that students can demonstrate as evidence that they have acquired some form of knowledge. It is used to classify and monitor the development of cognitive skills. By adapting this framework to a specific area of instruction, increasing levels of competence can be described. For example, students who have been taught how to use PowerPoint to give a presentation on their project work may demonstrate increasing levels of competence, as indicated in Table 2.4.

Table 2.4 *A simple hypothetical progression using Bloom's Taxonomy and adapted to one aspect of the use of PowerPoint in a presentation*

LEVEL	BEHAVIOUR TO DEMONSTRATE KNOWLEDGE OF POWERPOINT APPLICATION
5.0 Evaluate	Checks the quality of their PowerPoint presentation against teaching and evaluates the strengths and weaknesses of the choices made
3.0 Apply	Executes a PowerPoint presentation of their project work
1.0 Remember	Recalls key features of PowerPoint

Note that the table does not use all of Bloom's levels. The class may not contain students operating at all six levels, and it is easier for teachers to identify progress if fewer levels are used for assessment purposes. It is unlikely that all the students in any class will be at any one of the levels indicated. It is more likely that sub-groups of students will be operating at each of the levels. This means that there may be three different groups of students at different stages of readiness to learn, or ZPDs. What a student at the lowest level is ready to learn is different from what a student at the middle level is ready to learn, and also different from what a student at the highest level is ready to learn. Vygotsky emphasised the extension or stretching of individuals. Stretching every student means that every student's ZPD needs to be known.

If teaching is targeted at the higher-level students, the students at lower levels will become frustrated, restless and possibly even disruptive to the class, as they may not be able to understand the material presented. Likewise, if teaching is targeted to the lower-level students, the students at higher levels may become bored, which may also lead to restlessness and disruption to the class. Finally, if teaching is targeted to the middle level, students at both higher and lower levels may become frustrated, bored, restless and disruptive.

The SOLO taxonomy

Another example of a developmental taxonomy which describes increasingly sophisticated levels of cognitive performance is Biggs and Collis's (1982) Structure of the Observed Learning Outcome (SOLO) taxonomy, shown in Table 2.5. The SOLO taxonomy examines the ways in which ideas are connected in the work students produce. It can be applied to written text, design or artistic work, performance or dramatic endeavours, sport or cultural events. The taxonomy begins with simple individual ideas that are not connected and culminates in the description of a sophisticated way of exploring multiple ideas, elements or characteristics of work and the way they blend together into a cohesive whole.

Table 2.5 *SOLO taxonomy*

5. Extended abstract	There is recognition that the given principle is an instance of a more general case. Hypotheses about examples *not* given are entertained, and the conclusions are held open.	○ ○ ⦻⦻⦻⦻ ○ ○
4. Relational	Most or all of the evidence is accepted, and attempts are made to reconcile. Conflicting data are placed into a system that accounts for the given context.	○ ○ ⦻⦻⦻⦻ ○ ○
3. Multi-structural	Several consistent aspects of the data are selected, but any inconsistencies or conflicts are ignored or discounted so that a firm conclusion is reached.	○ ○ ○ ⦻⦻⦻ ○ ○
2. Uni-structural	An answer based on only one relevant aspect of the presented evidence so that the conclusion is limited and likely dogmatic.	○ ○ ○ ○ ⦻ ○ ○ ○
1. Pre-structural	Cue and response confused. Student avoids the question, repeats the question, a firm closure based on 'guesstimate'.	○ ○ ○ ○ ⊠ ○ ○ ○

A simple hypothetical progression using the SOLO taxonomy and adapted to the task of a book review is shown in Table 2.6.

Table 2.6 *SOLO adapted for the task of a book review*

5. Extended abstract	Review synthesises elements of the text and evaluates it in the context of other literary works by the same author or within the same genre.	○ ○ ⦻⦻⦻⦻ ○ ○
4. Relational	Review draws relationships between the different elements of the text to provide an over-arching evaluation.	○ ○ ⦻⦻⦻⦻ ○ ○
3. Multi-structural	Review discusses discrete elements of the text.	○ ○ ○ ⦻⦻⦻ ○ ○
2. Uni-structural	Review focuses on one element of the text – for example, plot or characters.	○ ○ ○ ○ ⦻ ○ ○ ○

Dreyfus's model of skill acquisition

Another commonly used developmental taxonomy is Dreyfus's model of skill acquisition, which describes levels of increasing expertise. A summary of this developmental taxonomy is presented in Table 2.7.

Table 2.7 *Dreyfus's model of skill acquisition*

Expert	No longer relies on rules, guidelines or maxims; operates from a deep understanding of the total situation; analytical approaches are used only in novel situations or when a problem occurs; vision of what is possible.
Proficient	Sees situations holistically and identifies goals or salient aspects intuitively; perceives deviations from the normal pattern and possesses perspectives on a situation; decision-making is less laboured.
Competent	Perceives actions at least partially in terms of longer-term goals; conscious, deliberate planning and use of standardised and routinised procedures; makes reasoned decisions about new situations without being sure of appropriateness of decision.
Advanced beginner	Minor adjustments to rules or plans can be carried out in some situations under supervision.
Novice	Rigid adherence to taught rules or plans; no store of contingency plans for when circumstances vary from the expected.

Source: Adapted from Dreyfus & Dreyfus (1980).

Like Bloom's Taxonomy and the SOLO taxonomy, Dreyfus's model can be adapted to describe the development of learning within a specific instructional skill area. The Dreyfus model is particularly effective when used to evaluate the performance of practical skills – for example, cooking, as shown in Table 2.8.

Table 2.8 *A simple hypothetical progression using the Dreyfus model adapted for cooking skills*

Expert	Invents own recipes
Proficient	Adapts recipe to suit situation
Competent	Attempts changes to recipe (e.g. substitutes an ingredient, adjusts amounts/times) when necessary
Novice	Follows a recipe

Krathwohl's Taxonomy of the Affective Domain

Another developmental taxonomy, Krathwohl's Taxonomy of the Affective Domain, describes attitudinal stages through which people move when acquiring new ideas or behaviours. In developing an understanding of how to work within an affective frame-work, teachers can put strategies in place to scaffold student engagement. This can be powerful, as it means that realistic and attainable goals are more likely to be set, and consequently progress is more likely to be achieved. The generic version of Krathwohl's Taxonomy is presented in Table 2.9 (note that the levels appear in the opposite order from the levels in Bloom, SOLO and Dreyfus – top down rather than bottom up).

Table 2.9 *Krathwohl's Taxonomy of the Affective Domain*

Characterising	A learner who has become an advocate of new information or procedures
Organising	A learner who is incorporating new information and procedures into their existing schema. New information and procedures can be implemented with understanding in a regular and effective manner.
Valuing	A learner who is able to see the worth of new information and procedures
Responding	A learner who is actively participating in and interacting with new information or procedures without agreeing with or endorsing them. This could also be described as compliance.
Receiving	A learner who is willing to receive or listen to information and ideas, but has not made decisions about the worth of the information
(Rejecting)	A learner who is not willing to receive or listen to information

Note: An extra lower level, 'Rejecting', has been added to Krathwohl's framework to cater for those individuals who are so set in their ways that they are not willing to listen to new information.
Source: Adapted from Krathwohl, Bloom & Masia (1964).

Table 2.10 features an adaptation of Krathwohl's Taxonomy, which demonstrates how it can be used to show students' engagement with or attitude towards the development of study skills.

Table 2.10 *A simple hypothetical progression using Krathwohl's Taxonomy and adapted for study skills*

Receiving	Listens passively to information provided to assist students with the development of effective study skills
Responding	Completes set tasks designed to develop study skills
Organising	Independently organises time and materials to implement study skills routine
Characterising	Voluntarily leads peer-mentoring study skills program

---

Reflective questions

Select a task you might use with students.

* Which developmental framework best fits the task?
* Could the use of this developmental framework assist you in planning or assessing this task in the future?

These developmental taxonomies can assist with the assessment of student learning. They can be applied to different tasks, and an extensive examination of how these are used in the development of rubrics is provided in Chapter 7.

Curriculum progressions

Curriculum progressions – like the Australian Curriculum or AusVELS in Victoria – describe the predicted development of learning in a particular learning area. These are often linked to expected developmental levels for grades or age groups. They can be constructed using a combination of theory and expert opinion. The advantage of this type of developmental construct is that it is more specific than a developmental framework, and does not require the large amounts of data necessary to construct an empirical progression (see below). The disadvantage is that it can be influenced by the usual practices of those constructing it, and may not reflect the actual order in which students acquire skills or knowledge.

Derived progressions

Derived progressions are empirical. They are constructed using data drawn from large numbers of people. Statistical methods are applied to the data to determine the likely order in which skills, knowledge or attitudes will be developed. Examples of derived progressions are the scales used in NAPLAN (see Figure 2.3) and in the PISA and Trends in International Mathematics and Science Study (TIMSS) international studies. Derived progressions represent a typical rather than an absolute pathway for students, and can therefore provide a useful frame of reference for teachers without being prescriptive. Though not deterministic, they can be used constructively in the process of planning learning goals for students. They can assist teachers to select goals that are developmentally appropriate and that maximise the rate of learning of their students.

The authors at the Assessment Research Centre at Melbourne University have also produced a number of derived progressions: a set for students working in the standard curriculum and another for students with additional learning needs. The purpose of these progressions is to help teachers make decisions about learning goals for students. Copies of the progressions for a standard curriculum are provided in the appendices at the end of this chapter. An example of a progression for students with additional needs is provided in Chapter 12. The progressions for a standard curriculum are:

Assessment for Teaching

Band	Reading	Persuasive writing	Language conventions	Numeracy
9	Processes and interprets ideas that are implicit in a range of complex narrative and information texts. Analyses and evaluates evidence in persuasive texts and identifies language features to infer an author's intended purpose and audience.	Incorporates elaborated ideas that reflect a world-wide view on the topic. Makes consistently precise word choices that engage and persuade the reader and enhance the writer's point of view. Punctuates sentence beginnings and endings correctly and uses other complex punctuation correctly most of the time. Shows control and variety in paragraph construction to pace and direct the reader's attention.	Identifies errors and correctly spells words with difficult spelling patterns (*miniature, severely, technological, label*). Demonstrates knowledge of grammer and punctuation conventions in more complex texts, such as the correct use of possessive pronouns (*its*).	Applies knowledge, skills and strategies to interpret and solve multi-step word problems involving: volume of an irregular object, scale, location and symmetry on a grid, mass and geometric properties of squares and triangles. Interprets complex rules involving diagrams and time-series graphs.
8	Interprets ideas and processes information in a range of complex texts. Understands how characters' traits and behaviours are used to develop stereotypes. Analyses and interprets persuasive texts to infer a specific purpose and audience. Uses the context to interpret vocabulary specific to a text or topic.	Writes a cohesive text that begins to engage and persuade the reader. Makes deliberate and appropriate word choices to create a rational or emotional response. Attempts to reveal attitudes and value and to develop a relationship with the reader. Constructs most complex sentences correctly. Spells most words, including many difficult words, correctly.	Identifies errors and correctly spells most words with difficult spelling patterns (*echoes, principle, angrily, encouraged*). Demonstrates knowledge of grammar and punctuation conventions in more complex texts, such as appropriate sentence structure, the correct use of pronouns, pairs of conjunctions (*neither, nor*), forms of adverbs (*more deeply*), complex verb forms and quotation marks for effect.	Applies knowledge, skills and strategies to interpret and solve multi-step problems involving: proportion, fractions, length, cost, time, mass and probability. Solves number operations with decimals to two decimal places.
7	Applies knowledge and understanding of different text types to process ideas, draw conclusions and infer themes and purpose. Identifies details that connect implied ideas across and within texts including character motivation in narrative texts, the values of a writer in persuasive texts and the main ideas in information texts.	Writes a persuasive text with a developed introduction, an elaborated body and a clear conclusion. Develops plausible arguments through use of logic, language choices and effective persuasive devices. Joins and orders ideas using connecting words and maintains clear meaning through the text. Correctly spells most common words and some difficult words, including words with less common spelling patterns and silent letters.	Identifies errors and correctly spells words with common spelling patterns and some words with difficult spelling patterns (*temporary, ineffective, excellent, circulated*). Demonstrates knowledge of grammar and punctuation conventions in more complex texts, such as the correct use of compound verbs (*could have*), apostrophes for possession (*nobody's*) and quotation marks for speech.	Interprets rules and patterns to solve problems involving number operations. Solves a problem using information from a divided column graph. Calculates time using hours and days. Solves a multi-step problem involving simple proportion and money. Finds the value in a pattern modelled on triangular shapes.
6	Makes meaning from a range of text types of increasing difficulty and understands different text structures. Recognises the purpose of general text features such as titles and subheadings. Makes inferences by connecting ideas across different parts of texts, interprets figurative language and identifies the main difference between characters in narrative texts.	Organise a persuasive text using focused paragraphs. Uses some effective persuasive devices and accurate words or groups of words when developing points of arguments and ideas. Punctuates nearly all sentences correctly with capitals, full stops, exclamation marks and question marks. Correctly uses more complex punctuation marks some of the time.	Identifies errors and correctly spells most words with common spelling patterns (*soldiers, address, meant, activity*). Demonstrates knowledge of grammar and punctuation conventions in more complex texts, such as appropriate and clear sentence structure, and the correct use varied conjunctions (*whether*).	Applies suitable strategies to solve problems using skills including: knowledge and attributes of 2-D shapes and calculation of time. Solves a multi-step reasoning problem involving number calculations. Recognises prime numbers less than 20.
5	Uses clearly stated information in familiar text types to draw some conclusions and inferences. Draws conclusions about a character in narrative texts. Connects and sequences ideas in longer information texts and identifies opinions in persuasive texts.	Structures a persuasive text to include an introduction and a body containing some related points of argument. Includes enough supporting detail for the writer's point of view to be easily understood by the reader, although the conclusion may be weak or simple. Correctly structures most simple and compound sentences and some complex sentences.	Identifies errors and correctly spells one- and two-syllable words with common spelling patterns (*grown, drafting, message*). Recognises grammer and punctuation conventions in standard sentences and speech, such as the correct use of verb forms, synonyms, connecting words (*however*), brackets and apostrophes for contractions (*he's*).	Calculates the missing value in a decimal multiplication equation and adds and subtracts decimals to one decimal place. Solves a money problem involving division. Uses information from a pie graph to solve a simple problem. Uses knowledge of 2-D shapes and 3-D objects to identify particular shapes.
4	Locates clearly stated information in factual and narrative texts to connect ideas and make inferences. Identifies the meaning of some unfamiliar words from their context and finds key information in longer texts including tables and diagrams.	Writes a persuasive text in which paragraphs are used to group like ideas and persuasive devices are used to attempt to convince a reader. Correctly punctuates some sentences with both capital letters and full stops. May demonstrate correct use of capitals for names and some other punctuation. Correctly spells most common words.	Identifies errors and correctly spells some one- and two-syllable words with common spelling patterns. Recognises grammar and punctuation conventions in standard sentences and speech, such as consistency within sentences, the correct use of verb forms and appropriate order of phrases.	Identifies a specific 3-D object from a diagram. Solves a problem involving elapsed time. Finds an unknown number in number sentences involving simple addition and subtraction. Uses knowledge of probability to predict an outcome. Reads a scale to find a change in temperature.

Figure 2.3 *NAPLAN progressions (derived)*

a. Progression of Problem Solving Development

b. Progression of Reading Comprehension Development

c. Progression of Numeracy Development

d. Expanded Numeracy Progression for Number

e. Expanded Numeracy Progression for Measurement

f. Expanded Numeracy Progression for Data and Chance

g. Expanded Numeracy Progression for Geometry.

For students with additional learning needs (see Chapter 12), the progressions are:

a. Pathway of Cognitive Development for Students with Additional Needs

b. Pathway of Cognitive Development for Students with Additional Needs (Autism Spectrum Disorder)

c. Pathway of Communication Development for Students with Additional Needs

d. Pathway of Emotional Development for Students with Additional Needs

e. Pathway of Interpersonal Development for Students with Additional Needs

f. Pathway of Literacy Development for Students with Additional Needs.

These progressions are derived from the data collected from the assessment of thousands of students. The development of these progressions, and the use of the assessments linked to them, are covered in the chapters to come.

Reporting against the developmental progressions

Once a developmental progression is linked to tests, reports can be generated to identify student skill levels and ZPDs. One such report is the Learning Readiness Report, which is one of three reports that can be generated using the Assessment Research Centre Online Testing System (ARCOTS). Sample questions from this system can be accessed via www.cambridge.edu.au/academic/arcots. An example of a Learning Readiness Report is shown in Figure 2.4. The report shows a series of level descriptions arranged from the lowest level at the bottom to the highest level at the top. The black bar shows the student's level on the progression. The text beside Level H outlines the skills that are currently in the student's ZPD. The lower seven 'nutshell' statements (A to G) describe the skills that this student has a greater than 50:50 chance of using correctly. The upper four 'nutshell' statements (I to L) describe the skills that the student has a less than 50:50 chance of using correctly.

The skills in the 'nutshell' statements are the skills that a student at that level is on the verge of learning, and are therefore those with which the student will benefit most from scaffolding. This is the point of intervention for teaching. More detail on the Learning Readiness Report is provided in Chapter 10.

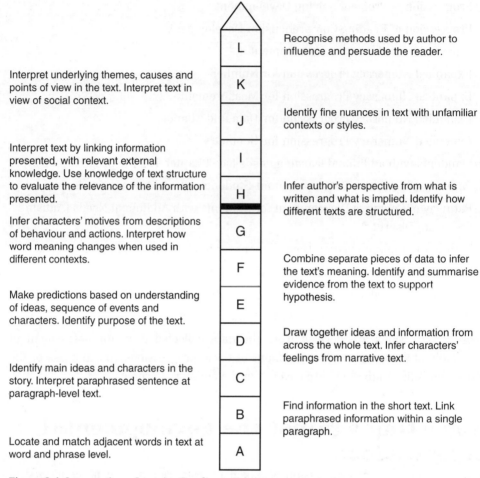

Recognise methods used by author to influence and persuade the reader.

Interpret underlying themes, causes and points of view in the text. Interpret text in view of social context.

Identify fine nuances in text with unfamiliar contexts or styles.

Interpret text by linking information presented, with relevant external knowledge. Use knowledge of text structure to evaluate the relevance of the information presented.

Infer author's perspective from what is written and what is implied. Identify how different texts are structured.

Infer characters' motives from descriptions of behaviour and actions. Interpret how word meaning changes when used in different contexts.

Combine separate pieces of data to infer the text's meaning. Identify and summarise evidence from the text to support hypothesis.

Make predictions based on understanding of ideas, sequence of events and characters. Identify purpose of the text.

Draw together ideas and information from across the whole text. Infer characters' feelings from narrative text.

Identify main ideas and characters in the story. Interpret paraphrased sentence at paragraph-level text.

Find information in the short text. Link paraphrased information within a single paragraph.

Locate and match adjacent words in text at word and phrase level.

Figure 2.4 *Interpreting a Learning Readiness Report*

During PLT discussions, teachers use these developmental progressions to assist in the selection of appropriate learning goals for students. If the teacher sets goals below the student's ZPD, the student will not be challenged by the tasks. If the teacher sets goals above the student's ZPD, the student may become frustrated or demoralised. Learning goals are most effective when they are designed to address those skills that the student is on the verge of learning – at the point where they are ready to learn.

In addition to the more formal assessments, teachers can use their own observations, student work samples and other forms of assessment to place students on developmental progressions. The key is to find evidence of the skills that the student will need scaffolding to perform correctly. When attempting to target their teaching, teachers can ask which skills the student is on the verge of learning and which skills they are using but confusing. The answers to these questions often denote the skill level of the student – the ZPD.

Knowing which skills a student can routinely use correctly (the ZAD) gives some information about their level, but is not enough data for teachers to target their teaching where it has the potential to have the most impact. The ZAD is used as a basis for scaffolding. Collecting evidence of what students do, say, make or write, and interpreting it to find the ZPD, are essential skills for teachers to develop if they want to teach their students at the point at which they are most ready to learn.

Reflective question

Consider the evidence of student learning that you might be asked to use in your teaching practice. How effectively would this evidence allow you to determine the ZPD of a student?

Apply to practice

We suggest that teachers and students, ideally within a PLT or tutorial group, look for evidence of a student's developing skills to locate the ZPD and plan teaching interventions to help the student make progress. To help with this process, it is necessary to understand the typical path students take in their learning. That is, we need to know not only what they can do, but what skill they are ready to learn. The Assessment Research Centre (ARC) has studied these developmental pathways and constructed derived progressions in problem-solving, reading comprehension and numeracy (Appendices 2.1–2.4). The following exercise provides you with the opportunity to practise using classroom evidence to locate a student's ZPD on one of the ARC's derived progressions.

Task

1 Based on Appendices 2.1–2.4, select one of the progressions listed below:
   • problem-solving development
   • reading development
   • numeracy ('nutshell' statements and expanded progressions).
2 Select three samples of work from different students completing the same task in the learning area covered by the chosen progression. In selecting the pieces of work, you should choose samples that are considered to exhibit high, medium and low degrees of accomplishment.

3 Compare the work samples and analyse the elements or skills evident in each of them. Pay particular attention to distinguishing differing levels of complexity or sophistication in the samples.

4 Identify the skills that each student has demonstrated consistently. These represent the student's ZAD. Based on the skills demonstrated in the work samples, locate each student's ZAD on the selected progression.

5 Re-examine each of the work samples. This time, focus on identifying each student's emerging skills to determine their ZPD. This can be found by looking for the skills the student is getting right about half the time – the 50:50 point. Based on the skills demonstrated in the work samples, locate each student's ZPD, or point of readiness to learn on the selected progression.

6 Write a brief summary of the process prompted by the numbered instructions and questions below. The summary should include consideration of the following:

- the progression selected
- the skills evident in each of the three work samples
- how the skills in evidence have been used to locate each student's ZPD on the chosen progression
- the suitability of the evidence used for locating each student on the progression.

7 After choosing a progression and considering the selected work samples, separately list the observable actual skills for each student.

8 Using the evidence, state the ZAD for each of the three students, giving reasons for your choices.

9 After considering the selected work samples, separately list the observable emerging skills for each student.

10 Using the evidence, state the ZPD for each of the three students, giving reasons for your choices.

11 Review the suitability of the evidence used to determine the ZPD for each student. Does the need for observable evidence of skills affect the types of evidence (work samples) that might be used to locate a student's ZPD?

12 What questions has this process raised?

Check your progress

Below is a set of rubrics to help you reflect on your answers to the Apply to Practice task and assess your understanding of this chapter. These can be used to help scaffold learning.

2.1 When considering student skills, you:

    a identified skills from the work samples

    b analysed the difference between the skills in the work samples

    c evaluated the validity of the selected work samples to demonstrate skills at varying levels of complexity.

2.2 When considering the ZAD, you:

    a located the students on the related learning progression

    b explained the placement of the students on the progression in terms of their ZAD

    c evaluated the PLT's use of the evidence to place the students on the progression in terms of their ZAD.

2.3 When considering the ZPD, you:

    a located the students on the related learning progression

    b explained the placement of the students on the progression in terms of their ZPDs, including what the student is most ready to learn – that is, where intervention for the student will have the most impact

    c evaluated the PLT's use of the evidence to place the students on the progression in terms of their ZPDs, including what the student is most ready to learn – that is, where intervention for the student will have the most impact.

2.4 When considering the suitability of the evidence (work samples), you:

    a identified whether the evidence was suitable for the purpose of locating student ZPD

    b evaluated, using examples, the suitability of the evidence for the purpose of locating student ZPD

    c generated a hypothesis, based on the examples, about the ways in which you might ensure that the future selection of evidence is suitable for the identification of student ZPD.

Appendix 2.1: Progression of problem-solving development – nutshell statements

Level I	Develop multiple strategies connecting abstract representations of objects and situations.
Level H	Generalise rules and/or re-evaluate possible strategies in light of information provided.
Level G	Draw on variety of skills to develop strategies required to solve complex problems.
Level F	Identify complex logical relationships in a problem. Develop non-routine problem-solving strategies.
Level E	Select appropriate multi-step strategy to solve problems. Translate problem into a rule.
Level D	Apply a range of up to two-step strategies to solve problems.
Level C	Apply one-step strategies to solve problems in less familiar contexts.
Level B	Use one-step strategies to solve problems.
Level A	Follow instructions to solve problems in familiar contexts.

Appendix 2.2: Progression of reading development – nutshell statements

Level L	Recognise methods used by author to influence and persuade the reader.
Level K	Interpret underlying themes, causes and points of view in the text. Interpret ambiguous text in view of social context.
Level J	Identify fine nuances in text with unfamiliar context or styles.
Level I	Interpret text by linking information presented with relevant external knowledge. Use knowledge of text structure to evaluate the relevance of the information presented.

Level H	Infer author's perspective from what is written and what is implied. Identify how different texts are structured.
Level G	Infer characters' motive from descriptions of behaviour and actions. Interpret how word meaning changes when used in different contexts.
Level F	Combine separate pieces of data to infer the text's meaning. Identify and summarise evidence from the text to support your hypothesis.
Level E	Make predictions based on understanding of ideas, sequence of events and characters. Identify purpose of the text.
Level D	Draw together ideas and information from across the whole text. Infer characters' feelings from narrative text.
Level C	Identify main ideas and characters in the story. Interpret paraphrased sentence and paragraph-level text.
Level B	Find information in the short text. Link paraphrased information within a single paragraph.
Level A	Locate and match adjacent words in text at word and phrase level.

Appendix 2.3: Progression of numeracy development – nutshell statements

Level L	Use factorisation to simplify quadratic equations. Find function domain and intercept with the axes, minimum/maximum and turning point. Use logarithmic and exponential functions.
Level K	Use Pythagoras in 3D application. Calculate probability of multiple events.
Level J	Interpret trends in charts and data. Apply algebra to solve measurement problems.
Level I	Solve linear equations. Apply angle facts for triangle. Calculate using rational and real numbers.
Level H	Analyse problem and apply strategies to find solution. Calculate area and volume of 3D objects. Equivalent fractions.
Level G	Calculate perimeter and volume, averages, probabilities and equations of a straight line. Convert between fractions and percentages.
Level F	Add and convert fractions. Use scale to calculate distance on maps.

Level E	Identify number patterns and solve simple equations. Use Cartesian plane.
Level D	Add and subtract fractions. Use percentages, congruence, plans and nets.
Level C	Simple money calculations. Convert between standard-length units. Identify unlikely events.
Level B	Recognise place values and common fractions. Read common graph types. Use +, – and x. Use appropriate volume units.
Level A	Add and skip count numbers less than 20. Recognise 2D shapes.

Appendix 2.4: Expanded progression of numeracy development

The expanded version of the numeracy progression consists of separate progressions for number, measurement, chance and data, and geometry. These are presented below.

Expanded progression of numeracy development – number

Level L	Use polynomial identities and properties of exponents to simplify algebraic expressions. Use exponential and logarithmic functions. Find function domain and intercepts with the axes, minimum, maximum and turning point. Calculate with exponential, polynomial, rational, logarithmic and periodic functions.
Level K	Generalise patterns using explicitly and recursively defined functions. Perform arithmetic operations on polynoms. Use factorisation to simplify quadratic equations. Analyse function using different representations. Extend properties of integer exponent to rational exponent.
Level J	Use linear equations and systems of linear equations to represent and solve both maths and real-life problems. Generate tables, graphs, rules, expressions and equations to model real-world situation. Construct a function to model a linear relationship between two quantities. Classify function as linear or non-linear.
Level I	Use algebraic notation to represent and solve quantitative relation between dependent and independent variable. Find rational number as a point on the number line. Calculate using rational and real numbers. Use properties of arithmetic operations to generate equivalent expressions. Compare rational numbers and find prime factors. Calculate with integer exponents.

Level H	Use proportional relationship to solve problem, including discounts, taxes and interest rates. Represent, analyse and generalise different patterns using tables, graphs and symbolic rules. Relate and compare different forms of representation for a relationship. Solve an inequality involving fractions.
Level G	Use properties of equivalent fractions to add and subtract fractions. Compare fractions with different numerators and denominators. Multiply and divide fractions. Understand the concept of unit rate and use ratio reasoning to solve problems. Rates and percentages (find a percentage as a rate over 100). Apply properties of operations to generate equivalent expressions. Estimate and calculate absolute and relative error of rounding.
Level F	Represent fractions on number line. Recognise and generate equivalent fractions (denominator 2, 3, 4, 6, 8). Add and subtract fractions with same denominator. Use decimal notation for fraction (convert between decimals and fractions). Use four operations and their properties to solve word problems involving calculations with distances, money and time.
Level E	Use properties of operations as strategies to multiply and divide. Round numbers using the knowledge of place value. Represent whole number on the number line, find segment length and understand concept of unit segment. Recognise unit fractions in both numerical and geometrical form (express area of a part of a shape as a fraction). Compare fractions with same denominator or numerator. Describe and extend geometric and numeric patterns.
Level D	Add and subtract with whole-digit numbers up to 1000 using knowledge of place value, properties of operations and relationship between addition and subtraction. Represent and solve word problems involving multiplication and division. Recognise fractions $\left(\frac{1}{2}, \frac{1}{3}, \frac{1}{4}, \frac{1}{5}\right)$ as a part of a whole.
Level C	Perform addition and subtraction operations on whole digit numbers with and without trading. Multiply by 10. Knowledge of place value (units, tens and hundreds). Solve one-step addition and subtraction word problems. Find unknown single-digit number in addition or subtraction equation.
Level B	Classify numbers as odd and even. Understand meaning of base 10. Read and write numbers using base-ten numerals. Count within 1000 (skip count by 5, 10 and 100). Addition/subtraction of two-digit numbers without trading. Extend numeric and symbolic patterns.
Level A	Add and skip count numbers less than 20. Match number names with numerals. Recognise numeric patterns (skip count forward 2s, 4s and 5s). Carry out single-digit addition and multiplication as repeated addition.

Expanded progression of numeracy development – measurement

Level L	Distinguish between scalar and vector measure (recognise that to specify velocity or force you need to define both direction and magnitude). Solve problems involving calculation of constant, relative speed and distance. Use units as a way to understand problems and to guide the solution of multi-step problems.
Level K	Use radian measures/calculate arc of a circle. Convert between radians and degrees. Use Pythagoras's theorem and trigonometric ratios (sine, cosine and tangent) to find unknown lengths of sides, unknown angles or the area of right-angled triangles.
Level J	Calculate measures that are derived or composed from other measures, such as density, which is composed of mass and volume. Use appropriate units consistently in formulae.
Level I	Apply angle rules for parallel lines and triangles to determine unknown angle size. Solve real-world and mathematical problems involving finding an unknown side length given the perimeter and area. Find area and perimeter of complex shapes.
Level H	Use multiplication by whole number or fraction to solve scaling problems. Convert measurement units within given measurement system. Report a measurement result as a value that lies within a given interval of measurement error. Make judgements about acceptable or reasonable error in a measurement context.
Level G	Relate measurement of area and volume to the operations of multiplication and addition. Estimate the accuracy of a measurement and report lower and upper bound. Measure and compare different angles in whole-number degrees using a protractor. Recognise that angle measure is additive.
Level F	Apply mental maths and estimation strategies using whole numbers, decimals and fractions when estimating the size of measurable property of an object. Distinguish between linear, area and volume measurement. Measure area and volume by counting unit squares/cubes.
Level E	Estimate the size/length of an object and express the result in appropriate metric units. Convert between standard length units (larger to smaller). Add and subtract times and calculate elapsed time. Recognise area as an attribute of plane figures and understand concepts of area measurement.
Level D	Understand concept of scale and the measurement units. Use number and unit to report result of measurement of directly measurable quantities such as weight, length and time.
Level C	Use ruler to compare objects of different lengths and express the difference in appropriate units. Add length to find perimeter of regular 2D shapes. Measure time intervals in minutes. Solve word problems involving addition and subtraction of time intervals in minutes.

Level B	Use ruler to measure and estimate length. Select appropriate unit (cm, m and km) to report, compare or estimate length. Read digital and analogue time to the nearest minute.
Level A	Count objects in sets and report result associated with the unit – for example, three apples, two pies … Compare and order length of shapes using direct comparison and informal measurements. Tell time in hours and half-hours.

Expanded progression of numeracy development – data and chance

Level L	Analyse scatter plots for outliers and positive or negative association. Interpret the effect of the outliers on measures of centre. Investigate sample population to explain or detect any bias in statistical inferences. Critically analyse statistical reports in media.
Level K	Use relative frequencies and sample size to explain difference between theoretical and experimental probabilities. Use measures of centre and of spread obtained from random samples to draw inferences about two populations.
Level J	Specify sample (event) spaces for single and straightforward compound events. Analyse, interpret and make inferences from data presented in double-column graphs, stem and leaf plots and box plots. Find and interpret relationships among variables in the data.
Level I	Use mean, median, inter-quartile range and range to summarise and describe numerical data. Use box and whiskers plots to interpret and compare distributions. Identify possible causes of variation in the data. Select the most appropriate way to represent, analyse and interpret collected data.
Level H	Use ratios to compare probabilities. Make predictions based on probabilities. Find mean, median, mode and range for data. Formulate research questions that can be answered by collecting data.
Level G	Use invented strategies to list outcomes of compound events – for example, count all possible outcomes instead of using formulae. Compare likelihood of events using numerical representation. Distinguish between categorical, discrete and continuous data and use variety of representations to represent it.
Level F	Interpret and display data using column graphs, line plots, and stem and leaf graphs. Select appropriate graphs for a given data set and its context. Evaluate inferences and predictions based on data. Compare likelihood of chance events.

Level E	List all possible outcomes of familiar events involving chance – for example, tossing a coin or rolling a die. Make predictions and justify conclusion based on collected data. Describe fairness of events in qualitative terms. Understand relationship among tables, graphs and data.
Level D	Order events from least likely to happen to most likely to happen – for example, events arising from social situations. Collect categorical and numerical data and represent results using column graphs (to represent frequencies).
Level C	Distinguish between likely and unlikely events based on day-to-day experience. Make predictions about likelihood of the events – for example, what is possible and what is not. Collect data related to their own activities and represent with appropriate labelling.
Level B	Classify objects according to properties such as shape, colour, size or some other observable property and present results using a tally table.
Level A	Classify objects (up to 10) according to colour, shape or size. Compare number of items in each category and recognise which category has more or fewer items. Read and interpret pictograms where there is 1:1 correspondence.

Expanded progression of numeracy development – geometry

Level L	Use of coordinates and absolute value to find distance between points in the plane. Equation of the line and interpretation of slope as a constant rate of change. Describe geometric shape using equations. Find/visualise solution to set of equations in a form of geometric curve.
Level K	Solve inequalities graphically. Calculate the length of an arc of a circle and area of a corresponding section. Find the area of a trapezium. Use formulae for volume of cylinder, cone and sphere to solve both mathematical and real-life problems. Apply Pythagoras's theorem in both 2D and 3D to determine unknown length. Use trigonometry in both 2D and 3D to determine unknown length.
Level J	Solve simultaneous linear equations graphically and algebraically. Apply Pythagoras's theorem to find distance between two points on the plane. Describe the 2D figures that result from slicing 3D figures.
Level I	Name and classify different polygons. Use formulases for the area and circumference of a circle. Solve problems involving scale drawings of geometric figures requiring computing their actual lengths and areas from a scale drawing.

Level H	Identify parts of similar and congruent shapes and use proportional relationship to find missing measures. Identify and use different properties of quadrilaterals. Classify 2D shapes in hierarchical order based on their geometrical properties. Reflect, translate and rotate figures by using appropriate tools and methods.
Level G	Find the area of right-angle triangles, regular triangles, regular quadrilaterals and regular polygons (pentagon, hexagon, octagon ...) by composing into rectangles or decomposing into triangles or other familiar shapes. Identify similar and congruent shapes. Draw rectangles/triangles in the coordinate plane given coordinates for the vertices.
Level F	Apply rotational and line symmetry – for example, flip, slide, reflecting and turn. Recognise and identify right-angle triangle as a special category amongst other triangles. Represent 3D figures using nets made up of rectangles and use the nets to find the surface area of these figures. Draw angles in whole-number degrees using protractor.
Level E	Define and use coordinate system as two perpendicular lines with the intersection at the origin. Use coordinates (ordered pairs of numbers) to locate point in the plane. Recognise and draw all lines of symmetry for 2D figures. Draw angles (right, obtuse, and acute).
Level D	Compare shapes according to their geometric properties (shape, length, angle). Identify and draw points, perpendicular and parallel lines, line segments, rays and angles in 2D figures. Classify and measure angles (right, acute, obtuse).
Level C	Classify different shapes and identify their parts (vertices, edges, angles) and spatial relationship between the parts – for example, sides of the rectangle are parallel and perpendicular. Name basic 3D shapes. Identify their defining properties. Use coordinates to locate an object in a grid and describe its position. Identify pairs of parallel lines.
Level B	Classify shapes by number of corners or sides. Name shapes such as diamonds, ovals, rectangles, pentagons and hexagons. Describe position of an object in the space – for example, top right, bottom left – using grid. Recognise line of symmetry for a 2D shape.
Level A	Name basic shapes – for example, circle, square, rectangle and triangle. Distinguish between defining properties – for example, triangles are closed and three-sided – versus non-defining properties – for example, colour, size, orientation. Draw basic 2D shapes, correctly recording the defining features.

Chapter 3

Conducting assessments

Masa Pavlovic, Nafisa Awwal, Roz Mountain and Danielle Hutchinson

This chapter provides an introduction to the administration of assessments that can be used for teaching. It emphasises that assessment in this context demands a clear understanding of its purposes as the identification of a level of readiness to learn in all students, and examines the use of this to make teaching decisions about appropriate interventions. The chapter expands on some of the ideas about the use of 'skills not scores' discussed in Chapter 1 – ideas that contrast assessment for teaching with summative testing. It provides practical examples of how to maximise each student's opportunities to demonstrate their skills and knowledge, and discusses online assessment.

Learning objectives

In this chapter you will learn to:

- conduct assessments while controlling potential sources of inaccuracy
- target assessments to maximise their usefulness
- recognise the advantages of online assessment, looking at a specific example
- further your understanding of the need to confirm assessment results with other sources of evidence.

Introduction

The focus of this chapter is on issues related to the administration of assessments and the interpretation of data to achieve the goal of supporting the planning of targeted teaching strategies for immediate implementation in the classroom. It builds on ideas about the subject of developmental learning introduced in Chapter 2. Teachers need to know about the administration and interpretation of assessments if they are to use data to inform teaching. This chapter provides a foundation for teachers to build knowledge, experience and judgement in administering and interpreting assessments, and linking them to teaching in the classroom through collaborative work in a teacher team. The collaborative teacher team cycle, or professional learning team (PLT) cycle described in Chapter 4 shows where this work fits within a broader process. The use of assessment as it is presented in this chapter provides a springboard for targeting teaching interventions to the right level on the progression for all students. In addition, there is discussion of how teachers can go about examining critically the progress their students have made over time, so this information can be used to evaluate the success of their teaching strategies in the classroom.

The 2011 Organization for Economic Co-operation and Development (OECD) review of evaluation and assessment in Australia (Santiago et al. 2011) concluded that while overall assessment and evaluation were well conceptualised at systemic and national levels, there was no clear agenda or framework on how assessment should be used to inform classroom practices and improve student learning outcomes.

Classroom assessment

Classroom assessment has two forms: summative and formative. Summative assessment represents an end-point of instruction, and provides the teacher with information on students' past learning. Typically, summative assessment results are provided as scores, so have reduced direct value to teachers for instructional planning because scores do not include information on the specific skills demonstrated by students. This is an important distinction, as it highlights that scoring – which is really only a type of coding system – has (like all codes) little or no meaning until it is decoded. At best, summative assessments may provide teachers with a checklist of desired outcomes or serve as a means of comparing students with each other, or against some other normative group. However, summative assessments often have a purpose in the context of project-, program- or policy-based information. They do not necessarily help teachers, because they are an after-the-fact report, but policy-makers, school principals, subject coordinators and those in decision-making roles will use summative assessment data to change programs, policies, and perhaps even research and resource information. These assessments are important, and have a great deal of utility when the assessment data is aggregated at class, school, system or even national levels. A characteristic of summative assessment data is that they inform decisions related to programs or large groups of students. Summative assessment occurs at a specific point in time, and treats assessment as an event rather than a process.

Formative assessment provides feedback during the process of learning so that action can be taken to improve teacher and student performance. It is continuous, and requires that the score is decoded to interpret the underlying skill. When formative assessment is conducted in a developmental framework, the skill description provides a basis for scaffolding learning. Apart from the requirement that it must be qualitative, formative assessment is distinguished by the purpose for which the assessment results are used, rather than by the format of the assessment. Any assessment that provides meaningful information for the improvement of teaching during the course of learning can be used formatively. In a restaurant, when the cook tastes the soup, the assessment is formative. When the customer tastes the soup, the assessment is summative.

The teacher's role is one of monitoring and supporting student growth. When assessment data are interpreted via a criterion-referenced framework or developmental progression, the emphasis is on skills, not scores. The skills or knowledge of the person being assessed are explicitly stated. Not only does the teacher know the current skill level, they can also see which skills are typically developed next, providing rich information that can be used for decision-making. This information is much easier for teachers to use than raw scores or normative interpretations. Such data interpretation is also useful for informing resourcing and policy decisions. Because the data are expressed as skills, not scores, their meaning is clearer and the decisions can be targeted more effectively.

Developmental assessment

Developmental assessment is a way of interpreting assessment data. It is not a set of assessment instruments, but rather a way of using data that instruments yield. It assumes that people grow in ability, sophistication, knowledge and understanding because of opportunities to learn, and that assessment can be used to track their growth. In this book, when using the term 'developmental' in connection with assessment, we are not referring to a cognitive, Piagetian style of development but to the accumulation of skills, knowledge and attitudes that accrue as a result of exposure to new ideas, new procedures and new opportunities to learn. Adopting a developmental approach to assessment enables an interpretation in terms of the progressive accumulation of knowledge, skills and attitudes from simple to complex, easy to difficult and so on. It assumes that we can interpret this growth or accumulation by observing the changes in indicative behaviours linked to assessment task completion, and that people can be ordered in terms of their capacity to respond to increasingly difficult or demanding tasks. It also assumes that the assessment of a person's ability or growth is independent of the set of tasks used. This is one of the most crucial aspects of the approach. For this assumption to hold, the personal attribute assessed (the construct) must be measurable by different sets of assessment tasks, which independently yield the same conclusion or inference about the person's development. For example, regardless of which test of reading comprehension is used, the same conclusion about a student's level of reading comprehension should be reached. This is a property called 'specific objectivity of assessment'.

Capturing an accurate representation of student knowledge and skills

As discussed in Chapter 2, the theories of Glaser, Rasch and Vygotsky can be combined to form a developmental model of learning, which offers an alternative to the deficit model. If teachers are to adopt a developmental model and use assessment to inform their teaching, it becomes important that students are given the opportunity to demonstrate their knowledge and skills to the best of their ability. This shifts the aim of assessment towards an ongoing process of learning and away from a snapshot of the spread of student performance at a particular point in time under a particular set of circumstances. This snapshot approach to assessment administration is typically used if the purpose of the assessment is norm-referencing (for example, matriculation frameworks, such as the Australian Tertiary Admission Rank, or ATAR) or if the intention is to sample the student population at a point in time (e.g. international testing programs, such as the Program for International Student Assessment, or PISA). In these circumstances, the assessment procedure has a specific intended and summative purpose. The results of these assessments are not used to inform teaching, and so do not need to provide timely information about what a student is ready to learn. They are mostly used to inform policy and to make predictive decisions about students' probable learning in new contexts and new programs. For these purposes, it is reasonable that students be tested at the same time and under the same circumstances. However, even matriculation examination structures recognise that when a student is extremely unwell, has experienced a serious misadventure or has some other impairment, there is a need to make reasonable adjustments so that the student has the opportunity to truly demonstrate the knowledge and skills they possess.

As the purpose of developmental assessment is to determine a student's zone of proximal development (ZPD) and to serve as a frame of reference for teachers to set learning goals, some accommodations are not only possible, but desirable. This is because when accommodations are made the risk of collecting inaccurate information about student ZPD is reduced. For example, if student understanding of the influence of immigration on culture is assessed via an essay, a person with highly developed essay-writing skills might achieve a higher score than a person with the same understanding but less skill in essay writing. If people with the same understanding receive very different scores, the usefulness of this assessment in determining the level of understanding of the influence of immigration on culture is limited. A similar problem arises when the reading demands of an assessment interfere with comprehension of the task, and when an assessment is undertaken under extreme time restrictions.

However, it is also important that accommodations do not inadvertently alter the nature of the main idea or construct being measured. For example, if a student were given the opportunity to present their knowledge orally rather than in written form in order to eliminate potential measurement error related to writing difficulties, it would be important that the student were not marked on their presentation abilities. Doing this would introduce a different construct – namely presentation skills – which might distract from the original purpose of the assessment task, which is to collect information about the student's understanding of the influence of immigration on culture.

This type of situation is said to have a 'prejudicial effect' on the assessor. That is, one set of conditions – such as the quality of the student's presentation skills – distracts the marker from their task of collecting and interpreting data about the student's understanding of the subject of the assessment. This is similar to the 'halo effect' (Thorndike 1920) of positive bias, with which teachers are very familiar. Just as teachers must remain mindful about letting their negative or positive perceptions of a particular student interfere in their assessment of that student's performance, so too they must be sure that accommodations or adjustments to an assessment do not inadvertently generate invalid or unreliable data about student performance.

The factors that contribute to the collection of inaccurate data, or the making of inaccurate inferences, are collectively referred to as 'noise'. The ability of teachers to understand and reduce noise becomes critical in their use of evidence-based teaching practices. Without it, teaching practices will be less effective. A detailed analysis of the ways in which task construction can minimise the potential for noise is provided in Chapter 10. The factors that contribute to assessor-related noise, such as bias and consistency, are addressed in Chapters 7 and 10. The ways in which teachers can account for and minimise noise while conducting assessments are considered here.

Controlling sources of noise

Knowledge of correct classroom practices and issues connected with assessment administration can improve the validity of inferences and interpretations made from assessment results. Some of these issues and recommended practices are summarised below.

Procedures

It is important to provide clear instructions to students, not only on the required format of their responses – including precisely how and where to record them – but also on how they can make corrections if they need to do so. In the case of paper and pencil assessments, students need to know if and when they are expected to provide an open-ended answer, a single selection (for multiple-choice items), a performance or a portfolio. For all types of assessment, students need to know the expected time limits, if applicable, and whether time is taken into account in assessing the quality of the student work. Specifically, for computer-based assessments, it is important to allow students enough time to familiarise themselves with the delivery system and to ensure that there are no technical glitches affecting the delivery. Also, accommodations for students with additional needs should be made to ensure that all students have the opportunity to demonstrate the skills being assessed. For example, students with motor impairment may need special assistance to record their answers, whether in paper and pencil or computer-based assessments, while students with visual impairment may need assistance in the form of larger print, a magnifying glass or a Braille version of the test. Alternatively, students may need assistance in reading and recording responses.

The administrator/teacher

All assessments should set out the responsibilities of the teacher to ensure that distractions, such as noise and movement, are kept to a minimum. The word 'standardised' applies only to the way in which an assessment is administered. This applies to any form of assessment, and in the case of computer-based assessment, administrators have an additional responsibility to provide help with any technical problems, such as internet connection or speed issues. It is also important that teachers are able to recognise when an assessment should be postponed or discontinued. This is particularly important when the circumstances will affect confidence in the accuracy of the test result, or if there is a risk of distress to students. For example, if teachers are conducting online assessments and there are repeated internet dropouts, they may ensure a more accurate result by postponing the test until the technical issue can be resolved.

Context

The scope of the assessment needs to agree with the purpose for which the test is to be used. For example, to evaluate student mastery of a specific topic or the last lesson taught, one would not use an assessment that covers the content for a whole year. Another example is the use of timed tests for classroom assessment, as they tend to measure test-taking speed and possible test-taking practices in addition to student knowledge and skills, therefore confounding the interpretation of test results. Also, if an assessment is conducted in severe conditions – too hot, cold, noisy, crowded or messy – or with incorrect equipment, insufficient space or poorly produced assessment materials, this can interfere with student performance.

Student characteristics and disposition

Students have individual characteristics, such as motivation, health, stress levels and fatigue, that affect their performance on any assessment task. While it is often difficult to adjust for these factors in high-stakes assessments, in the classroom it can be possible for the teacher to take them into account when making inferences from results. Also, teachers have the opportunity to confirm results through examining other forms of evidence, or designing their own assessment tasks to gather further evidence. Clear information about the purpose of an assessment and intended use of the results may reduce the stress associated with test-taking. This will assist students by providing a context in which they can interpret their results and make use of the feedback that will be generated from their participation. In addition, testing at the end of the day should be avoided, as students are often tired at that time, or impatient to go home. Students can also be less alert immediately after lunch or intense physical exercise. Teachers might also consider exercising flexibility to postpone a test if a student is unwell or stressed.

No matter how good the assessment, it is not always possible to fully engage the student to such an extent that they provide their very best performance. Sometimes students will perform at a maximum level when baseline assessments are undertaken at the beginning of the year and under-perform later in the year. Sometimes they will be totally disengaged from the assessment exercise. In general, teachers can help students perform at their highest level of capability, but it is difficult for a teacher to overcome the effect on a student who is feeling unwell, who comes from a home where breakfast is not available, whose language is not English, whose family is dysfunctional and distressing to the student, and so on. To some extent, these issues can be overcome by the culture of the classroom and the school, but not completely. So an assessment result must be considered as a measure at one point in time, which can often be influenced by these factors that operate in the background of the student performance.

The assessment task or test

The assessment task should be presented in a format that is familiar to students. Tasks and all associated information should be presented clearly and comprehensively. Computer-based assessments need to be designed to make it easy for students not to miss information required for the successful completion of the task. Size and resolution of the screen and layout of information all need to be taken into account.

Factors such as these contribute to measurement 'noise' because they interfere with the accuracy of the information that teachers are trying to collect or interpret. As teachers become more aware of the risk of such variation, they increasingly view individual test results as just one piece of the evidence puzzle. This growing understanding of the need to combine test results with other evidence collected over time facilitates the use of practices that allow teachers to make valid inferences about both student ZPD and the best teaching strategies. If the purpose of the assessment is to identify the students' ZPD, then it makes sense to administer the assessment when most or all of these factors can be controlled or eliminated.

Reflective questions

- How many forms or sources of evidence can you think of that would be useful for confirming an assessment result? See how your list compares with those of your colleagues or fellow students.

- Which of the factors listed above do you see as the most problematic, in your experience, in terms of the way in which it might affect interpretation of test results?

Online assessment

Increasingly, assessments are being delivered in an online environment. These computer-based assessments are rapidly replacing old-fashioned paper and pencil methods. One advantage of online testing is that it delivers instant responses and analysis of results to teachers and students, so that immediate information is available for intervention purposes. Such an approach to test administration controls many factors that introduce error into measurements. Online platforms for the delivery of assessments provide new and novel opportunities to gather data other than right/wrong coding procedures. Also, in the context of assessment for teaching, there are many advantages for teachers in the use of computer-based assessment delivered online. Computer-based assessments are engaging for students, and online assessments can be designed to match students' ability levels. In addition, teachers in an online testing environment often have access to test results in time to inform their teaching and monitor the progress of their students over time. Some online tests are also continually reviewed and updated, thus minimising practice effects and the possibility of teaching to the test.

The ARCOTS tests

A good example of an online assessment system is the Assessment Research Centre Online Testing System (ARCOTS). It is the system used in the research that underpins the approach recommended in this book. The ARCOTS assessment instruments consist of a series of reading comprehension, numeracy and problem-solving tests, delivered online together with an integrated reporting system. The tests are designed to locate students' ZPD on the developmental progressions provided in Chapter 2. They were developed using item response modelling. For a detailed explanation of the way in which item response theory was used to develop the tests, refer to Appendix A. For information on how item response modelling can be adapted for classroom use, refer to Chapters 9 and 10.

The ARCOTS assessments are interactive, and responses are recorded, scored and reported at individual and class levels in real time. The use of such a system allows teachers to get same-day feedback about the point of readiness to learn, or ZPD, of each of their students. A sample version of ARCOTS is provided on a website that can be accessed at www.cambridge.edu.au/academic/arcots.

The ARCOTS reports

Reports generated by ARCOTS are presented to maximise their use within a developmental model of learning. Examples of the various types of reports available are presented in Chapters 2, 10 and 11. The first is a learning readiness report; the second is a student profile report; and the third is a class profile report. You will notice that none of these reports highlights a score or a grade. Each of them focuses on the skill level at which the student is ready to learn.

Like all individual pieces of assessment, these reports should be considered as a starting point, or within the context of other available evidence. Doing this will increase the accuracy of the inferences you draw from them by ensuring one-off performances do not usurp a broader understanding of each student's learning. These reports are discussed in detail in Chapters 10 and 11.

Test targeting

To get the most accurate test results and indicators of student improvement over time, the selection of the correct test for each student is important. This is called targeting the test. Tests designed from a developmental framework provide maximum information at one level on a developmental progression. If a student receives a result that is either too high or too low, the usefulness of the result will be limited. For example, if the student answers 100 per cent of the questions correctly, the test result is of little use, as it indicates only the skills that the student has already developed. It does not provide an indication of the point at which new skills are beginning to emerge. Similarly, if the student answers none of the questions correctly, the teacher again has no information about the student's ZPD. In this case, they also have no information about the skills that the student is capable of demonstrating.

As discussed in Chapter 2, the developmental model of learning advocates the use of the 50:50 point to identify student ZPD. The ideal test will enable a student to answer approximately 50 per cent of questions correctly. This is sometimes difficult for teachers and students to understand and tolerate. Even so, badly targeted testing is a major source of assessment error. More information about constructing targeted in-class tasks is provided in Chapter 9.

Some online assessment systems are adaptive, which means that the ability level of students is determined during the course of the assessment and the test is adapted accordingly. ARCOTS, for example, provides extra questions during a test if a student is performing above or below the expected level. This can be an attractive option, particularly for teachers who are new to online testing. There is a danger, however, that the use of adaptive tests will discourage teachers from using classroom evidence and observations to estimate student ability and select the most appropriate test for the student. While it can initially involve more work, targeted assessment is often ultimately more informative for the teacher than computer adaptive testing. More detail on how to target testing within ARCOTS is provided in Appendix A, and more information on evaluating the effectiveness of teaching practices across a range of student abilities is provided in Chapter 11.

Summary

When teachers use a developmental model to improve student learning, it is important that their assessments give an accurate picture of the level at which their students are operating. When conducting assessments, it is therefore crucial that they remain mindful of factors that may distort the data collection and interpretation process, collectively referred to as 'noise'. Teachers must actively plan to minimise noise – particularly if they are using assessments to plan teaching. Data that are contaminated by noise will be significantly less useful for planning, as they may not be an accurate representation of a student's capacity. In being prepared for this, teachers will become increasingly adept at using multiple sources of evidence to verify the veracity of assessment results and the quality of inferences drawn about student learning. One increasingly popular source of evidence is online testing, which can provide timely and accurate information on student progress. An example of an online assessment program is ARCOTS, which produces both individual and class reports that provide teachers with timely and accurate information about student ZPD. This information can then be used as part of the evidence base against which teaching can be planned.

Apply to practice

1 Consider three assessments that you have seen or used. Describe how the assessment was or could have been used in a formative way. What impact does, or would, using assessment in this way have on your practice?

2 Consider the ways in which you conduct, or have been taught to conduct, assessments. Describe the kinds of factors that contribute to 'noise' in your environment. What strategies do you use, or could you use, to minimise this noise?

3 Consider ways in which you have seen results presented. What information did they provide about student learning? How useful would they have been in a learning environment that was using a developmental model of learning?

Check your progress

Below is a set of rubrics to help you reflect on your answers to the Apply to Practice questions and assess your understanding of this chapter. These can be used to help scaffold learning.

3.1 Your description of the use of three assessments:

    a identified why they were formative

    b explained how they could be used formatively

    c identified how the formative use of the assessments could change classroom practice.

3.2 When identifying strategies to minimise noise, you:

    a considered strategies in isolation

    b considered strategies in relation to one another

    c synthesised the strategies to make generalisations that can inform school policy or protocols for assessment.

3.3 When considering the ways in which results have been represented, you:

    a considered whether they were scores or skills

    b considered the type of information that was interpretable from the results

    c evaluated the interpretable information against the developmental model of learning to determine the usefulness of the results.

Chapter 4

Team-based interpretation

Michael Francis, Pam Robertson and Danielle Hutchinson

This chapter explores how teachers can work together in teams to discuss and interpret assessment data. The ways in which professional learning teams operate are discussed in detail, and the importance of lobbying for support and the allocation of resources within the school is addressed. The chapter examines the way in which learning goals are achieved through intervention based on the use of assessment data. Its purpose is to lead teachers to work with their PLT colleagues to set goals on developmental scales of student skill and understanding.

Learning objectives

In this chapter you will learn to:

- recognise the role of a PLT in improving both teaching and student learning outcomes
- understand the formation and operation of the PLT within an over-arching conceptual framework
- appreciate the use of the PLT cycle to inform the work of the PLT
- identify the factors that underpin the operation of the PLT
- use a PLT log to facilitate PLT planning, systematically record and reflect on decisions, and build a database of effective intervention strategies
- grasp how the PLT can support an evidence-based, properly resourced decision-making culture
- understand the way in which the PLT can identify its own ZPD and plan for its own development.

Introduction

A professional learning team (PLT) helps teachers to interpret assessment data, and hence to maximise student learning outcomes. In the ongoing Assessment and Learning Partnerships (ALP) project (see the Introduction), the greatest learning gains are being made in those schools where teaching strategies are shared and discussed by teams of teachers who challenge each other to provide evidence of the effectiveness of their teaching practices. These teams focus on data that indicate student abilities and skills. They function as collegial groups, apply best practice based on research, develop teamwork and collaboration skills, and accept joint responsibility for all students' learning.

As you are reading this chapter, you may be thinking about forming, joining or improving a PLT. What follows is advice shaped by research regarding best practice. Understanding this practice is as essential to a teacher who has never been a member of a PLT as it is to one already working in a PLT. High-functioning PLT do not just happen from inception. They *become* high functioning. For a PLT to become high functioning requires time and clarity – clarity about the purpose of the PLT, the role of the teacher, the processes to be followed, the actions to be taken and the support required.

The high-functioning PLT requires a conceptual framework and structure. It recognises why this is necessary – not just in terms of ordering PLT work, but also in terms of PLT sustainability, including the induction of new members. In this chapter, we provide a framework to help you build a PLT – one in which teachers learn to work collaboratively to discuss and interpret assessment data from reports of student

performance in skills-based testing. We also look at how to use the PLT cycle introduced in Chapter 1, which sits within this framework and is designed to support PLT
effectiveness.

A successful PLT uses a conceptual framework that sets out the steps to be taken
by the team and describes the relationship between those steps and the team's goals.
If followed, the framework provided by the five steps from measurement to policy
(Figure 4.1) will give new and existing PLT members a clear sense of direction and
purpose.

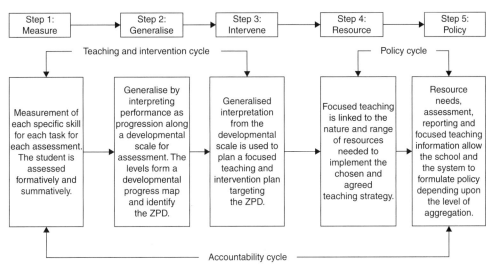

Figure 4.1 *Five steps from measurement to policy*
Source: Adapted from Griffin (2007).

Step 1 asks teachers to use evidence to assess student performance formatively
and to be able to justify their conclusions to the PLT. Step 2 asks PLT members to
generalise student performance as a skill level on a developmental progression, thus
identifying what the student can already do and what they are ready to learn. Step 3
requires the PLT members to collaboratively plan teaching interventions according
to student ZPD as indicated by the identified level on the relevant progression. Step 4
has the PLT identify the resources required to implement the targeted teaching plan.
Step 5 requires the PLT to evaluate evidence of the effectiveness of the teaching intervention to inform future action and to frame policy. When these steps are followed,
the effectiveness of the PLT is built in at every stage.

If some of the five steps in the framework are omitted, a PLT's work can be
undone. Consider, for example, the common practice of teachers moving directly
from assessment to teaching, skipping Step 2, in which student performance is
generalised as a skill level on a developmental progression. When this happens,
rather than spending time targeting teaching in terms of what the student is ready

to learn, the focus shifts back to the test, and to an apparent need to teach to the test. PLT that adhere to the framework avoid this error. There will, of course, be times when a PLT draws on existing resources and policy to implement the targeted teaching plan, so a cycle involving Steps 1 to 3 can be implemented successfully. It is a loop that allows for baseline assessment, interpretation of student development and targeted teaching, and it can be repeated regularly. But there are no other short-cuts that can be taken without compromising the five-step framework. Another common sequence that is avoided by an effective PLT occurs when school or system policy is made on the run, unsupported by evidence. When policy decisions about resource provision are made without the exercise of each of the preceding steps, then resources can be wasted and student improvement can suffer. This can create situations in which resource allocation is driven by political motives rather than need.

Chapters 2 and 3, which covered Steps 1 and 2 of the five-step framework, examined developmental teaching and assessment: how to administer assessments in order to determine a student's level on a selected developmental progression. These steps are prerequisites for the effective operation of a PLT. We now look at how the PLT makes use of the information they provide.

Collective planning of teaching interventions

When student performance is interpreted as a level on a developmental progression, teaching shifts to decisions about how the student can best learn at their current level of proficiency, or within their ZPD. This step involves decisions about which intervention strategy is best for the student, given their level of development. The PLT takes collective responsibility for this, determining the intervention for each developmental level, with the classroom teacher implementing the intervention. Griffin and Care (2009) found that taking collective responsibility in a PLT for the planning of targeted interventions enhanced teacher effectiveness. This is because working in a team within a framework, and following an implementation process, allow for the development of synergies. These include:

- pooling of expertise of a group of teachers who collectively possess a wide range of experience and knowledge
- analysis and evaluation of a range of teaching strategies, student activities and resources that can be used (and subsequent evaluation of their effectiveness)
- generalising of teaching intervention strategies targeted to groupings of students at the same level across different classes, where appropriate.

The PLT meeting and cycle

If teachers meet in a PLT to consider the progress of their students on a particular progression (see Chapter 2 appendices), each teacher should bring learning readiness reports and other evidence of learning for three of their students working at different levels on the progression. One teacher's selection of students should then be chosen for discussion. One of the selected students should be developing at a low level on the progression, a second should be at a middle level and a third should be at a higher level. As a group, the teachers share their expertise to work on learning and intervention plans for those students. They then discuss the generalisation of this plan in relation to other students in their classes who are working at the same levels, with minor adjustments made for individual student learning needs and styles. As part of this process, the PLT focuses on how classes may best be organised to address the needs of different ZPD groups. At the next meeting of the PLT, members work on learning programs for students from another teacher, and discuss the effectiveness of intervention strategies identified at the earlier meeting, and so on. At subsequent meetings, the PLT gradually cycles through students at different developmental levels. By following this process, the PLT progressively builds into its practice differential and targeted teaching interventions for the four or five groups of students at different developmental levels that typically appear in any class.

To maximise PLT effectiveness, meetings of the PLT need to have structure. Each meeting of the team should be organised by an agenda that leads team discussion through a planning, implementation and evidence cycle. This cycle includes the examination of student reports, the setting of objectives for student learning, the planning of a learning program targeted to the student's current level of learning, the implementation and review of the learning program, and the use of resources.

Five questions are central to guiding PLT discussion and prompting work at each stage. These are presented here as a guide for PLT discussion:

1 What is the student ready to learn, and what is the evidence for this in terms of what the student can do, say, make or write?

2 What are the possible evidence-based interventions and the associated scaffolding processes for each?

3 What is the preferred intervention, and how will it be resourced and implemented?

4 What is the expected impact on learning, and how will this be evaluated?

5 What was the outcome, and how can this be interpreted?

The cycle resulting from these questions is represented diagrammatically in Figure 4.2.

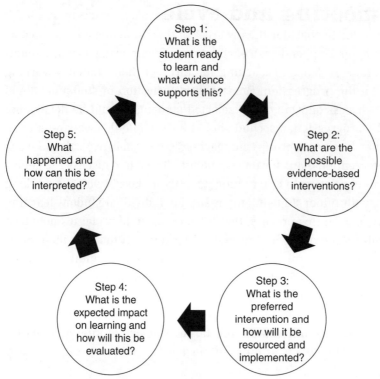

Figure 4.2 *The PLT cycle*

What is the student ready to learn, and what is the evidence for this in terms of what the student can do, say, make or write?

The purpose of reviewing student progress is to identify the student's ZPD. Before the meeting, the teachers nominating students for discussion assemble as much current evidence as possible to identify each student's ZPD. This can include a variety of assessments, from student reports to work samples and behavioural observations. The subsequent discussion should use the language of evidence (what the student does, says, makes and writes) to make inferences about student knowledge. Members of the PLT are encouraged to challenge these inferences by asking about what students can be expected to do, say, make or write at the developmental level being considered. The language of evidence is addressed in more detail later in this chapter.

The evidence presented about a student needs to be evaluated by PLT members asking:

- What can the student do independently?
- What is the student ready to learn?

In determining what the student is ready to learn, the teacher formulates learning intentions for the student. The PLT then considers both long- and short-term targets. Developmental learning progressions are critical in this step, as they can be used to describe the skills and abilities at both the student's current readiness level and the next level. PLT are encouraged to use the learning progressions to make decisions about consolidating a student's skills within a level or moving them to the next level.

What are the possible evidence-based interventions and the associated scaffolding processes for each?

Once student learning goals have been set, it is important for the PLT to work as a team to identify the best approaches to targeted intervention and the associated scaffolding processes. The key questions to ask at this point are:

- What explicit intervention strategies can be identified to help this student attain the learning targets set?
- On what basis are the identified intervention strategies being considered for implementation?

The whole PLT needs to be involved in this discussion. The reason for this is not just that there is a need for the load to be shared or that a higher number of contributors results in the identification of more effective strategies. The deeper reason is the need for PLT members to recognise that responsibility for student learning is shared, that students are 'our students, not mine' and that teachers are accountable to one another.

Intervention strategies should be considered only in the light of their ability to deliver the explicit learning intention identified in Step 1. Evidence of effectiveness needs to be tested by the PLT through a process of challenge. Questions that a PLT might ask of a suggested intervention strategy could include:

- With whom and for what purpose was the strategy used previously?
- What learning outcomes from that teaching intervention suggest that the strategy proposed would support the achievement of the current learning intention?

What is the preferred intervention, and how will it be resourced and implemented?

When the PLT recommends an intervention strategy for a student, it is important that the reasons for its adoption are explained clearly. This introduces peer accountability and a reflection point for the PLT to analyse its own thinking about what did and did not work when subsequently analysing the data on the effectiveness of the intervention strategy adopted.

A benefit of this over time is that the PLT will build up a bank of demonstrably successful strategies for a range of students at each developmental level. These can be drawn upon, reviewed and discussed to create developmentally appropriate learning programs.

A corollary of identifying successful strategies is the identification of relevant resources. In this process, teachers consider what resources are required to support the planned intervention program. Resources can include people (teachers, professional support staff and aides) and professional development programs, as well as time, space, equipment, materials, technology and so on. Some examples of the questions that can be focused on are:

- What resources were successful in the past with students at this level, and what is the evidence for this?
- What new resources and materials are needed?
- Are they available – or will they be? If not, what are the implications for the planned teaching strategies?

The teacher is an important resource that is sometimes overlooked or taken for granted. The PLT should check to see what skills and knowledge the teacher needs in order to implement the identified strategy. For example, the teacher may need:

- opportunities to work in tandem with other teachers
- specific professional development, resources or materials
- support in class
- mentoring from more experienced colleagues
- curriculum materials
- additional information about the student
- specific expertise or experience.

What is the expected impact on learning, and how will this be evaluated?

The PLT must be outcome oriented. Intended student learning outcomes – what the student will do, say, make or write – must be stated clearly. The process of how and when these will be checked must also be explored by the team. A firm date is necessary for the review of student learning outcomes. When this information is made explicit, the work of teachers is better targeted and the PLT is better able to evaluate the effectiveness of the teaching intervention.

What was the outcome, and how can this be interpreted?

At the completion of the teaching intervention, and on the date set aside to review the results, the PLT discusses the evidence of its effectiveness. This evidence is considered in relation to expected impacts. By planning thoroughly from the outset, teachers will be prepared far better for the review meeting.

Questions asked in this session should also include 'What worked?' and 'What did not work?' These questions must cover strategies employed, activities undertaken and resources utilised. What was the impact and what are the implications for future teaching?

The PLT log

The PLT log is the means by which the PLT organises and documents its work. The PLT records in the log each decision it takes in implementing the steps outlined in the PLT cycle. This process provides both the structure of PLT meetings and the documentation against which the team can evaluate the success or otherwise of its actions. The PLT log can be used to scaffold the thinking of the members of the team during each meeting. A further advantage is that the ongoing use of the log and its maintenance, in hardcopy or electronic form, will enable the PLT to build their own evidence base of effective, developmentally targeted teaching strategies.

Templates for two PLT logs appear in Figures 4.3 and 4.4. Figure 4.3 shows a basic log, identifying the key elements that need to be examined and documented. As the team becomes more sophisticated in its understanding of the PLT process and analysis of the data, detail becomes more important. This is reflected in the PLT log template in Figure 4.4 and in the sample of a PLT log for literacy in Figure 4.5, which addresses Level E of the ARCOTS Progression of Reading Development.

The PLT log template shown in Figure 4.4 was developed, trialled and refined by teachers in literacy and numeracy working groups drawn from existing PLT. It was developed to both guide and record planning of teaching interventions at specific levels on a developmental progression. The log should be used for a student who is representative of the students grouped at a developmental level, to plan an intervention that can be targeted to the group. The use of a student representing a level helps the PLT focus on evidence in relation to each step of the process.

The design of the PLT log template reflects the questions that inform the PLT cycle. It assumes that the PLT is working on a developmental progression. It numbers the actions the PLT should take in order. The PLT:

1   identifies the student's ZPD and describes the evidence on which this is based

2   records on the log the specific skill or concept being targeted. This is described as the learning intention(s). Depending on the developmental level being targeted, there may be one or more of these.

3   considers what the student will be able to do, say, make or write to demonstrate that the learning goal has been achieved

4   makes a clear distinction between intervention strategy and learning activity. The emphasis here is on teacher action: what the *teacher* will do, say, make or write to facilitate teaching.

5   considers the nature of the learning activity to ensure that it aligns with the learning intention and selected strategies

Professional learning team log

School/team: .... Date log produced: .... Review date: ....

Name/s:	Developmental progression:	Evidence (do, say, make, write) ARCOTS/SWANS level:	ZPD:
		Other evidence:	

Learning intentions	Teaching strategies	Resources	Evidence to be collected
1.			
2.			
3.			

Figure 4.3 *A basic PLT log template*

PLT Log - Template

Student/Student Group						
Data:						
Developmental Domain:						
Where are the students? **Developmental Level & Nutshell Statement**						
1. Evidence for this level? (What makes you say this?)						

Where do they need to go?		*How will they get there?*			*What is needed to get them there?*	*What worked? What did not work?*
2. Learning Intention/s (Specific skill or concept or part thereof to be learned)	**3. Evidence** (What the students will be able to do, say, make or write).	**4. Teaching strategy** (What the *teacher* says, does, makes or writes)	**5. Learning activity** (Describes what the students are actually going to do)		**6. Resources** (People, place or things used in the activity to realise the learning strategy)	**7. Review & Reflection**
2.1						Review Date: Reflection:
2.2						Review Date: Reflection:
2.3						Review Date: Reflection:

Figure 4.4 *An advanced PLT log template*

PLT Log - Literacy

Student/Student Group			
Data:			
Developmental Domain:	Progression of Reading Development		

Where are the students?
Developmental Level & Nutshell Statement
Level E: Make predictions based on understanding of ideas, sequence of events and characters. Identify purpose of text.

1. Evidence for this level? ARCOTS testing student ZPD was Level E. Analysis of work samples against the progression confirmed this.
(What makes you say this?)

> **Keep it simple!** Order your strategies in terms of how you intend to roll out the lesson.

> Develop this learning intention next.

> *Consider, for example, delivery, student response, task complexity or appropriateness, student engagement, suggested changes, content, resources, etc.*

Where do they need to go?	*How will they get there?*		*What is needed to get them there?*	*What worked? What did not work?*
2. Learning intention/s (Specific skill or concept or part thereof to be learned).	**3. Indicators** (What the students will be able to do, say, make or write).	**4. Teaching Strategy** (What the *teacher* says, does, makes or writes)	**5. Learning Activity** (Describes what the students are actually going to do)	**6. Resources** (People, place or things used in the activity to realise the learning strategy)	**7. Review & Reflection**

Learning intention/s	Indicators	Teaching Strategy	Learning Activity	Resources	Review & Reflection
2.1.1 Students will understand the concept of 'prediction'.	The student will be able to explain what is meant by 'prediction'.	Backwards design process – student reading of complete comic strip sequence. Convergent questioning on final frame: How did we reach this point? What, who, when, why and how? Collation of student responses for subsequent reference	The students will engage with illustrated text in the form of a series of comic strips to explore 'prediction' and identifying the clues that assist in the making of predictions.	Ms Jones Mr Brown Rooms 12 & 13 Three comic strip sequences, one complete, two incomplete	**Review data:** *How long will this teaching sequence take? When will you need to meet to consider the evidence?* **Evidence:** *What evidence indicates student improvement?*
2.1.2 Students will make plausible predictions from an illustrated text about what will happen next.	The student will be able to make, write/illustrate or tell a plausible next instalment of the story.	Prediction – introduce concept using incomplete comic strip sequence Model for students the search for clues in preceding frames on which to make a prediction Use think/pair/share for students to predict what happens.	The activity will involve students looking for clues in a series of comic strip sequences and then deciding what should go in the next 'blank' frame of the sequence.	Data projector Paper copies of incomplete comic strips for each student	**Reflection:** *Was the teaching intervention successful? What is the student's developmental level now? What, if anything, would the PLT do differently? If not, why not? What next?*
2.1.3 Students will be able to recognise and justify the evidence on which their predictions are based.	The student will incorporate ideas, events and/or characters to justify the prediction being made.	Facilitate whole group discussion and consideration of predictions based on clues that can be identified in the illustrated text. Identification of possibility of multiple plausible outcomes – search for best fit based on evidence. Iteration – Repetition of exercise using different types of text emphasising prediction and evidence (clues).	Students will explain their reasons for making their prediction.		
2.2 Students will be able to identify different sorts of clues in a text and make a prediction based on those clues.					**Review Date:** **Reflection:**
2.3 Students will draw on understanding of ideas, sequence of events and characters to identify overall purpose of text.					**Review Date:** **Reflection:**

Figure 4.5 *An advanced PLT log for literacy*

6 identifies resources, asking what support the teacher needs and whether any resources need to be sourced from elsewhere. If materials have been developed, a sample of each should be attached to the log for later reference by the PLT

7 checks whether or not the intervention resulted in improvement in the student's ZPD, reviewing the intervention strategies and their impact. The review is at the heart of the PLT inquiry and learning cycle.

Maximising the usefulness of PLT meeting time

The minimum recommended time for a PLT to meet is one hour every two weeks. This meeting time should be free of all other commitments. Ideally, another hour should be set aside for each teacher to prepare for the meeting. Other commitments need to be surrendered in order to make time for the PLT meeting – it should not be added to an already busy schedule. Experience shows that there is no point in adding a PLT meeting to a teacher's schedule without creating time for it. For this reason, the availability of meeting time becomes a responsibility of the school leadership.

Each teacher should come to the PLT meeting prepared with examples of three student reports, together with work samples. The discussion then remains focused on the PLT tasks and follows an agenda. A lot can be accomplished in a one-hour meeting. The focus on three students at different levels allows teachers to generalise to other students in their class who are working at the same levels, with adjustments made for individual learning styles.

Generalising interventions

Often the same learning targets can be used for students at the same or similar developmental levels. One way to identify groups of students operating at the same level is to use a class report such as the one generated by ARCOTS. This kind of report will be discussed in more detail in Chapter 11.

The example in Figure 4.6 shows how planning within PLT meetings can be applied to groups of students. The figure shows a segment of a class. It identifies four instructional groups. Three groups – separately identifiable within the three grey boxes – contain several students who are performing at the same level. One student – indicated by the oval – does not belong to a group with common learning targets in that class but may be identified by the PLT as part of a group from other classes. When this happens, commonalities within and across classes can be found and synergies can be identified.

Language of evidence

In order to implement the successful elements of a PLT, the team needs to draw on the language of evidence to make inferences about student understanding, knowledge, thinking or feeling. What a student understands, thinks or believes is not directly observable. As teachers, we observe students' overt behaviours or actions – that is,

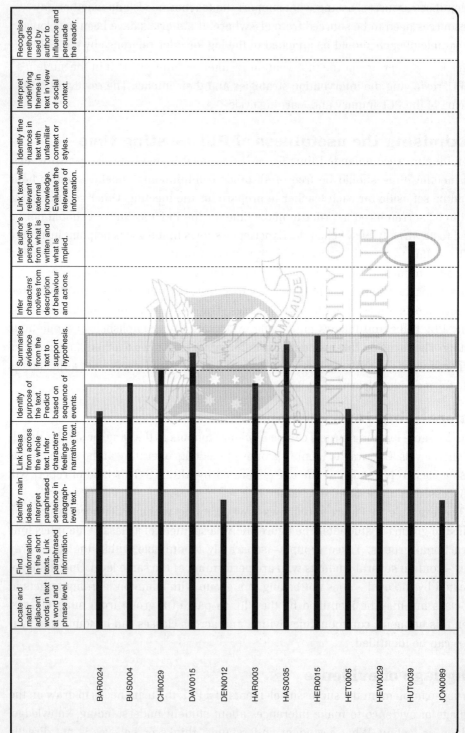

Figure 4.6 *Class report used for grouping students*

what they do, say, make or write. It is from these that we infer student knowledge or skills, and it is these actions that should be the focus of discussions in the PLT.

Examination of each form of evidence should focus on what a student can do and what they are ready to learn. The language is important. It reinforces the developmental framework that underpins learning. Discussions that focus on what the student is *not* able to do only encourage a deficit approach, leading to 'fixing' gaps in students' learning rather than focusing on moving them forward by scaffolding – direct intervention by a teacher or collaboration with a more skilled student.

Language of challenge

Successful PLT need a language of challenge. Team members should support their statements about student learning by providing evidence of the things they have observed the students do, say, make or write. Effective challenge reduces sources of error that may otherwise result in incorrect determination of student ZPD. PLT members should also be encouraged to challenge themselves and each other to ensure that any inferences are based on sound evidence. Some examples of the questions that can be asked to challenge statements are:

- If we implement this strategy with our students, what are we likely to see them do, say, make or write? If this strategy was previously successful with our students, what specific changes did we observe?
- How should any observable change in behaviour be interpreted in terms of learning? Did any previous changes constitute evidence of improved quality of learning?
- Would we recommend the use of this strategy?

It is important to note that the aim is to challenge the evidence rather than to criticise or judge the team member who presents it. The focus is on the student behaviour as evidence of learning. Challenge should never be personal. Attention should also be paid to vocal tone and body language. It is important that all members of the PLT work collaboratively and in support of one another. The PLT leader must be strong enough to act as a facilitator and establish rules of participation. The leader must also help draw out the concerns of all the PLT members. This is achieved through establishing a norm of listening, reflecting and challenging, rather than criticising.

Vocabulary of evidence

Student behaviours or observable evidence (things the student may do, say, make or write) can be organised into layers of increasing proficiency. For example, Bloom's Revised Taxonomy, as discussed in Chapter 2, offers a way in which teachers can frame the discussions in their PLT. In Table 4.1, the use of the words in the right-hand column of the table allows us to describe the student behaviours we observe. This in turn helps us to infer the proficiencies in the left-hand column.

Table 4.1 *PLT vocabulary linked to the Anderson and Krathwohl taxonomy*

Know	**Do**: reads, matches, selects, views, identifies **Say**: names, states, describes **Make**: reproduces **Write**: labels, records, lists, enumerates, defines
Understand	**Do**: converts, describes, estimates, generalises **Say**: cites, discusses, explains, paraphrases, restates (in own words) **Make**: traces, classifies **Write**: gives examples, makes sense out of, summarises
Apply	**Do**: acts, administers, collects, controls, determines, develops, discovers, implements, participates, produces, shows, solves, uses **Say**: articulates, contributes, informs, instructs, predicts, projects, relates, teaches **Make**: charts, constructs, includes, prepares, preserves, provides, transfers **Write**: assesses, computes, establishes, extends, operationalises, reports
Analyse	**Do**: breaks down, correlates, focuses, recognises, separates **Say**: differentiates, discriminates, distinguishes, points out **Make**: illustrates, creates diagrams, subdivides, prioritises **Write**: infers, limits, outlines
Evaluate	**Do**: critiques, defends, interprets **Say**: appraises, concludes, criticises, justifies **Make**: reframes, weighs, draws, judges **Write**: compares, contrasts, decides, supports
Create	**Do**: adapts, anticipates, categorises, collaborates, combines, compiles, compares **Say**: communicates, expresses, contrasts **Make**: creates, composes, designs, devises, facilitates **Write**: formulates, generates, incorporates, individualises, initiates, integrates, intervenes, models, modifies, negotiates, plans, progresses, rearranges, reconstructs, reinforces, reorganises, revises, structures, substitutes, validates

These verbs help PLT focus their discussions on student actions and responses rather than on their own activities. While this sounds simple, when PLT discuss student results, the discussions often turn to opinions about students and to what the teacher has done rather than giving a clear description of student achievement. This shift in language requires the conscious effort of every team member to keep the focus of attention firmly on students, by bearing in mind the impact of all decisions on the observable evidence of learning.

Establishing protocols

Developing and using set protocols when discussing student work provide an effective way to help PLT members develop the language of evidence. Protocols structure the discussion and give all PLT members a chance to talk and a chance to listen. They can focus the attention of the PLT on the task at hand, assist teachers to use language appropriate for the task and ensure that all members engage in the discussion.

Reflective questions

What protocols might be followed by the PLT to support:

- presentation of evidence by the classroom teacher at the PLT meeting
- staying 'on task' during the meeting
- covering the range of developmental levels represented in the classes taught by members of the PLT
- reflecting on the success or otherwise of targeted teaching interventions?

Resourcing the work of the PLT

As discussed, a PLT has one overriding purpose: to maximise student learning and thus to enable all students to realise their potential. The identification and prioritisation of resources by the school play an important role in the achievement of this purpose. Without appropriate resources to support the effective operation of the PLT, and the design and delivery of teaching interventions, outcomes are likely to suffer.

Time spent in PLT meetings should be counted formally as part of a teacher's workload, and it is a powerful form of professional development. Where proper provision is made, the ability of the PLT to deliver intended improvements in student learning is enhanced, as is the sustainability of the PLT itself. Properly resourcing the work requirements of the PLT is the first of many resource decisions that a school must make when establishing PLT. Others relate to the resourcing of teaching strategies and the provision of targeted professional development so teachers can build their knowledge base.

Where resources are scarce, it is inevitable that policy decisions will be compromised. Awareness of this problem is important for PLT leaders, even in schools where the implementation of PLT has been planned carefully. At its most basic level, this problem creates a need for some PLT to lobby for staff support and resource allocation – especially the time needed for the meeting. This requires broadening the PLT conversation, which can be done through regular progress reports at staff meetings and formal reports to school leadership. These reports might indicate progress in terms of the PLT cycle: test reports (evidence); identification of the range of developmental levels in the student cohort; actions taken, including examples of strategies used; resources employed and needed; and outcomes. When this conversation takes place regularly, the need for lobbying recedes and is replaced by an evidence-based decision-making culture.

Characteristics of effective PLT

Most PLT are 'works in progress', and the level of success at which a PLT uses developmental continua to inform teaching and learning plans relies on a number of things. The experiences of PLT across a range of settings suggest that, ideally, they are made up of between four and eight members. This permits the support of a team of colleagues while making sure that everybody in the team has an opportunity to contribute to the discussion. Important characteristics of successful teams are:

- strong, learning-focused leadership supported by committed and engaged school leadership
- the engagement and interest of all team members
- a willingness to collaborate and support each other
- acceptance of shared responsibility for all students, informed by a shift from thinking in terms of 'my class' to 'our students'
- a commitment to the belief that every child can learn
- a commitment to realising every student's potential
- the practice of challenging rather than sharing ideas
- an understanding of the use of student assessment reports to inform decision-making
- an emphasis on evidence rather than inference.

Progression of PLT activities

Not all of these characteristics will be present in a PLT, especially at the start of its operation. The characteristics will often need to be fostered by team leaders and the school leadership. Unless the school leadership is supportive and engaged in the PLT approach, it will not succeed. In the same way that the PLT identifies the ZPD level of the students for whom it is responsible, and is required to describe the evidence on which this decision is based, the PLT should consider its own development, and the evidence for this, in relation to the progression of PLT activities (Table 4.2). The term 'PLT activities' here refers to the work the PLT undertakes to advance student learning.

Table 4.2 *Progression of PLT activities*

LEVEL	DESCRIPTION
A	**Viewing existing student achievement information** PLT at this level look at information that describes the achievement of their students.
B	**Sharing practices** PLT at this level discuss and consider teaching and assessment practices based on familiarity, ease of use and curriculum expectations.
C	**Exploring student evidence to inform teaching** PLT at this level combine evidence of student learning to determine areas of need and make associated teaching plans. They discuss the suitability of assessment data to inform teaching. They seek evidence to resolve disagreement.
D	**Changing professional practices** PLT at this level combine evidence of student skills to identify what students are ready to learn, developing teaching plans collaboratively. They review data to determine teaching effectiveness. They discuss plans for improving their teaching and assessment practices and assist each other to implement new and relevant practices.
E	**Taking shared responsibility for student and teacher learning** PLT at this level take responsibility for improving the professional practices of members so they can enhance the learning of all students. They discuss difficult issues in a frank and professional way.
F	**Synthesising evidence-based practices** PLT at this level review all practices in terms of their explicit consequences for student learning. They take responsibility for developing the professional practices of all members by addressing the skills each member is ready to learn in an evidence-based manner.
G	**Conducting research to inform practice** PLT at this level conduct action research into the effectiveness of teaching and assessment practices in order to contribute to the knowledge of teaching and learning, both within the PLT and in the wider educational community.

Having considered its own ZPD, the PLT can plan the next step in its own development.

Summary

This chapter has examined the formation and operation of the PLT. The need for PLT to be formed within an over-arching conceptual framework has been emphasised. Similarly, it has been stressed that the PLT cycle helps to formalise the work of the PLT and to retain its focus on a step-by-step approach incorporating evidence, developmental goals, strategies and resources, before starting again with evidence of progress. Advice has been provided on the need to establish the protocols and duration of PLT meetings and the use of the language of evidence and challenge. Two PLT log templates have been provided to facilitate PLT planning, to record decisions for review and reflection, and to help PLT build a database of effective strategies. Advice has also been given regarding how PLT can support an evidence-based, resourced decision-making culture. Finally, characteristics of effective PLT have been described and a progression of PLT activities has been provided to assist the PLT in identifying its own ZPD and planning for its own development.

Apply to practice

Using data to plan teaching interventions is central to the idea of targeted intervention. Initially, PLT find that this process takes time. Like any complex task, it requires practice. Using the step-by-step approach outlined in this chapter and the PLT log will help.

Using data to make instructional decisions involves five questions that form the PLT cycle. These are:

1 What is the student ready to learn, and what is the evidence for this in terms of what the student can do, say, make or write?
2 What are the possible evidence-based interventions and the associated scaffolding processes for each?
3 What is the preferred intervention, and how will it be resourced and implemented?
4 What is the expected impact on learning, and how will this be evaluated?
5 What was the outcome, and how can this be interpreted?

Task 1

1 Working as a PLT, use one of the reading, numeracy or problem-solving progressions (see Chapter 2 appendices) to plan a teaching intervention for two or three groups of students, each of which is operating at a different developmental level. Use the steps outlined in this chapter and either of the PLT logs as a guide. Restrict your plan to one learning intention per group and keep it simple. At this stage, it is more important to develop an understanding of the process rather than to develop a detailed plan.
2 Reflect on the process. Use the Check Your Progress rubric below to aid PLT planning and subsequent reflection on how you went about this process in this practice exercise.

Task 2

Review the language advice in Table 4.1.

1   In an application of the higher-order categories from Bloom's Taxonomy, *analyse* the allocation of verbs to the do, say, make and write taxonomy.

2   *Evaluate* the allocation. *Create* a new table with verbs that reflect the evidence you would be likely to *apply* in one of your teaching subjects.

3   Share these with a peer and *challenge* the classification.

4   Then *collaborate* to *create* a new table and *check* it at your next classroom opportunity for assessment of student learning readiness.

Check your progress

Below is a set of rubrics to help you reflect on your answers to the Apply to Practice questions and assess your understanding of this chapter. These can be used to help scaffold learning.

4.1   How did you identify the student level on the developmental progression?

   a   Test data alone were used to identify the student's developmental level.

   b   Test data were combined with (or replaced by) a range of observable data to identify the student's readiness for learning.

   c   Anomalies or discrepancies between pieces of evidence were investigated in order to make a decision about the student's readiness to learn.

4.2   How did you set learning intentions for the student?

   a   The learning intentions were independent of a level on the developmental progression.

   b   The learning intentions were defined by a level on the developmental progression.

4.3   How did you set strategies to be used to achieve the learning intentions?

   a   A list of possible strategies was produced.

   b   Strategies were selected with the aim of closing the gap between the current and target levels.

   c   Strategies were selected on the basis of evidence of their effectiveness in moving towards the next target level.

4.4   How did you decide on resources to be used to achieve the learning intentions?

   a   Resources were listed.

   b   Resources were selected with the aim of closing the gap between current and target levels.

   c   Resources were selected on the basis of evidence of their effective use in closing the gap between the current and target levels.

4.5 What type of evidence did you decide to collect to show that the learning intention has been achieved?

a Evidence sought is general in nature.

b Evidence sought is specifically targeted.

Chapter 5

Cultural change and assessment

Esther Care and Patrick Griffin

This chapter expands on the previous chapter to describe in more detail the culture of challenge and collaboration linked to the peer accountability that is required to implement an evidence-based approach to teaching through the PLT structure. For those beginning their teaching careers and those new to a school where PLT operate, the chapter serves as an introduction to a new organisational structure and to what a new teacher can expect from school and team leadership within this structure. It introduces styles and levels of leadership that influence PLT functioning, from the first steps of implementing the collaborative approach through to managing and peer mentoring attitudinal change, technical capabilities and integration of the developmental learning approach into the teaching culture. Accountability at the leadership and team levels is explained, and an account is given of how different aspects of leadership – symbolic and cultural, technical, human and educational – are all required for successful cultural change.

Learning objectives

In this chapter you will learn to:

- identify the characteristics of a school culture where decisions are evidence based and dependent on quality assessment
- identify the level of commitment among the school leadership and the PLT leaders, and estimate the likelihood of success of innovative programs in a school
- identify those individuals committed to change through ownership of procedures
- understand how your expertise in this new approach to assessment can be linked to change activities in schools through an understanding of prime movers and leadership characteristics
- differentiate between emotional support among teachers and professional support for teaching
- identify the main features of taxonomies that can be used to characterise levels of leadership and of team functioning
- appreciate the complexity of the processes required to contribute to change in attitude, accumulation of technical knowledge and implementation of the consequences.

Sharing is a good thing, both in the action and in the consequence, as can be seen in coffee breaks and lunchtimes in schools, which are characterised by teachers sharing their experiences. This helps to build a community of teachers who feel supported by each other through sometimes difficult interactions in the classroom. In contrast to this time of sharing, the culture within the PLT is characterised by objective discussion of student progress in learning. Such discussions are an opportunity for you as a novice or beginning teacher to put on record your collections of evidence about student performance, and to work to make sense of the diverse perspectives that might be apparent among teacher colleagues. While shared stories can build rapport, in this context you need to become a critical appraiser of others' inferences and interpretations concerning the implications of the available evidence.

Data for decision-making are based on what students do, say, make and write as evidence. It is the inferences drawn from this evidence that you and your colleagues need to learn how to challenge. But this must be done in a non-confrontational way. It does not matter whether you are a new or experienced staff member of a PLT – everyone needs a non-confrontational approach to challenging colleagues. There are many different ways of interpreting data, and in a PLT or tutorial group, decisions should be defended using evidence supported by the team. This means that group members need to be equipped to challenge each other's interpretations. As discussed in Chapter 4, we refer to this as a culture of challenge. It contrasts with a culture of endorsement, which can characterise the campus, the corridor or the lunch-room chat, and can even be present in advice given to and by teachers. That is the culture of sharing the 'good idea' and endorsing it uncritically. Both cultures have their place, and each serves a different function. For teachers, the culture of challenge can be a significantly different way of functioning. Challenge is potentially confronting, and can be taken badly. Learning both how to challenge interpretations of evidence and how to respond to challenges concerning your own interpretations equips you to analyse evidence professionally.

Group culture

Cultural change requires multiple inputs from multiple sources. It includes change in attitudes, values and social norms. In this context, 'culture' refers to the common understandings within a group about their perspectives, their conventions and their identity. These understandings drive characteristic behaviours of the group. A group may be a school, a family, a tutorial group, a business organisation or, as in this case, a professional team. Where one member of a group acts in a way that conflicts with the culture of the group, there are several possible outcomes. The member can be isolated by the group, excluded, disciplined or assimilated gradually back into the group culture, or the culture itself can integrate the minority perspective. The group can bring formal or extrinsic factors into play, such as incentives or punishments, or it can use the group dynamics in an effort to resolve the potential conflict created by its members acting outside of the group norm.

Group culture varies in the degree to which it is dynamic. Some groups appear to be inflexible and resistant to integration of new ideas, while others are more open. Where a group exists due to a formal structure – as in a school – it is more likely to be homogeneous with regard to its purpose. In turn, purpose dictates many of the norms characteristic of the group, and its operating framework may not only be well understood but may also be made explicit in terms of formal documentation and consequent procedures.

Notwithstanding the formal nature of school committees and the functionality implied by their naming, the primary goals and functions of committees are not always made clear. At the most elemental level, committees, or meetings of committees, are structured in order to communicate and/or to make decisions. These are the two primary functions, although they are not always made explicit. How does this relate to our proposed cultural change within professional learning teams and teacher education programs? Our argument is that the purpose of PLT is to use data to improve teaching, and hence to facilitate student learning. Where schools have previously included a professional learning team structure, the purpose, functions and practices of these teams may have been diverse. Many teams focus on administration issues. We argue that teams should primarily focus on student learning outcomes. When individuals come together under a new name or label but with a perception that the same work is to be done as in the past, they bring with them the culture of the past. How is the slate to be wiped clean? How do teams change their focus from administration to student learning outcomes?

Achieving cultural change: Leadership

Multiple inputs and multiple sources are needed to change a culture from one of endorsement to one of challenge; from a focus on administration to student learning outcomes; from an individual teacher and a class to a group responsibility for student learning; from a focus on inference to one dependent on evidence; from whole-class teaching to targeted and differentiated instruction. At the base level, the school leadership needs to be involved and engaged, and to take ownership of the approach. This can be implemented through a set of connected activities that include participation in professional development activities, providing resources for professional development and for meeting time, engagement in the PLT processes and involvement in cyclic evaluation activities. It is possible to describe school leadership in terms of eight levels of involvement (Table 5.1).

Table 5.1 *Eight levels of school leadership involvement*

	DESCRIPTOR	QUOTABLE QUOTE
1	Uninterested	Leadership is preoccupied with other, unrelated matters and takes no interest in the innovation. Sometimes not even aware of the existence of the program in the school. The program is likely to wither and fail.
		This is a story about four people: Everybody, Somebody, Anybody, and Nobody. There was an important job to be done, and Everybody was asked to do it. Everybody was sure Somebody would do it. Anybody could have done it, but Nobody did it. Somebody got angry about that because it was Everybody's job. Everybody thought Anybody could do it. Nobody realized Everybody wouldn't do it. In the end, Everybody blamed Somebody when actually Nobody asked Anybody. (Anonymous, *Financial Times* 1988)
2	Aware	Leadership knows the program exists but cannot show any awareness of its details, goals or structure. The program has a high probability of failure.
		What is necessary to change a person is to change his awareness of himself. (Abraham Maslow)
3	Interested	The leadership is aware and keen to know more but has difficulty in finding time to be involved any more than listing its goals and knows who is involved but plays no part in the program.
		You may not be interested in war, but war is interested in you. (Trotsky)

	DESCRIPTOR	QUOTABLE QUOTE
4	Supportive	Provides resources, and encourages staff to be involved; has praise for those promoting and leading the program. Too busy to be directly involved. Not a central concern or high priority of the school. If we do not hang together, we will all hang separately. (Benjamin Franklin)
5	Involved	Attends meetings, observes classes, shows excitement about the project and highlights the efforts of those leading the project but still lacks a full understanding of its detail and approach. When the people become involved in their government, government becomes more accountable, and our society is stronger, more compassionate, and better prepared for the challenges of the future. (Arnold Schwarzenegger)
6	Engaged	Actively involved in all parts of the project and appreciates its needs and possibilities, promotes the project to those not involved and regards self as a part of the project. We are all dependent on one another, every soul of us on earth. (George Bernard Shaw)
7	Committed	Puts resources and long-term strategy in place to ensure the sustainability and leadership of the program has succession plans. Ensures the success of the project and reinforces the gains achieved. We may have all come on different ships, but we're in the same boat now. (Martin Luther King)
8	Ownership	Takes a lead and identifies with the project as a flagship exercise for the school. Promotes it to stakeholder groups and in the school community. Takes the role of leader and champions the program and identifies self as the initiator and promoter. Actively participates in and understands the nuances of the project. It surprises me how disinterested [Hawking means uninterested] we are today about things like physics, space, the universe and philosophy of our existence, our purpose, our final destination. It's a crazy world out there. Be curious. (Stephen Hawking)

Schools with leadership that takes an uninterested, aware, interested or supportive stance are unlikely to succeed in the implementation of a PLT culture, primarily because leaders do not become involved in the implementation itself. Schools in which the principal and school leadership teams are involved, engaged and committed to the program, so that their ownership is apparent, are likely to succeed not only in changing student outcomes but also in changing attitudes and beliefs of teachers about student learning potential. Sometimes school leadership groups or principals will show different levels of engagement for different programs in the school. Those innovations and programs where the greatest engagement or ownership are present will succeed, while those at the lower end of awareness will fail.

There are specific activities that school leadership can undertake to implement the approach. The first step is for leaders to enrol themselves in linked professional development programs (see Appendix C). This ensures an understanding of what the cultural change comprises in terms of beliefs about learners, knowledge about the principles of the use of assessment data to inform teaching and familiarity with expectations of PLT. Beyond the teacher, tutorial group or team level, it provides you with an appreciation of the importance of the leadership team and an understanding of the required framework for how staffing structures are decided upon, how the resource needs are rationalised in terms of time, and the support needed for guiding you and your peers through the cultural change. PLT may be constructed across year levels or across subjects within a year level. PLT need professional learning time and associated resources. Schedules for school meetings must accommodate the PLT time required in order to ensure that appropriate time is provided for functional implementation of a PLT-led student learning review cycle. Simultaneously, the need for tiered accountability comes into play.

Accountability and cultural change

What is accountability? It is the obligation of an organisation or individual to account for their activities, accept responsibility for them and disclose the results in a transparent manner. Accountability is the extent to which individuals or groups discharge their responsibilities. It is self-evident that the school principal and leadership team are accountable to their community for the learning outcomes of those students for whom they are responsible. This accountability is evaluated and measured in many ways, due to the various natures of the stakeholders, but the final endorsement will rest in student learning outcomes. Teachers in a PLT, however, are also accountable to each other.

Reflective question

Consider the quote relating to 'Uninterested' in Table 5.1. Have you experienced a similar situation involving Everybody, Somebody, Anybody and Nobody? What were the outcomes of this situation and how could a PLT avoid such a mess?

Leadership within the professional learning team mirrors that within the school leadership team – with full participation by all in professional development and in ensuring that the working environment facilitates the work. The PLT leader is responsible not only for the daily functioning of the team, but for mentoring and guiding it.

In order for this to occur, the PLT leader needs to have access to additional support, which may be sourced through the school leadership team and through PLT leaders' groups, both from within and external to the school. Team leaders need to conduct their business in the following ways:

- promote a focus on teaching and learning
- encourage communication within the team and across the curriculum
- focus discussion on evidence, not inference
- link data to developmental learning
- ensure that the PLT is accountable to the school leadership for student learning outcomes
- ensure that links between PLT leaders enable a culture of accountability to other team leaders both within and between schools
- take responsibility for the professional development of team members
- protect the culture of change. A focus on this requirement is ensured by the accountability of the PLT leader to the school leadership.

Within the PLT, the notion of accountability is maintained. Putting aside the business emphasis on accounting for one's actions and instead adopting a focus on responsibility to and for each other, team members function collaboratively. That is, they have one shared goal: enhancing student learning. Each brings to that goal their various resources – evidence bases and skills. These resources are combined in order to achieve an understanding of student progress that members might find impossible to achieve separately. Accountability for student learning is shared within the culture of the PLT. This precept is responsible for the notion, introduced in Chapter 1, that teachers accept joint responsibility for their students rather than claiming ownership of students or groups of students.

The principles outlined in Chapter 1 summarise the main targets of the cultural change within schools. These are the use of evidence as the first step in targeting instruction, the practice of challenging interpretations of the evidence and the adoption of joint responsibility for student outcomes. The underlying principles are that assessment should be used as a driver for teaching, in the knowledge that all students can progress in their skills. Discussion within the team is to focus on what the students do, say, make or write in the context of the construct or topic of interest.

One of the reasons for our focus on the evidence (what people do, say, make or write) is that it can be changed in the classroom using explicit teaching. Explicit and directed teaching can help focus what students say. Teachers can also help students to improve what they make (work samples). And teachers spend a lot of time helping students with their writing. It is through improvements in what students do, say, make and write that we can infer what they have improved in terms of their knowing and understanding. Although there is a great deal of simplicity in this approach, its introduction requires a coordinated and comprehensive change process. In order to guide this process, the school and PLT leaders bring to bear diverse leadership skills.

A leadership framework

Sergiovanni (1992, 2006) describes five domains of leadership. His framework firmly emphasises collaborative decision-making, and is based on a 'consensual' model of power that is manifested *through* other people instead of *over* other people (Leithwood 1992). The development of purpose is a key concept in Sergiovanni's theory. This driver is at the core of implementation of the change approach described in this chapter, and provides the vision that the leader promotes. This leadership model contrasts with instructional leadership, which carries a connotation of hierarchies and top-down delegation. It relies on collective responsibility and continuous improvement, the fostering of teacher development and collaboration in problem-solving (Leithwood 1992). Sergiovanni's five domains are described in Table 5.2. In changing the culture of the PLT and the school, we focus on two types of leadership domains: the symbolic and the cultural.

Table 5.2 *Sergiovanni's (1992) five leadership domains as described by Griffin and Care (2012)*

DOMAIN	DESCRIPTION
Technical	An effective leader demonstrates the capacity to optimise the school's financial, human and physical resources through sound management practices and organisational systems that contribute to the achievement of the school's vision and goals.
Human	An effective leader demonstrates the ability to foster a safe, purposeful and inclusive learning environment, and a capacity to develop constructive and respectful relationships with staff, students, parents and other stakeholders.
Educational	An effective leader demonstrates the capacity to lead, manage and monitor the school improvement process through a current and critical understanding of the learning process and its implications for enhancing high-quality teaching and learning in every classroom in the school.
Symbolic	An effective leader demonstrates the capacity to model important values and behaviours to the school and community, including a commitment to creating and sustaining effective professional learning communities within the school, and across all levels of the system.
Cultural	An effective leader demonstrates an understanding of the characteristics of effective schools and a capacity to lead the school community in promoting a vision of the future, underpinned by common purposes and values that will secure the commitment and alignment of stakeholders to realise the potential of all students.

Griffin and Care (2012) describe successive developmental levels of the symbolic and cultural domains for PLT leaders and members, as shown in Table 5.3. You can use this to ascertain how likely it is that you, as part of a team, will succeed in changing the culture of a school through a developmental approach to assessment.

Table 5.3 *Hierarchical levels in symbolic and cultural PLT leadership*

DOMAIN		DESCRIPTION
Symbolic	1	Steers the PLT focus on student learning outcomes, growth and impact of intervention strategies; maintains focus on the well-being of students and the goal of self and PLT improvement.
	2	Commits to modelling their own learning development within the PLT and the well-being of PLT members; communicates the PLT goals and school expectations based on learning outcomes.
	3	Commits to the process of evaluating broad opportunities and differentiated intervention strategies with a focus on learning outcomes and growth in student development.
	4	Mentors members of the PLT on their own emotional and professional well-being; encourages professional learning and exploration of new ideas and strategies associated with growth of student learning; promotes a shared understanding of the culture of PLT.
Cultural	1	Has a vision of the PLT and its success; celebrates successes and shares evaluations of various strategies with team members.
	2	Involves the PLT in a shared vision and uses this to establish PLT culture using the experience of teachers in the classroom and student data as evidence of successful interventions.
	3	Uses public communication within and between schools with other PLT leaders and school leadership groups to inform and educate as well as to implement peer-to-peer accountability within the PLT.
	4	Adapts the school and PLT planning cycles to achieve short- and long-term goals within the target group of students; emphasises the importance of professional development and celebrates development of each PLT member.
	5	Acts as a mentor in the PLT and for other PLT leaders; contributes to the school culture of learning outcomes in evidence-based decision-making and models this behaviour in their own work; communicates the successful activities of the PLT to other schools and other PLT leaders.

The levels outlined in Table 5.3 do not occur as discrete and coherent stages. As with most development, PLT leaders – like you as a member of a PLT – will move fuzzily between levels as they deal with the challenges inherent in progressing. At the same time, movement through the levels of the technical, human and educational domains will be occurring. The PLT leaders will be managing the technical aspects of their roles in ensuring appropriate allocation of resources; the human aspects of their roles in modelling appropriate ways to challenge the evidence brought to PLT meetings by members; and the educational aspects of their roles in applying the learning derived from relevant readings on differentiated practices, identification and evaluation of appropriate pedagogical strategies to targeted groups of students. A central responsibility for the PLT leader in the change-management process is to facilitate team members' understandings of the use of assessment data as evidence. Managing the team's progress rests not only on the PLT leader's own technical understanding but on their human leadership abilities. This brings into play the PLT leader's affective capacity and the readiness of the PLT members – including you – to embrace the culture of development.

Changes in attitude

There are several taxonomies that can be used by PLT leaders to help structure their monitoring and facilitation of changes in attitude among the team members. One is the affective taxonomy developed by Krathwohl, Bloom & Nasia (1964), as outlined in Chapter 2. The taxonomy is ordered according to the principle of internalisation. In brief, this describes a process where an individual moves from being aware of something – for example, an attitude or opinion, a belief or a value – to a state in which that attitude, opinion, belief or value is internalised. Once internalised, these affective characteristics guide or control the person's behaviour.

The taxonomy has been reframed in Table 5.4 to describe teachers' attitudes towards the use of data to make instructional decisions, illustrating the approach detailed in this book. The PLT leader might initially self-assess against this taxonomy and then encourage the team members to do the same.

Table 5.4 *Krathwohl and developmental assessment*

STAGE	DESCRIPTION
Rejecting	Avoids discussion of merits of developmental assessment; highlights flaws; contrasts with personally favoured approaches; criticises proponents and cites other approaches as superior; ridicules, disagrees, argues against the approach; avoids involvement.
Receiving	Listens passively; shows awareness of the importance of learning about the approach; shows sensitivity to the needs and learning problems of students and teachers; accepts differences in school culture and approach; attends activities designed for learning about developmental assessment.

STAGE	DESCRIPTION
Responding	Complies with formal requirements; participates in discussions about developmental assessment; completes assigned tasks; is compliant with rules and procedures.
Valuing	Demonstrates a belief in the link between assessment and the learning process; appreciates applications of developmental assessment; demonstrates a problem-solving attitude to issues in developmental assessment; demonstrates a commitment to the improvement of assessment practice; suggests new ideas and activities; tries to help others; looks for opportunities to learn more about the role of assessment in teaching.
Organising	Adopts procedures voluntarily; uses systematic approaches to solve assessment interpretation issues; accepts responsibility for own assessment decisions and behaviour; adjusts behaviour to accommodate the requirements of the situation; formulates a professional development plan in harmony with abilities, interests, and beliefs about developmental learning and assessment; demonstrates self-reliance through working independently.
Characterising	Displays consistent consciousness of developmental approaches to assessment; uses an objective approach to problem-solving using assessment data and evidence; models assessment habits and attempts to influence others to adopt these; prepares convincing and sound arguments in favour of developmental assessment practices.

To promote practices within your PLT or tutorial group that will deliver the desired teacher development learning outcomes, it can be helpful for you to review your group's implementation of these practices. This process helps the members to monitor progress and to plan their professional development. Dreyfus's model of skill acquisition (Dreyfus & Dreyfus 1980 – see Chapter 2), which is based on the contribution of formal instruction and then practice, is a useful tool for this purpose. In Table 5.5, we illustrate this approach to reviewing some of the technical skill capacities resident in the PLT.

Finally, the PLT leaders need to be able to make decisions about their own knowledge development and their understanding of the use of data. Checking one's own understanding is essential for a continuous learning cycle. Both informal metacognitive activities (thinking about one's own professional learning) as well as formal checking processes can provide a platform for identifying needs for professional development in the use of data. This book makes a start in this direction. However, you will need to formalise your understanding of data-use opportunities and limitations and plan your own professional development appropriately. The role of the team leader in this planning is critical. Not only must the PLT leader understand the learning needs of the team; they must also ensure that there is systemic support for

Table 5.5 *Dreyfus and developmental assessment*

STAGE	DESCRIPTION
Novice	Shows rigid adherence to known assessment procedures and plans; applies procedural rules to interpretation and use of assessment processes and data; adheres strictly to the use of scores and grades in a normative framework.
Advanced beginner	Follows guidelines for action in known situations; confines activity within short-term and immediate steps; recognises global characteristics of a situation only after prior experience; identifies surface rather than subtle features.
Competent	Follows standardised and routine developmental assessment procedures; consciously plans for use of developmental assessment; locates assessment strategies and practices in context of long-term professional goals; uses assessment data in a formal manner.
Proficient	Sees developmental assessment situations holistically rather than in terms of parts of the process; identifies salient and critical issues in a situation; identifies deviations from the normal pattern and develops broad perspectives on a situation; uses and relies on rules, guidelines or mantras for guidance but allows their meaning to vary according to their own perception of the situation.
Expert	Operates from a deep and intuitive understanding of the total assessment and teaching situation and the application of assessment to teaching intervention; able to deal with anomalies in assessment data; has a vision of what is possible in developmental assessment and takes action to realise this through networks of peers; can demonstrate the effect of developmental assessment on students; adapts analytical approaches in novel situations or when problems occur.

this learning, and this is achieved through the PLT leader's participation at school leadership level. In this context, the focus is on the assurance that every member of the PLT understands how data are used to drive instructional intervention decisions. Bloom's (1956) action-based taxonomy, revised by Anderson and colleagues in 2001 (see Chapter 2), identifies the activities or behaviours that are important for learning. Table 5.6 illustrates how each type of learner, from confused to creative, might act while moving along a developmental progression that characterises professional learning teams.

These progressions are tools for examining an individual's attitudes, skills and knowledge about the use of assessment data. Table 5.7 contains a progression describing the levels of engagement of individuals in the PLT itself. The progression was derived using data collected from teachers working in PLT that use the approach described in this book. It is known as the progression of PLT engagement, and the term 'PLT engagement' refers to the degree to which teachers participate in the activities of the PLT, as described in Chapter 4.

Table 5.6 *Anderson and Krathwohl and developmental assessment*

CLASSIFICATION	DESCRIPTION
Confused	Merges the deficit and developmental approach, and links remedial intervention and diagnosis to developmental assessment; promotes teaching to the test rather than teaching to the construct; interprets evidence in terms of problems students are having and ignores evidence of readiness to learn.
Remembers	Recalls ideas about developmental assessment and its definition; recognises the elements of developmental assessment and lists its properties; describes the process of developmental assessment; identifies the appropriate instruments and uses the language of evidence-based assessment; follows guidelines and procedures; can name, define and use the language of developmental assessment.
Understands	Explains ideas or concepts of developmental assessment; interprets assessment terms and explains types of assessments; explains the use of progressions in reports and nutshell statements; links assessment data to curriculum and instruction; classifies instruments and evidence; summarises, infers and paraphrases ideas of developmental progressions; compares and explains various approaches to developmental assessment.
Application	Implements and uses developmental assessment in a range of situations; carries out, executes, uses and interprets developmental assessment strategies and ideas; constructs assessment instruments and reports based on developmental evidence-based assessment and intervention.
Analytical	Discriminates and explains differences between developmental and other approaches to assessment; compares approaches; defines and identifies the discrete attributes of the developmental assessment approach; organises materials according to purpose and unpacks ideas about developmental assessment.
Evaluative	Justifies course of action taken in developmental assessment; checks and critiques evidence and its validity; judges the accuracy of data and deals with anomalies; makes decisions about the appropriate use and value of the data; links assessment to appropriate strategy and resource allocation.
Creative	Generates new approaches and ideas about the use of developmental assessment; formulates and tests hypotheses about data interpretation and use; generates and tests solution strategies where anomalies occur; designs and builds instruments and interventions as well as resource allocation approaches.

Table 5.7 *Progression of PLT engagement*

LEVEL	DESCRIPTION
A	**Receiving** Teachers at this level meet together to learn about PLT activities.
B	**Responding** Teachers at this level comply with PLT activities in meetings. They participate in discussions and listen to the views offered.
C	**Accepting the value of the PLT** Teachers at this level engage in PLT activities because they believe they help improve learning for some students. They report back on the implementation of teaching plans and complete PLT-related activities outside the meetings when other priorities allow.
D	**Committing to the value of the PLT** Teachers at this level are committed to participating in PLT activities. They complete them to the best of their ability and support others to do so if they seek help. They take opportunities to inform others of the benefits of their work and make plans to ensure their teams are successful.
E	**Aligning actions to PLT expectations** Teachers at this level organise their individual actions so the actions are consistent with PLT expectations. They take joint responsibility for the success of their PLT activities by participating in discussions and reporting back on their work outside meetings. They seek feedback from other members and provide feedback and encouragement to each other. They make efforts to build the success of the PLT in order to enhance the learning of their students.
F	**Prioritising the PLT** Teachers at this level prioritise PLT activities over other school demands, as the activities enhance the learning of all students. They communicate openly about the effectiveness of their teaching, use their time productively and are proactive in their support of each other to ensure they are successful at improving student learning. They take actions to ensure the sustainability of their PLT both within the team and with school leadership.
G	**Characterising PLT practices** Teachers at this level act in accordance with PLT practices in all aspects of their work. They coordinate their actions to ensure they improve student learning and seek opportunities to advocate their approach to others.
H	**Exerting influence** Teachers at this level use their links with people or organisations outside their PLT to influence policy and strategic planning in ways which characterise their PLT practices.

Summary

In this chapter, we have outlined several taxonomies that provide useful management and mentoring tools for PLT leaders and members. From the initial steps taken
by the school leadership team to adopt the assessment and learning model, a tiered
accountability approach is recommended where team members are accountable to
each other, team leaders meet and exchange ideas and also check their own leadership, being accountable to each other among the team leaders in the school, and
team leaders are then accountable to the school leadership. Through this approach,
school leaders, PLT leaders and PLT members are all accountable to each other at
the professional level, but ultimately accountable to the students for whose progress
they are responsible.

Apply to practice

Change in schools relies on developing the skills, knowledge and attitudes of staff.
This chapter presents many different developmental progressions that can be used
when assessing and planning for the development of teachers.

1   Select one of these progressions to assess yourself and one of your colleagues
    (with their agreement).

2   Use evidence to place yourself and your colleague at progression levels and then
    use this information to collaboratively plan professional development to take
    both of you to a higher level in the domain.

3   As you go through this process, practise the ideas presented in this chapter by
    considering the appropriateness of inferences (challenging them if necessary)
    and taking opportunities to enhance engagement and accountability.

Check your progress

Below is a set of rubrics designed to help you reflect on the process you undertook
while completing the Apply to Practice task and assess your understanding of this
chapter. These can be used to help scaffold learning.

5.1   During the discussion, you considered the appropriateness of inferences by:

    a   accepting them at face value

    b   asking questions to ascertain whether they were supported by evidence

    c   considering them in the light of the supporting evidence provided.

5.2   During the discussion, you built opportunities to enhance accountability by:

    a   trusting that you and your colleague would follow through

    b   verbally agreeing on a monitoring process for the plans you put in place c documenting a monitoring process for the plans you put in place

    d assigning time to follow up on the monitoring process you documented.

5.3 Your engagement in the assessment and planning process is best described as:

    a compliance (I only did it to complete the task)

    b interest (I found the process interesting, but I don't know whether it will change anything)

    c commitment (I found this process useful and intend following through with the plan).

Chapter 6

Judgement-based assessment

Patrick Griffin and Pam Robertson

Many forms of assessment have pre-determined right and wrong answers. Familiar examples are multiple-choice questions and matching activities. When a teacher is marking these forms of assessment, there can be no doubt about whether a student has answered correctly or incorrectly. Other kinds of assessment, such as essays and art folios, require different marking methods. For these, there is no pre-determined answer and teachers must use their professional judgement to assess the work. These assessments are sometimes dismissed as subjective because they rely on the judgement of individual teachers, but there are ways for this kind of assessment to be formalised and codified to reduce the dangers of subjectivity. This chapter explains the process via which this can be achieved.

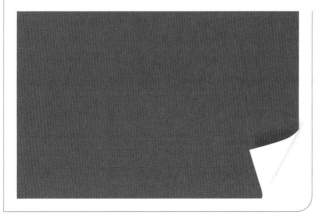

Learning objectives

In this chapter you will learn to:

- identify the strengths and weaknesses of judgement-based assessment
- understand how the use of a developmental assessment framework can minimise the weaknesses of judgement-based assessment so it can be used to better inform teaching decisions
- build a developmental assessment framework that describes the domain, strands and capabilities to be taught in a unit of work.

Objective and subjective assessment

The terms 'objective' and 'subjective' in the context of assessment refer to the manner in which assessments are scored. Assessments are referred to as 'objective' if they can routinely be marked as correct or incorrect. This is generally applied to multiple-choice questions, or questions for which there is only one correct answer. Subjective assessments involve judgement. In general, they require an assessment in which the teacher weighs up or judges the value or quality of a performance or an answer and differentiates between higher and lower quality student work. This process of weighing up the quality of a performance is used in this chapter to develop a series of criteria that will help teachers make these subjective judgements.

In fact, there are no purely objective assessments. All assessments can be classified as qualitatively subjective – it is a matter of where the judgement takes place in the process of planning, implementing and scoring assessments. Even a multiple-choice test involves a lot of subjective judgement in terms of which skills to assess, how many questions per skill, how long the test will be, how to sample the work of the class and so on. So the objectivity of the test defines only the method of scoring. It does not address the issues of planning, developing, implementing, administering, providing feedback and making decisions about what to do with the assessment data. These are all subjective decisions because they involve judgement at every point.

This chapter focuses on the subjective process of judging the quality of the student performance. In a multiple-choice test, there is no judgement of quality required. Hence it is called objective. In other forms of assessment, such as essays, projects, worked solutions, short-answer questions, products, folios and so on, the teacher is faced with the issue of how to make a judgement about the quality of learning that can be inferred from the quality of the evidence presented by the student. This is subjectively marked assessment and involves judgement. Hence we call this form of assessment judgement-based assessment. This refers only to the process of discriminating between levels of quality in the evidence presented by the student. It does not address the issue of what to assess, how to assess or how to provide feedback.

This chapter provides a model of assessment and measurement that enables highly reliable and accurate information to be used by a teacher or PLT, based on subjective assessments rather than routine online, multiple-choice tests. It builds trust among teachers about their judgement, and supports the use of professional decision-making in a PLT.

Judgement-based assessment in a developmental context

Judgement-based assessments are the most common assessments in education. It is common for teachers to give a mark on an essay, a score on a solution to a maths problem or a mark out of five for a short description. In all these cases, a mark or code is assigned that depends on the teacher's judgement of the relative quality of the student's response or performance.

Fundamentally, all assessments are variations of a stimulus response exercise. The student is challenged by, presented with or asked to respond to a stimulus – an instruction, a task, a problem, a comment. In responding, the student ticks a box, or provides a short text or figure, a sample of work, an extended response, a performance, a folio and so on. The assessment task can be divided into two parts – a stem and a response, as illustrated in Figure 6.1. The stem usually contains some information: an instruction regarding the purpose of the task and a further instruction regarding what the student must do to demonstrate their skill, understanding or knowledge. In Figure 6.1, the amount of judgement needed to assess the response is represented on the bottom axis, which lists response types, and increases from left to right. Objective forms of assessment, which have predetermined answers, are indicated at the left-hand end of the axis. The development of methods for objective testing, otherwise known as multiple-choice or objectively scored tests, is discussed in Chapter 8.

Item structure and assessment types

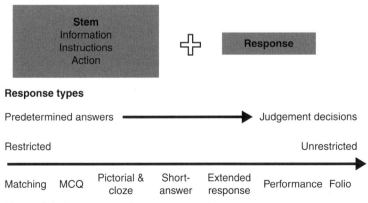

Figure 6.1 *A taxonomy of assessment and response types*

Judgement-based assessment approaches vary in their shapes and formats. Some teachers use checklists; some use sticky notes on an observation board; some use a pen to write comments in the margins of student work; some use technology to record verbal feedback; some use marks, grades or rating scales. The diversity among methods is enormous but some things are common to all: they all depend on the teacher's professional judgement, and they are all valued by teachers as a fair and valid form of assessment and trusted as the best appraisal of a student's work.

Part of the allure of judgement-based assessment is that it is based on direct observations of a performance, a product or a procedure. It enables assessment to be carried out within real-world contexts, including complex performances that involve decision-making and higher-order skills – skills for which the relative quality of a response is not easy to assess in an objective manner. In addition, judgement-based assessment allows the opportunity to broaden the type of feedback given from the dichotomous, right or wrong, black and white restrictions of objective assessment to one in which different levels of quality can be described, thus adding to the richness of the information gathered via assessment.

Judgement-based assessment has been criticised as subjective, susceptible to bias, lacking in rigour and so on. There are also difficult challenges in linking technical measurement aspects such as reliability and validity to the process of observation and judgement of complex behaviours, products and procedures. In some educational jurisdictions, concerns about the reliability and validity of judgement-based assessment have led to greater value being placed on externally provided testing than on classroom assessments – especially where the assessment data is used for top-down accountability processes. Such beliefs can lead to a narrowing of the focus of education from those things that are important to those things that are easy to measure.

Reflective questions

In your own education as a student or in any opportunities as a classroom teacher, what are your experiences of judgement-based assessments? What do you think are the strengths of judgement-based assessments compared with objective assessments? Do the strengths outweigh the weaknesses? What procedures have you used, or seen used, to make such assessments more consistent and accurate?

The issues of consistency of judgements, suitability of evidence and validity of inferences are important ones. When using judgement-based assessment in such tasks as essays, reports, short-answer questions, performances and portfolios, we recommend the use of assessment rubrics and moderation (checking in the PLT or tutorial session) to improve the consistency of judgements.

The following are typical assessment tasks with typical weaknesses:

- Describe in five sentences the importance of the Magna Carta (five marks).
- Write an essay that describes a recent holiday you had.
- Solve these simultaneous equations and show your working.

$$3x + 4y = 22$$
$$2x + 10y = 22$$

- Improvise the role of a street busker miming for donations from passers-by (graded from A to E).

These are all examples of a common form of assessment, in which exercises are set and a number of marks are assigned to them. Each of these examples lacks instruction for the student or for the teacher regarding how the task might be assessed or how to discriminate between higher and lower quality responses. Little or no advice is given to the student regarding what constitutes a minimum or a maximum performance, or a partially correct response. In their simplest form, rubrics can indicate how an answer, performance or product is partly correct, as illustrated below:

Simple rubrics

Fully correct answer = Skill demonstrated = 2

Partly correct answer = Skill partially demonstrated = 1

Incorrect answer = Skill not demonstrated = 0

These rubrics provide some information to the teacher about how to assign scores, but they do not solve all the problems in the above assessments because they give no information regarding the rationale for deciding whether a response is fully correct, partially correct or incorrect. They offer little or no assistance to the teacher in terms of intervention. Imagine the discussion of these particular assessments in a PLT. The culture of challenge would offer a rich opportunity for teachers to explain how the marks are to be assigned and why particular scores are assigned to particular performances or pieces of work.

Scores and codes

The point that is often lost in assessments is that to assign a score to student work is to do no more than assign a code to represent the relative quality of the work. Sometimes in very junior primary classrooms, a series of stamps is used. A Grade 1 student providing work that pleased the teacher might be given an elephant stamp. When the teacher wants to encourage the student to do better work and aim for an elephant stamp, the teacher might place a flatworm stamp on the student's work. If the work is particularly good, the teacher might put a star on it, or sometimes two or three stars. Stamps and stars are replaced in later years with numbers. When this happens, the number zero might indicate that the quality of the work is unacceptable and the number five might indicate that it is excellent. These numbers are just like the elephant stamp or the star. They are codes – part of the language between the teacher and the student that indicates the relative quality of the work.

A parent who sees their child's work covered in stars would be very pleased to know that the teacher thought that the student's work was excellent. A parent who sees that the student's work score is typically 5/5 or 17/20 or 95 per cent would be equally pleased to know that the student's work was regarded as excellent. What the parent never learns with these codes is *why* it is considered excellent. As parents, we are happy to see two or three stars, 17/20 or 95 per cent in the margins of our child's work. Sometimes, if we are really lucky, the teacher might even write the words 'good work'. Then we are particularly pleased.

But why are we happy to know that our child is producing relatively good work if we don't know what the good work represents? We can look at our child's artwork in Year 1 and see that it shows all the characteristics of a Year 1 student's artwork and that it has been given four stars, telling us that the teacher was very pleased, but do we know from this how the student has learned to control line and colour? Do we know how well the student is learning to represent reality or understanding the basics of abstract art? If a Year 9 student's essay receives the comment 'Great work, Patrick!' do we know from this that Patrick has mastered the arts of paraphrasing, including direct speech, paragraphing in sequence, correct spelling or the interrelation of multiple ideas and issues? If we know about the skills of writing, we might infer some of these things, but if we do not know very much about writing, we can only conclude that the teacher thought this was good work – or in this case, 'great' work. Under these circumstances, we would not know why the teacher thought the work was great, or how to help the student improve.

The important point is that all these comments, scores or stamps represent a coded language that the teacher shares with the students to communicate the teacher's satisfaction with the work and the relative quality of the student performance. They are codes, and every time we use a code we need to know how to decode it. In this chapter, we learn how to recognise the relative quality of work, how to define levels of relative quality, how to code and communicate with students about their cognitive competence and how to decode that information in a way that enables targeted intervention by the teacher in order to improve student performance. This is a process of coding and decoding in such a way that teachers are enabled to infer the quality of learning, the point of development on a progression and the zone of proximal development (ZPD) and targeted intervention. All of this is based on judgements of relative quality, and coding in a way that can be decoded.

Judgement-based assessment needs to be used to inform inferences and predictions about learning. Once assessment data are collected, they need to be considered as only a sample of possible outcomes, and this sample needs to be generalised in order to be used to inform teaching (see Chapter 2). Generalisation relies on an understanding of an underlying variable (continuum, progression or criterion-referenced framework). It is generally assumed that the performance, the process, the observation and interpretation (assessment) are undisturbed by outside factors. We usually assume that our observations are sufficient, our records accurate, our criteria clear, our judgement correct, our decision-point stable and the decision reproducible. However, these conditions are often not met. Judgement-based assessments generally are characterised by uncertainty of decision, a lack of generalisation process, distortion or absence of a continuum or criteria, confusion about appropriateness of evidence or observations, ambiguity, inconsistency of interpretation, suspicion of judgement-based assessment, loosely phrased rubrics and unclear rules of judgement for teachers. These factors weaken the ability to infer, predict and plan. They lead to the development of bad rubrics, and bad rubrics weaken a teacher's capacity to improve student learning. Generally, these are why the public mistrusts teacher judgement and relies instead on large-scale standardised tests or commercial products.

The authors of this book have developed a method that can be used to ensure assessments are sufficiently matched to an underlying variable so that generalisations can be made. Chapter 7 describes how to improve the accuracy of assessments and ensure that data collected using judgements of relative quality is best suited to help the process of generalisation. Chapters 9 and 10 show how criterion-referenced frameworks can be devised to provide detailed descriptions of progressions in order to support teaching decisions. A proper approach to judgement-based assessment depends to a great extent on the assessor's capacity to formulate a developmental framework for the learning they are assessing. All of these methods and processes are based on a series of principles underpinning a developmental assessment approach, as set out below:

- A set of underlying developmental continua describing growth in specific domains of learning *can be constructed*. The continua describe constructs that are measurable, and that have direction and units of measurement.
- The continua do not exist in and of themselves, but are empirically *constructed to assist in explaining observations* of learned behaviour.
- Each *continuum can be defined* by a cohesive set of indicative behaviours representing levels of proficiency in the area of learning. These behaviours can be demonstrated through the performance of representative tasks, and can be regarded as either direct or indirect indicators of proficiency.
- Not all behaviours can be directly observed. *Related, indirect observations* can be used, along with directly observable behaviours, to describe competency or ability.
- The indicators (*behaviours*) may be ordered along a continuum according to the amount of proficiency, competence or ability required for satisfactory performance or success on each task.

- *People* can be ordered along the continuum according to the behaviours they are able to exhibit or the tasks they are able to perform. The behaviours, in turn, can be interpreted to provide a substantive representation of the level of proficiency or ability.

- It is not necessary to identify or to observe all possible behaviours or indicators in order to define the continuum. The continuum can be defined by any *representative, cohesive sample* of indicators that covers a range of levels on it.

- There is *no one correct sample* of indicators, tasks, test items or pointers that exclusively defines the continuum or the domain, although there may be a set of indicators that is generally agreed upon as important in defining the continuum.

- While the indicators used to define the continuum are related, there is no causal or dependent relationship between them. It is neither necessary nor obligatory to observe lower-order indicators in order to observe higher-order behaviours. The existence of higher-order indicators implies the ability to demonstrate lower-order indicative behaviour. The relationship is *probabilistic, not causal.*

Working within this assessment approach allows many weaknesses of judgement-based assessment to be overcome. More detailed discussions of how this approach can deal with issues of validity and reliability are provided in Chapter 9. The approach provides an assessment model that has a range of important properties:

- It is *criterion-referenced.* The performance is not qualified by comparison with any group or expectation of group membership, as is the case with normative assessment. The performance is described purely for its level of quality, by reference to criteria that are situated within a continuum of increasing competence. It provides a series of thresholds that enables the student's development to be tracked and monitored. In its best form, it identifies the ZPD.

- It is *developmental.* The levels identify the next step in development for a student, allowing teaching efforts to be focused.

- It is *analytical.* Each element of the performance is defined and assessed in terms that are recognisable by any judge, and there are strict rules that must be applied when measuring performances. The rules allow for consistent judgements to be made by different assessors.

Reflective question

Analyse a topic in your teaching subject and describe how you would use a criterion-referenced, developmental and analytical assessment to support the notion that assessment is for teaching.

Building developmental assessment frameworks

The starting point for conducting high-quality judgement-based assessment is to define the construct to be assessed. As explained in Chapter 2, a construct is something we invent or 'create' to help us make sense of what we observe. Even if teachers are not familiar with the word, each teacher has an idea of the yardstick against which they measure their students. You can hear this in the everyday language of teachers: 'She is great at maths', 'He struggles with spelling'. They attribute the observations they make of students to differing amounts of ability or capacity in some underlying trait. This underlying trait is the construct. A construct can be defined simply by describing students with 'high', 'medium' and 'low' abilities in the area under consideration (e.g. capability in maths or spelling), or by adapting a developmental taxonomy to form descriptions of typical behaviours at different levels of the construct. The use of a developmental assessment framework, as described below, further defines the construct.

The term 'framework' is used to incorporate all the elements of an instructional unit or domain of learning. It can apply to any learning environment, including vocational contexts and school settings. Examples are hospitality, medical clinical skills, school leadership, inorganic chemistry for Third Year undergraduates, a reading program for Year 3 and a social studies unit in Year 6. A framework can also be a generic area of learning such as English language proficiency, or a set of generic skills such as teamwork or collaborative problem-solving. Within a framework, there are usually broad strands of learning, sometimes referred to as modules or units of instruction. Examples of these are customer relations, patient diagnosis, classroom management, equations, vocabulary, fluency and pronunciation. Strands can also be more generic skills, like social or cognitive skills. Within each of these strands there are learning outcomes, also known as 'capabilities', 'attributes' or 'competencies', that students are expected to develop. In this discussion, for simplicity, these are collectively described as 'capabilities'.

In summary, a learning domain can be described as consisting of various strands, and each strand can include various capabilities that students should possess. The development of these capabilities in students can be seen via behavioural indicators, and criteria can be used to judge the quality of each indicative behaviour. The relationships between the parts of the framework are shown in Figure 6.2. Some of the alternative terminology is presented at the base of the figure. From this figure, we can see that the domain consists of strands, which are broken down into capabilities (the things we want the students to be capable of), while the amount of each capability a student possesses can be assessed by considering the indicative behaviours and quality criteria.

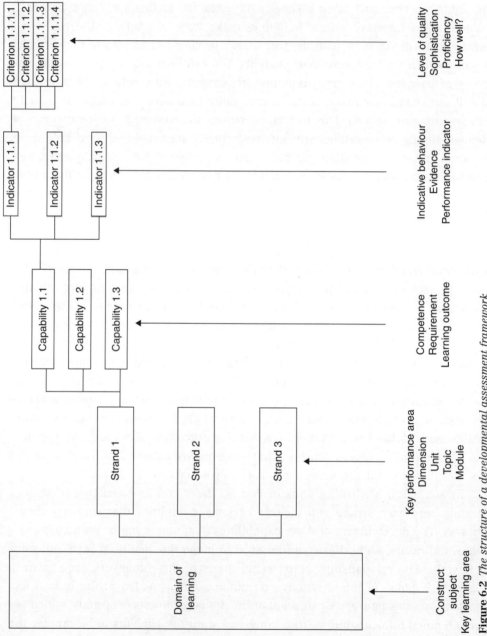

Figure 6.2 *The structure of a developmental assessment framework*

Construct
subject
Key learning area

Key performance area
Dimension
Unit
Topic
Module

Competence
Requirement
Learning outcome

Indicative behaviour
Evidence
Performance indicator

Level of quality
Sophistication
Proficiency
How well?

Domain of
learning

Strand 1

Strand 2

Strand 3

Capability 1.1

Capability 1.2

Capability 1.3

Indicator 1.1.1

Indicator 1.1.2

Indicator 1.1.3

Criterion 1.1.1.1
Criterion 1.1.1.2
Criterion 1.1.1.3
Criterion 1.1.1.4

For each capability, there is a series of indicative or typical behaviours – performance indicators – that should collectively provide the evidence to satisfy an observer that a capability has been developed. However, indicative behaviours can be demonstrated at different levels of quality. The tiler who lays the floor of a bathroom can be an artist or a worker who barely manages to make a serviceable floor. Both have provided evidence of the indicator – tiling the floor – but the level of quality is very different in the two cases. Similarly, the mechanic who fixes a car can be brilliant at diagnosis or can fail to identify a problem and leave things undone. In the same way, a doctor can diagnose a specific problem but fail to recognise symptoms of other ailments; a teacher might watch a child read aloud but fail to realise that the child does not comprehend the words read; and a student might acquire a language structure through a series of formulaic expressions but fail to express the nuances of the language. Each of these cases represents a person who has demonstrated an indicative behaviour that can be used as evidence of a capability, but these indicative behaviours alone do not address the quality of the performance assessed. A final piece of the framework structure is added to make it possible to describe the relative quality of performance. This piece consists of quality criteria. The indicative behaviours and associated quality criteria combine to become a rubric.

The point of departure of this approach to judgement-based assessment from any other assessment model is the hypothesis that competence is defined by a continuum rather than based on the 'can/cannot' dichotomy. The approach retains the can/cannot dichotomy, but seeks information at further levels of performance in a simple step: for each indicative behaviour, we ask the question 'How well was it done?' That additional step codifies the concept of relative quality. By doing so, the judgement-based assessment can be used to place a student on the relevant construct.

Table 6.1 presents examples of domains, strands, capabilities, indicative behaviours and quality criteria. It shows that these can be used to provide an assessment framework for traditional learning domains, as well as for general capabilities, such as personal and social capacity. Each example is an isolated snapshot of a complete assessment framework. The framework means that a range of assessment modes can be used to assess students. For example, a student's ability to calculate the area of rectangles can be determined using a test, teacher observation, a problem-solving task, homework questions and so on. Therefore, teachers have the flexibility of deciding how to assess this capability.

Generally, domains, strands and capabilities come from curriculum documents, although they can also be informed by research literature. Indicative behaviours and quality criteria, too, may be included in curriculum and assessment documents, but usually they draw on the practical experience of teachers in the classroom.

Table 6.1 *Examples of the components of developmental assessment frameworks*

	DOMAIN	STRAND	CAPABILITY	INDICATIVE BEHAVIOUR	QUALITY CRITERIA
Explanation	Subject, construct or learning area	Strand, dimension or key performance area	Expected outcome	What evidence shows that somebody has the capability?	What are possible levels of quality of the indicative behaviour?
Example 1	English	Reading	Make inferences from written materials	Make inferences from a narrative passage	Make inferences using implied information
Example 2	Maths	Measurement	Calculate area of rectangles	Calculate area of rectangles given the length and width	Calculate area by counting square centimetres
Example 3	Personal and social capacity	Self-management	Self-discipline	Completion of homework	Response to reminders to complete homework

Reflective question

Think about a learning domain with which you are familiar. Sketch out an example of a strand, capability, indicative behaviour and quality criterion within this area. How would a comprehensive framework for the domain benefit teaching? What restrictions does the use of such a framework impose?

Case study: The Assessment and Teaching of 21st Century Skills project

Tables 6.2 and 6.3 provide examples of a developmental assessment framework. The domain for this framework is collaborative problem-solving as developed for the Assessment and Teaching of 21st Century Skills (ATC21S™) project (<http://www.atc21s.org>), which characterised twenty-first-century skills as those essential for navigating contemporary education and workplaces. In the collaborative problem-solving part of the project, two or more students work together to solve a problem (Hesse et al. 2012). The structure of this framework is shown in Figure 6.3.

For each of these capabilities there are a number of indicative behaviours. Each indicative behaviour is accompanied by quality criteria. These have been defined by Hesse et al. (2012) and are shown in Tables 6.2 and 6.3.

Table 6.2 *Social skills in collaborative problem-solving*

ELEMENT	INDICATOR	LOW	MIDDLE	HIGH
Participation				
Action	Activity within environment	No or very little activity	Activity in scaffolded environments	Activity in unscaffolded environments
Interaction	Communicates with collaborators	Acknowledges communication	Responds to cues in communication	Prompts communication
Task completion/ perseverance	Undertakes task	Commences task	Attempts to solve task	Perseveres in task as indicated by repeated attempts or multiple strategies

Table 6.2 *Continued*

ELEMENT	INDICATOR	LOW	MIDDLE	HIGH
Perspective-taking				
Responsiveness	Responds to contributions of others	Ignores contributions of others	Acts in response to contributions of others	Incorporates contributions of others to suggest possible solution paths
Audience awareness	Adapts contributions to increase understanding for others	Makes contributions	Modifies contributions for others based on explicit feedback	Tailors contributions to others based on interpretation of their understanding
Social regulation				
Negotiation	Negotiates to accommodate differences	Comments on differences	Attempts to reach a common understanding	Achieves resolution of differences
Self-evaluation	Recognises own strengths and weaknesses	Is aware of own strengths and weaknesses	Communicates own strengths and weaknesses to collaborators	Utilises knowledge of own strengths and weaknesses
Transactive memory (knowledge about strengths and weaknesses of collaborators)	Recognises strengths and weaknesses of collaborators	Is aware of strengths and weaknesses of collaborators	Incorporates knowledge about strengths and weaknesses of collaborators	Harnesses the strengths and weaknesses of collaborators
Responsibility/ initiative	Takes responsibility for progress of group tasks	Responds to others regarding progress of individual activities	Reports to others on progress of activities	Monitors group's progress

Table 6.3 *Cognitive skills in collaborative problem-solving*

ELEMENT	INDICATOR	LOW	MIDDLE	HIGH
Task regulation				
Problem analysis	Analyses a problem	Takes problem at face value	Divides problem into sub-tasks	Identifies necessary sequence of sub-tasks
Goal-setting	Sets goals for task	Sets general goal such as task completion	Sets goals for sub-tasks	Sets goals that recognise relationships between sub-tasks
Resource management	Manages resources	Uses resources	Allocates resources to be used	Decides on use of resources to complete tasks
Flexibility and ambiguity	Responds to ambiguous situations	Inaction in ambiguous situations	Explores ambiguous situations	Uses ambiguity to inform decision-making
Information collection	Collects information	Collects all available information	Recognises the nature of the information needed for the immediate activity	Assesses the need for information related to current, alternative, and/or future tasks
Systematicity	Implements possible solutions to a problem	Uses trial and error	Creates purposeful sequence of actions	Systematically exhausts possible solutions
Learning and knowledge-building				
Relationships (representation and formulation)	Identifies connections and patterns between and among elements of knowledge	Focuses on isolated pieces of information	Links pieces of information	Formulates patterns among multiple pieces of information
Cause and effect (rules 'If ... then')	Uses understanding of cause and effect to develop a plan	Activity is undertaken with little or no understanding of consequence of action	Identifies sequences of cause and effect	Plans strategy based on a generalised understanding of cause and effect

Table 6.3 *Continued*

ELEMENT	INDICATOR	LOW	MIDDLE	HIGH
Adaptation (reflection and monitoring)	Adapts reasoning or course of action as information or circumstances change	Maintains a single line of approach	Tries additional options in light of new information or lack of progress	Reconstructs and reorganises understanding of the problem in search of new solutions
Knowledge acquisition	Acquires knowledge	Accepts information as given	Searches for and interrogates information	Creates and evaluates; tests generalisations

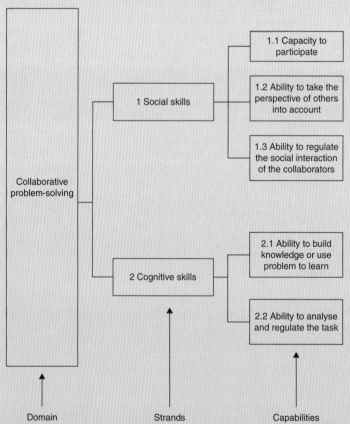

Figure 6.3 *Framework for collaborative problem-solving in ATC21S*™
Source: Griffin, McGaw and Care (2011).

Reflective questions

- How do the curriculum documents currently available to you compare with an assessment framework?

- Analyse their structure to see if domains, strands, capabilities and indicators can be easily identified.

- Do they also provide an indication of the possible levels of quality?

- Would it be more helpful if curricula were provided in the form of a developmental assessment framework, or are there greater advantages in teachers collaboratively building their own frameworks?

Summary

The requirements for subjective or judgement-based assessment are made clear by specifying indicative behaviours and levels of quality. Assessment tasks – stimuli or prompts – must be capable of eliciting the indicative behaviours. While it is often impractical to assess every indicative behaviour, it is reasonable to expect that when all the assessments of a domain are taken together, the indicative behaviours are representative of the range of capabilities within the domain. Developmental assessment frameworks provide a set of rules for coding and decoding different levels of quality in performance. They also ensure that there are explicit links between teaching and assessment. By using the approach presented in Chapter 7, indicators and quality criteria can be written in such a way that they do not function as a codebook, and so they maximise their usefulness for informing teaching interventions, encouraging differentiated instruction and supporting future development. We illustrate this further in Chapter 12 by using assessments of learning development for students with learning difficulties.

Apply to practice

Daily life presents many opportunities to observe people involved in collaborative problem-solving. Use the developmental assessment framework provided in Table 6.2 to assess the social skills of somebody in a collaborative problem-solving situation. You may do this by remembering a previous situation, or by conducting an assessment during a collaborative problem-solving exercise.

1. Reflect on your experience of using the framework to guide the coding of behaviours.

2. From the assessment, select one capability and devise a targeted teaching plan to develop it, based on the assessment data collected. It may be helpful to refer to the PLT cycle and PLT log (especially the distinction between teaching strategies and learning activities) discussed in Chapter 4. The teaching plan should articulate the learning intentions and the teaching intervention(s) that will be used to develop the capability.

3 Discuss how the use of the developmental assessment framework influenced the process of writing learning intentions.

4 Discuss how the use of the developmental assessment framework influenced the selection of teaching interventions.

5 Consider the impact on teaching practice of using developmental assessment frameworks.

Check your progress

Below is a set of rubrics designed to help you reflect on your answers to the Apply to Practice questions and assess your understanding of this chapter. These can be used to help scaffold learning.

6.1 Your reflection on your experience of using the developmental assessment framework to guide the coding of behaviours:

    a was general in nature

    b identified advantages/disadvantages of using the framework for coding

    c synthesised the implications of using the framework for coding.

6.2 Your discussion of the influence of the developmental assessment framework on the process of writing learning intentions:

    a was general in nature

    b identified how the use of the framework influenced the process

    c evaluated the influence of the framework on the process, based on a synthesis of the experience of writing the learning intentions.

6.3 Your discussion of the influence of the developmental assessment framework on the selection of teaching interventions:

    a was general in nature

    b identified how the use of the framework influenced the selection

    c evaluated the influence of the framework on the selection, based on a synthesis of the experience of choosing the intervention.

6.4 Your consideration of the impact on teaching practice of using developmental assessment frameworks:

    a was general in nature

    b addressed aspects of teaching practice that might be affected

    c predicted the implications for teaching practice based on an evaluation of using the framework.

Chapter 7

Writing assessment rubrics

**Patrick Griffin and
Pam Robertson**

Rubrics usually are written as a form of a rating scale, and often
fail to help teachers improve student performance or product.
This chapter presents a new approach to writing rubrics, which
fits within the developmental assessment framework described in
Chapter 6. An approach to the evaluation of rubrics is presented,
and several case studies and examples are presented as a
rationale for writing rubrics. The focus of the approach is on how
rubrics and judgement-based assessment can help teachers to
improve student performance.

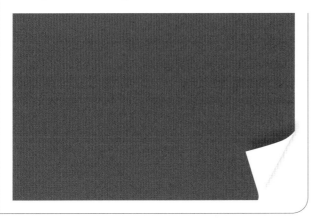

Learning objectives

In this chapter you will learn to:

- understand the role of assessment rubrics in the scoring of judgement-based assessments
- evaluate the quality of rubrics
- write rubrics that can be used within a developmental model of assessment.

Introduction

Teachers using judgement-based assessment need to operate within a criterion-referenced framework. In order to do this, they need rubrics – or rules to guide their judgements. The term 'rubric', however, is much over-used and misunderstood. Websites are available providing sets of rubrics for almost every conceivable area of learning, but much of what they offer is unhelpful and some of it is simply wrong. Although some of the rubrics offered on those sites are useful, almost none is under-pinned by a model of measurement and very few appear to be underpinned by a learning theory. Consequently, one of the first things we need to do when considering rubrics is to have criteria for evaluating them. Then we need to know how to write our own rubrics in such a way that they are useful and of high quality, with minimal risk of misleading students, teachers or PLT members. Rubrics written and interpreted in a criterion-referenced framework are generally underpinned by both a model of measurement and a learning theory or taxonomy. This chapter describes how to write rubrics within such a framework.

We define a rubric used within a criterion-referenced framework in the following way:

> An assessment rubric is a rule for scoring or coding the quality of an observed performance. It is the combination of an indicative behaviour and its associated set of quality criteria.

An assessment rubric combines the final two parts of the framework structure described in Chapter 6: indicative behaviours and quality criteria. When a rule is used for scoring, directly observed evidence becomes the focus of the rubric and errors associated with subjectivity can be reduced. As we have argued in the preceding chapters, evidence must take the form of what a person can do, say, make or write. The focus on evidence scored according to a rubric allows judgement-based assessments to be considered reliable and consistent, thereby providing a starting point for valid inferences.

In a developmental assessment framework, the capabilities are the skills, knowledge, attitudes and/or expectations that might be established within a domain or strand of learning development. They are 'big ideas', sometimes stated in abstract terms, which represent the overall development of a person in an area of learning. They answer such questions as:

- What can a teacher expect of a pupil in a learning area?
- What can a principal expect of a teacher in classroom practice and pedagogy?
- What can an employer expect of a worker in a workshop practice?
- What can be expected in professional development in order to improve practice?

The capabilities might define the curriculum for teaching and learning within each of the strands or domains of a developmental assessment framework. They do not need to be directly observed and can describe understanding, knowing, competency, thinking or feeling. Capabilities can be described and defined by addressing the following questions:

- What are the big ideas, expected outcomes or issues that need to be developed within the learning area?
- Is it possible to identify evidence for these ideas, skills, knowledge or attitudes? What might the evidence consist of?
- How many capabilities are needed in order to define learning development within the relevant domain? What is adequate, authentic and appropriate, and what provides accurate information about the development?

This approach to writing rubrics uses the expert judgement of teachers to identify and refine statements of capabilities. Other approaches emphasise how *many* indicators are used to describe learning rather than how *well* learning is demonstrated. The crux of our approach is an emphasis on the quality rather than the quantity of evidence. It is true that the number of indicators is sometimes important: it is always important to decide how much evidence is adequate to draw a conclusion. But it is also necessary to decide what kind of evidence is appropriate to use, and rules are needed about how to determine the authenticity of evidence. The three aspects of adequacy, appropriateness and authenticity of evidence are always important. They have also to be considered in the light of the accuracy of the available information.

Descriptions of indicators define the evidence required to show the existence or development of capabilities. They show what someone would need to do to demonstrate that they have the capability in question. By observing the presence or absence of these indicators, or indicative behaviours, it is possible to make a generalised judgement about whether or not someone has the associated capability.

The essential characteristic of the evidence for an assessment is that it makes possible an unequivocal inference about the capability or the personal attribute of interest. The evidence must be appropriate, adequate, accurate and authentic.

- *Appropriate.* Is the evidence the right kind of evidence for making the decisions that need to be made? Is it supportive of the inference that is to be drawn from the data? Is it ethical to gather these data?

- *Adequate.* Do we have enough evidence to make the conclusion that we wish to make? This is a matter for the teacher to decide, but one observation is not enough. A test score needs to be moderated by other data. Other sections of this book focus on using multiple measures and multiple observations.

- *Accurate.* What efforts are being made to control 'noise' in the data? Have the influences of student behaviour been controlled? Are teacher attitudes to the assessment taken into account? Are other factors involved, such as heat or cold, time available, context in which the assessment is conducted? Has the process of collecting the assessment data been controlled?

- *Authentic.* Can it be verified that the evidence being used to make the decision is linked directly to the person being assessed? Is there a method or process of authentication to ensure that the evidence in the portfolio, test or other assessment device is actually produced by that person?

Once indicators have been defined and can be argued to meet the requirements of adequacy, appropriateness, authenticity and accuracy, the remaining issue is addressed: how *well* each of these indicative behaviours is demonstrated. This is important for identifying the underpinning developmental continuum. Thus quality criteria are ordered descriptions of how well the indicative behaviour may be demonstrated. They can illustrate increasing sophistication, difficulty, elegance or another measure of quality. Criteria represent a series of thresholds that differentiate people in terms of their ability to demonstrate development. The combination of an indicator and its associated quality criteria is called a rubric.

When assessing within a developmental framework, teachers need to code the performances (mark the assessments) of students to capture stages of development. For this reason, the quality criteria within assessment rubrics are written to describe increasing proficiency in the indicative behaviours. The first step when writing quality criteria, therefore, is to describe increasing stages of competency within each indicative behaviour. If you are writing rubrics for something you have taught a lot, you can draw on that experience to describe the typical stages through which students pass as they become more proficient. It may be helpful to collect samples of student work and sort the samples according to the stage of proficiency in the indicative behaviour you are trying to describe. You can then look at the similarities between the samples at each stage to formulate a description of the stage. The differences between samples at successive stages are also useful. Think about what is being done by students at a higher stage and not done by students at the next lowest stage. This can assist you to write descriptions that capture the distinct differences between each stage. Once you can do this, you are well on the way to writing a great assessment rubric.

If you are having trouble seeing or describing the stages of increasing competence, it is a good idea to refer to the developmental taxonomies introduced in Chapter 2. They provide invaluable support in highlighting the typical differences between stages, and they also suggest verbs that can be used to describe each stage. When using the developmental taxonomies, the first step is to decide whether increasing proficiency in the indicative behaviour is characterised best as an increase in knowledge, skill or attitude. Usually all the indicative behaviours within a set of rubrics relate to the same aspect. Select the developmental taxonomy to match the aspect you have chosen. Use the Dreyfus model of skill acquisition for writing skill-based rubrics, Krathwohl's affective taxonomy for attitudes and either SOLO or Bloom's Taxonomy for knowledge. As SOLO was developed specifically to describe learning outcomes, it is often the best taxonomy to use when writing knowledge-based rubrics. Once you have selected the most suitable taxonomy, decide which levels of the taxonomy can be adapted to describe levels of increasing competence in the indicative behaviour in question. Usually some levels are instantly recognisable, and it is best to focus on modifying these levels. It is not necessary (and in fact a disadvantage, as we will see later in this chapter) to write a quality criterion matched to every level in the taxonomy.

Once you have described the levels of increasing competence within each indicative behaviour, the next step is to tighten the way in which these are described, so you have quality criteria that can be used accurately to code the student performances. Accuracy is important so that the marking of student work is consistent and the rubrics provide a clear record of the student performance on which to make inferences to inform your teaching decisions. For this reason, it is helpful to utilise verbs to emphasise the differences between successive quality criteria. This focuses the rubric on student behaviours, making it easier to judge which quality criterion best captures the student's performance.

The language you use in the quality criteria should also be clear to all involved – your students and any other teachers using the rubric. Try to choose words that will communicate clearly and simply. Minimise the number of words in each quality criterion. It is a good idea to move the verbs to the start of quality criteria to emphasise the behaviours. It is also helpful to keep as much as possible of the language consistent between criteria within the same indicative behaviour and to only change words that describe the differences between criteria. This emphasises what is needed to move from one criterion to the next. Try to choose words that will be meaningful to all users of the rubric. Some disciplines involve a great deal of specific language. Where you need to use discipline-specific language, try to use terms that are familiar to the students. If you are writing rubrics for assessing young children, it may not be possible to express the rubrics simply enough for them to understand, so try to make the wording clear enough to show their parents. Whatever words you use, always remember that they should communicate clearly and succinctly.

The following rules outline what must be done to write quality criteria that allow different responses or performances to be recorded in a consistent and interpretable way. These rules have emerged over time, partly in response to problems encountered in assessment and data interpretation. Each rule has been tested in multiple situations, and has been found to improve assessment accuracy and/or interpretation. Too many rubric examples on the internet disregard these rules. Disregarding them can make assessment more difficult and time-consuming. It can also make assessment results less reliable and more difficult to use.

Rules for writing quality criteria

Good-quality criteria should follow these guidelines:

1 *There should be no counts of things right and wrong or pseudo-counts* (e.g. some, many). Counts and pseudo-counts do not give an indication of quality or sophistication, and their use can discourage students from testing their own limits. For example, a rubric that counts the number of words used incorrectly may encourage an ambitious student to play it safe by using only one-syllable words rather than trying to use more complex language. Example 3 (below) elaborates this idea.

2 *Avoid language that is ambiguous or contains comparative terms to define quality of performance* (e.g. don't describe the performance using terms like good, better, best, or appropriate, suitable, adequate, superior). Subjective terms can lead to inconsistent marking and disagreements during moderation about, for example, what constitutes 'appropriate' or 'suitable'. Even when teachers have a consistent view as to what these terms mean, it does not provide students with guidance about what is required.

3 *Avoid procedural steps describing a sequence of operations.* If steps are necessary in order to complete parts of a task, rubrics sometimes turn these procedural steps into criteria (completes Step 1, completes Step 2, etc.). This implies that the student who reaches the end of the sequence of operations has shown greater quality than the student who only completes Step 1. However, each of the steps can be performed with differing degrees of quality. Two students may perform Step 1 in different ways, and demonstrate different levels of performance. In many sequences, it is possible to observe some people performing a task or step in a sequence better than other people. So each step in the sequence should have its own quality criteria. This allows a judgement to be made about the difference between a student who completes Step 1 only, but does so to an amazingly high level, and a student who just scrapes through all three steps.

4 *Describe performances such that each successive description implies a progressively higher level of performance.* The difference in quality should be clear and observable. Developmental taxonomies can be very useful in helping

to identify progressively higher levels of quality. See Chapter 2 for examples. It can be helpful to make the 'jumps' in quality quite large and not worry about fine differences in quality. This ensures that the quality of the student's performance is recognised in the rubrics used to judge quality. If teachers find themselves realising when marking that the rubrics being used do not allow them to recognise the quality in the students' work, then there is something wrong with the rubrics and they should be reviewed.

5 *Contain one central idea that can be recognised through evidence – what the students do, say, make or write.* If more than one idea is contained in a criterion, it becomes difficult to judge which should be selected when a student has achieved one part but not the other. Example 1 (below) explains this in more detail.

6 *Be directly observable (do, say, make, write) – avoid negatives.* When criteria are directly observable, teachers are not required to make inferences in order to assess the work. Within a set of quality criteria, there is no need to specify what the student cannot do, as this is implied by the higher criteria.

7 *Reflect typical behaviours that cover a diverse range of qualities, including a stretch for the most proficient.* When assessment rubrics are interpreted in a criterion-referenced manner – rather than being converted to a percentage achieved, as is common practice – students are not penalised for not reaching the highest criterion. This allows teachers to set aspirational targets for the highest achievers, so all students are encouraged to stretch their capabilities. Often teachers are surprised when students achieve criteria that were considered aspirational, providing an important opportunity for teacher learning.

8 *Self-weight based on their capacity to separate by performance quality – that is, no weightings are to be used.* Many traditional assessments give greater weight to some rubrics than they do to others. Weightings are often used because teachers recognise that some rubrics are harder than others, and they wish this to be indicated when the rubrics are converted into a score or percentage. With a criterion-referenced interpretation, this reason for weighting some rubrics over others disappears, as the rubrics are mapped to levels on a developmental progression, not a percentage. This allows the assessment data to be used directly to plan teaching.

9 *Have four or fewer criteria for any indicator (to support consistency of judgements).* Experience in many instances has shown that when more than four criteria are used, teachers struggle to distinguish consistently the different levels of quality, because the differences between them are too difficult to recognise. Distinctions are more easily made when the jumps in quality are larger. This results in more consistent judgements.

10 *Be transparent so persons assessed can verify their assessment – don't use jargon.* It is ideal if all parties have a full understanding of the criteria. This allows students to have greater control over their own learning, and also facilitates open communication between students, parents and teachers. Transparent criteria allow students to self-assess, which helps them to make decisions regarding the way they utilise their time and energy.

Rules 1 to 3 are the core rules. Rubrics that do not follow these rules require learners to guess what the assessor is looking for. This is like asking learners to jump but providing no answer to the question 'How high?' Rules 4 to 10 are additional rules that increase the usefulness of rubrics. Intriguingly, Rules 1 to 3 are the easiest to use when evaluating existing rubrics, but are the hardest to apply when learning to write rubrics. You will find that rubric writing is a challenge that rewards persistent effort.

Reflective questions

Rule 7 requires rubrics to include criteria that are a 'stretch for the most proficient'. This is quite different from common assessment practice.

* What are the implications of such a requirement?
* How does the change from a score or percentage system of reporting to a criterion-referenced system challenge the traditional ideas of fairness?
* How could such a change best be introduced to students and parents?
* One way to think of criteria is to think about students you know. What does a highly capable student do? Use your answer to write a high-level criterion. Then write another, higher criterion to stretch the best students.
* What does a low-ability student do? Use your answer to write a low-level criterion. Then write another, lower criterion to allow all students to be recorded.

What is the difference between 'good' and 'bad' rubrics?

Like good rubrics, bad rubrics will provide information, but they cannot be synthesised and interpreted with reference to a developmental model. They may not facilitate teaching decisions: they cannot identify the point of readiness to learn. They are often written in arbitrary language that leads to multiple interpretations, which in turn necessitates a costly process of assessment moderation, with double or triple judgements. They offer little hope of self-assessment and they provide almost no transparency of assessment, so that candidates are led into a situation in which they must play the game of 'guess what the teacher wants'. This is unethical practice, and cannot lead to valid assessment interpretation. When examining rubrics provided by other people, the rules or meta-rubrics should be used to evaluate them. Unless a rubric meets these guidelines, it should not be used.

Below, a series of examples is provided to illustrate the use of the rubric-writing rules. Each example contains a rubric drawn from a real assessment which does not follow all the rules. The rubric is then rewritten to show how it can be changed to be more effective. A discussion of the two is also provided.

Example 1: Basketball

Table 7.1 shows one of a set of rubrics that has been used to assess the basketball skills of students. It is easy to see that the skills described represent increasing levels of quality in performance (Rule 4), that they are directly observable and that they are mostly described with positive language (Rule 6). The language used is unambiguous (Rule 2), there are fewer than four criteria (Rule 9) and the criteria cover a diverse range of performance qualities (Rule 7). In fact, the only real problem with this rubric is that it breaches Rule 5. Each criterion contains several ideas – dribbling, lay-ups and jump shots. This may cause difficulties for the assessor if the student has not developed consistently across the three different skill components. It is also hard for the student to interpret the feedback from this rubric. If the student is recorded as being at the accomplished level, is this because they have demonstrated all three skills at that level, or just two of the three? How would a student be scored who is able to dribble with head up using both dominant and non-dominant hands, shoot a lay-up with the dominant hand, but not shoot a jump shot?

Table 7.1 *Flawed rubric to assess basketball*

CATEGORY	BEGINNING	DEVELOPING	ACCOMPLISHED	EXEMPLARY
Form/skill execution	Needs to look down to dribble. Able to shoot a lay-up on dominant side but needs to use both hands. Uses both hands to shoot a jump shot.	Able to somewhat dribble with head up with dominant hand. Able to shoot a lay-up only with dominant hand. Able to shoot a jump shot but does not follow through.	Able to dribble with head up with both hands. Able to shoot a lay-up with both hands. Able to shoot a jump shot but does not meet all of the BEEF requirements (balance, eyes, elbow, follow through).	Able to dribble with head up with both dominant and non-dominant hand. Able to shoot a lay-up with both hands while taking off from the opposite foot. Able to shoot a jump shot with BEEF formation.

A version of the same rubric, written to comply with the rules, is shown in Table 7.2. In this set of three rubrics, the three components are separated so that each central idea has its own rubric (Rule 5). This removes the problem of poor feedback to students. The lower criterion, 'Insufficient evidence', is included to cater for those students not yet able to demonstrate the skills of dribbling, lay-ups and jump shots, or situations in which the student was not able to demonstrate these skills.

Table 7.2 *Improved rubric to assess basketball*

1.1 Dribbles	1.1.0 Insufficient evidence	1.1.1 Looks down to dribble.	1.1.2 Dribbles with head up using dominant hand.	1.1.3 Dribbles with head up using either hand.	
1.2 Shoots a lay-up	1.2.0 Insufficient evidence	1.2.1 Able to shoot a lay-up on dominant side using both hands.	1.2.2 Able to shoot a lay-up using only dominant hand.	1.2.3 Able to shoot a lay-up using either hand.	1.2.4 Able to shoot a lay-up using either hand while taking off from the opposite foot.
1.3 Shoots a jump shot	1.3.0 Insufficient evidence	1.3.1 Able to shoot a jump shot.	1.3.2 Able to shoot a jump shot with BEEF formation (balance, eyes, elbow, follow through).		

There are minor wording changes to improve the clarity of some criteria and ensure that there is a distinct difference in quality between successive criteria. It is possible that additional criteria could be added to dribbling and jump-shot rubrics to include a stretch for the most proficient. A criterion such as 'Hand dominance indistinguishable when dribbling' could be a useful addition. Note that the dribbling rubric describes three levels of quality and the jump-shot rubric describes only two. It is not necessary to have the same number of criteria in each rubric. It is more important that the differences in levels of quality are clear, and that the 'distance' in ability between criteria is reasonably large. Chapter 9 describes how rubrics with various numbers of criteria can be synthesised into level descriptions and how scores can be interpreted meaningfully using these levels.

Example 2: Written communication

Almost every form of written assessment (such as essays or reports) seems to include an assessment of the technical aspects of writing: grammar, spelling and punctuation. Assessors must consider whether this capability needs to be assessed in order to make inferences about proficiency in every topic or domain in which writing is used. The rubric in Table 7.3 is representative of many included in assessments of domains in which writing is used, such as history, science and geography.

Table 7.3 *Flawed rubric for assessing technical aspects of writing*

Mechanics	Limited skill in the use of conventions of spelling and grammar.	Some skill in the use of conventions of spelling and grammar.	Correctly uses conventions of spelling and grammar.

This rubric relies on the use of pseudo-counts (Rule 1), and as such is at the mercy of each assessor's own understanding of what each term (limited, some) may mean. The use of pseudo-counts makes it difficult to determine teaching interventions from the developmental data. What needs to be done to scaffold a student from having 'limited skill' to having 'some skill'? One way for students to improve their score on such a rubric is to stop trying to use more difficult words or grammatical structures, so the use of such rubrics may actually serve to dissuade students from trying new skills rather than encouraging their development.

An improved rubric for assessing written communication is shown in Table 7.4. This rubric avoids the use of pseudo-counts and asks the assessor to consider the *goal* of writing in subjects such as history and science – that is, communication. It uses the SOLO taxonomy (see Chapter 2). Criterion 2.1 is an application of the multi-structural level, where technical aspects are addressed, but not drawn together in a coherent whole, and Criterion 2.2 matches the relational level, where the various aspects are combined to address the primary purpose of communication. The differences in proficiency between each of these three levels are large, so the assessor can more easily identify the appropriate criterion.

Table 7.4 *Improved rubric for assessing technical aspects of writing*

2 Communicates with writing	2.0 Insufficient evidence	2.1 Technical aspects of writing permit the communication of content.	2.2 Technical aspects of writing facilitate the communication of content.

Example 3: Science

Many rubric writers understand the difficulties inherent in the use of pseudo-counts, and many go to great lengths to make rubrics clearer. In doing so, many resort to the use of precise counts, as shown in Table 7.5. Although this rubric would allow for more consistent assessment than those that use pseudo-counts, like the one in Table 7.3, it shares many of their limitations regarding informing teaching and changing student performance. It does not suggest the next step for the student, and may encourage students to restrict themselves to using skills and knowledge they have already mastered. As we will see in Chapter 9, we must also avoid the use of comparative terms and steps when writing criteria, if these criteria are to be used to derive criterion-referenced frameworks.

Table 7.5 *Flawed science rubric*

Scientific errors	Some 90–100 per cent of the answers have no scientific errors.	Almost all (85–89 per cent) of the answers have no scientific errors.	Most (70–84 per cent) of the answers have no scientific errors.	Less than 70 per cent of the answers have no scientific errors.

An improved science rubric is shown in Table 7.6. The rubric considers the sophistication with which the student has used scientific knowledge, rather than resorting to a count of right and wrong uses. Again, the SOLO taxonomy has been used, this time with the multi-structural, relational and extended abstract levels represented. Although the SOLO taxonomy has five levels, it is not necessary to have all five levels represented in a rubric. In fact, it is better to have fewer levels represented, as indicated in Rule 9. Although both of these improved rubrics are based on SOLO, the verbs used are quite different. The use of the standard verbs for any developmental taxonomy can wash out many interesting and distinguishing developments. It is better to consult the range of literature available on elaborations to the taxonomies (SOLO, Bloom (revised), Krathwohl and Dreyfus) and use the verb lists in the literature to write formal criteria.

Table 7.6 *Improved science rubric*

3 Uses scientific information	3.0 Insufficient evidence	3.1 Matches pieces of scientific knowledge to the question.	3.2 Identifies relationships between pieces of scientific knowledge.	3.3 Considers the robustness of the current scientific knowledge in light of scientific method.

The rubric in Table 7.6 may tempt teachers to record the highest level and all the levels below, as a student who considers the robustness of information also identifies the relationships between pieces of information and matches information to the question. Only the highest level observed needs to be recorded, as the hierarchy of the criteria implies that the student is also capable of the lower criteria. The best practice is to record the highest criterion and assume those underneath.

Example 4: Class presentation

The rubric shown in Table 7.7 is taken from a set of rubrics for assessing a class presentation. The writers of this rubric have tried to avoid comparative terms and in doing so have produced a rubric that would be impossible to use for assessment.

Table 7.7 *Flawed rubric on volume in a class presentation*

Volume	Volume is loud enough to be heard by all audience members throughout the presentation.	Volume is loud enough to be heard by all audience members at least 90 per cent of the time.	Volume is loud enough to be heard by all audience members at least 80 per cent of the time.	Volume often too soft to be heard by all audience members.

This rubric fails largely because it loses its focus on the actions of the presenter and begins to focus on the experience of others, which is difficult to judge (not to mention unfair if some audience members are hearing impaired). Classroom presentation rubrics often have this change of focus. Another example of such a rubric is one that assesses whether a presenter would be able to answer audience questions, without taking into account how difficult those questions might be. Such rubrics represent a subtle breach of Rule 4, as they describe the reaction of others rather than the performance quality of the person being assessed.

The improved rubric (Table 7.8) is structured using Dreyfus. The novice, competent and proficient levels are represented. Criteria 4.1 and 4.2 show the use of different verbs to describe the actions of the presenter, rather than qualifiers. This highlights the inherent differences in what the student is doing, saying, making or writing.

Table 7.8 *Improved rubric on volume in a class presentation*

4. Uses volume in a presentation	4.0 Insufficient evidence	4.1 Matches volume to the context of the presentation.	4.2 Emphasises parts of the presentation using changes in volume.	4.3 Uses volume to engage the audience in the ideas communicated.

While the examples shown in this chapter have been used with success, they do not represent an exhaustive list of possibilities. The important thing is to use a theoretical framework or one of the developmental taxonomies. These examples of the translation of a theoretical taxonomy to quality criteria show how it can be done. Of course, this introduces the danger that all criteria will start to look the same. This is only an initial danger, and it matters little if this is the case in the early stages of rubric preparation. As the capability matures, specialist rubric-writing skills will emerge and the style will depart from these models.

Reflective question

Rubrics such as the flawed examples above are easy to access. They can be readily written or sourced on the internet. Rubrics that follow the rules take time to write, but allow for easier marking, interpretation and use to inform teaching. What are the pros and cons of using each type of rubric? Given the time demands on teachers, what supports can teachers draw on to assist them to change from the former to the latter?

Although bad rubrics are easier to write than good ones, the information that can be obtained from good rubrics is well worth the effort of learning to write them. Well-written rubrics can be used to provide direct feedback that is of benefit to the student assessed. They can provide teachers with a direction regarding what to teach next and, as we will see in Chapter 9, can be a starting point for teachers to use when deriving criterion-referenced frameworks.

Templates for writing rubrics

Numerous templates can be generated to assist in the writing of rubrics. These templates serve as graphic organisers, reminding the writer of what must be included.

Key learning area	Subject
Module or unit name	Domain or unit
Capability or expectation	Capability
Indicative behaviour	Indicative behaviour
Criterion 1	Criterion 1
Criterion 2	Criterion 2
Criterion 3	Criterion 3
Criterion 4	Criterion 4

Figure 7.1a *A rubric-writing template for an individual rubric*

Any template should include the domain, strand and capability being assessed, as well as the indicator and quality criteria. It is often difficult to fit many rubrics into a single template, so templates can address each rubric individually, as in the example given in Figures 7.1a and 7.1b. Alternatively, a few rubrics can be included in a single template, as in the example in Figures 7.2a and 7.2b. In each of these examples, the template is given, followed by a completed example.

Collaborative problem solving	Subject
Social Skills	Domain or unit
Participation	Capability
Negotiation	Indicative behaviour
No attempt	Criterion 1
Comments on different perspectives	Criterion 2
Negotiates through differences in points of view	Criterion 3
Brings the issue to a mutual resolution and moves forward	Criterion 4

Figure 7.1b *Example of the use of the rubric-writing template for an individual rubric*

Domain: **Strand:**

Developmental taxonomy					
	Indicators				
	Capability				

Figure 7.2a *A rubric-writing template for multiple rubrics*

Domain: Visual communication – Information design **Strand:** 2 – Produces visual communications

Developmental framework: Dreyfus	Expert	2.1.1.3 Innovates with the use of design elements to create solution	2.1.2.3 Innovates with the use of design principles to create solution
	Proficient		
	Competent	2.1.1.2 Utilises rules/guidelines in the use of design elements to create solution	2.1.2.2 Utilises rules/guidelines in the use of design principles to create solution
	Advanced beginner	2.1.1.1 Uses design elements	2.1.2.1 Uses design principles
	Novice		
		2.1.1.0 Insufficient evidence	2.1.2.0 Insufficient evidence
	Indicators	2.1.1 Uses design elements	2.1.2 Uses design principles
	Capability	2.1 Designs visual communications	

Figure 7.2b *An example of a rubric-writing template for multiple rubrics*

The template in Figure 7.2 includes the numbering system introduced in Chapter 6 (see Figure 6.2), which can be useful when panelling rubrics and when synthesising rubrics from multiple templates. It also includes a place to record the developmental taxonomy that was used to guide the writing of the quality criteria. When writing quality criteria, it is important to use a learning taxonomy because this will help you focus on the differences between levels of quality. Further, it enables colleagues, as panel members (see Chapter 8), to check that the criteria address a useful range of possible levels of quality. Using developmental taxonomies helps to build in a relevant learning theory that underpins the assessment and in turn informs targeted teaching intervention and learning development. The taxonomy enables the link between learning theory on the one hand, and teaching and learning on the other, to be quite simple. The link is embedded in the assessment.

The mapping out of assessment rubrics produces descriptions of different levels of performance within the construct you are assessing. These descriptions can be used as a starting point for defining a hypothetical construct or progression. To define the construct from the assessment rubrics, you start with the rubrics laid out against a developmental taxonomy, as in the template provided in Figure 7.2. The criteria in each row are then synthesised to form a general description of typical behaviours present at a given level of development. When the synthesised descriptions are ordered by difficulty, they form a derived progression that outlines the typical behaviours at levels of increasing competence. A derived progression is one that is formed from data or professional judgement. This general process is described in Chapter 9, but there the order of items, or criteria, is provided by a statistical analysis or a pairwise comparison, whereas here the order is provided by the template.

Using the ordering of criteria provided by a developmental taxonomy is a helpful starting point for making a derived progression if the rubrics cover indicative behaviours that are of similar difficulty. Consider a set of mathematics rubrics that includes the indicators 'Adds two-digit numbers' and 'Solves quadratic equations'. Imagine that criteria for both rubrics have been written using Bloom's Taxonomy as a guide and that each indicator has a criterion at the 'Apply' level. If the ordering were to be used as the basis for describing a hypothetical framework, then it would imply that a student who is learning to apply their knowledge of two-digit addition is also learning to apply their knowledge of quadratic equations, which is absurd. This discrepancy arises from the vastly different difficulties of the two indicators. When the indicators within a set of rubrics are of similar difficulty, the problem is resolved. An example of a derived progression for a design process, using Bloom's Taxonomy, is provided in Figure 7.3.

Create	1.1.3 Synthesis of communication need demonstrated in development of solution		
Evaluate			1.3.3 Evaluates their own solution in terms of the design process
Analyse	1.1.2 Communication need informs solution	1.2.3 Determines usefulness of information for solution	
Apply	1.1.1 Establishes communication need	1.2.2 Applies information in solution	1.3.2 Demonstrates the use of the design process in development of solutions
Understand		1.2.1 Uses sources of information	1.3.1 Uses part of the design process
Remember			
	1.1.0 Insufficient evidence	1.2.0 Insufficient evidence	1.3.0 Insufficient evidence
Indicators	1.1 Definition of the communication need	1.2 Research – for information and ideas	1.3 Generation, development and refinement of ideas
Capability	1 Using the design process		

Figure 7.3 *Derived progression for a design process using Bloom's Taxonomy*

Direct observation and quality criteria

When the rubrics are written to align with a developmental assessment framework (domain, strands and capabilities), they can help teachers to determine the suitability of assessments by noting the extent to which the task elicits the direct observation of the desired indicative behaviours. However, the use of direct observation leads to another issue. If we observe only once, we run the risk of recording an inaccurate estimate of student learning.

The issue is whether the directly observed performance represents the highest level at which the student can perform or is an aberration demonstrated on this single occasion. The recording of the *typical* level requires a reflective procedure from the teacher, who needs to take several opportunities to observe content and context and make a balanced judgement. This means that observations must be made in several contexts – even in the most challenging circumstances – and a reflective decision must be made before recording the performance in a rubric. Competence is not about demonstrating a single task performance. A truly competent person has *the ability to adjust to the demands of the context*, allowing a skill to be demonstrated in a variety of circumstances. Variation needs to be sought by the teacher, and the decision on the highest typical level should be made on the basis of a range of observations. This is common sense in education and measurement – the making of multiple observations is a maxim of good measurement.

Developing rubric-writing skills

Good rubrics are difficult to write. Rubric-writing skills develop over time, and in the initial stages it may seem that they are not worth the effort needed to acquire them! With practice, it is possible to move from being a novice rubric-writer to competent, then proficient and perhaps even expert. Collaboration and practice are the two critical components in improving rubric-writing skills. Working with a PLT to write rubrics ensures a collaborative approach and peer accountability to help members persevere during the difficult early stages.

There is a series of steps that can be followed in developing good rubrics. The first step is to establish the draft ideas. Sometimes you will find the writing difficult. This writing paralysis often occurs because we think we need to write the perfect piece at the first attempt, but this is not the case. To begin, you should simply put down ideas for rubrics and not worry about whether they are good, bad or indifferent. From the resulting draft, it is possible to hone the rubrics and to pass them back and forth from one member of your team to another, in order to improve their expression, grammar, clarity and purpose. This important process is called 'panelling', and it will be explored in more detail in later chapters. An example of a panelled set of rubrics is shown in Figure 7.4. While it looks like colleagues have been terribly critical, the comments are important. Panelling is a process in which peers of the author critique and improve the rubric. They do not simply criticise it in a negative way.

Narrative Assessment

Component: Content and Organisation *Are these criteria for students or teachers? Have each of these been clearly developed with students?*

Elements:
Beginning
1. Does not provide initial details of time, place or character.
2. Includes <u>essentials</u> of time, place and character without elaboration. *What are essentials???*
3. Provides details about time, place and characters to establish context.
4. Provides detail to establish relationship between setting, major and minor characters. *May be only!*

What about a 'hook in'? A beginning that hooks the characte reader in from the opening?

Build Up
1. No build up. Straight into action. *(Would students understand this?)*
2. Writes a sequence of events which doesn't lead to complication.
3. Sequence of events including initiating event which leads to complication.
4. Includes events which lead up to problem, withholding/including information to maintain tension.

Problem
1. No problem. → *no problem/complication* → *no narrative????*
2. Identifies a problem.
3. Includes details about problem to build or maintain tension. *????*

Resolution *Some great narratives leave the final resolution to the reader???*
1. Doesn't include a resolution. *the*
2. Includes a resolution that links to other parts of the story. *?? What do you mean?*
3. Shows interaction between characters and conflicts and resolves the conflicts. *in an unexpected essay?*

It may not be a conflict *It may be one conflict!* *Conflicts (plural?)* *but- a complication*

Ending
1. Doesn't include an ending.
2. Story has an ending.
3. Ending includes reflection on story events. *Is this necessary????*

Characters
1. Names characters but doesn't elaborate.
2. Provides information about the characters using adjectives. *— Is this necessary?*
3. Uses devices such as dialogue, similes and <u>relationships</u> between characters to provide information about characters.

Plot
1. A series of events which are not linked.
2. A series of related events which occur in order. *What about when you start at the end & proceed through flashback*
3. A series of events which incorporate a problem which is solved.
4. Develops a cohesive series of events and elaborates and resolves each complication in episodes. *???? Minor & major complications?*

Setting
1. No mention. *Sometimes the setting is not crucial to the plot →*
2. Mentions the setting but does not describe it.
3. Describes the setting using <u>adjectives</u>. *?*
4. Uses similes, metaphors and/or word pictures to embed details about setting into the story. *metaphors are word pictures. & similes*

Beginning that grabs the reader — Students need models*

Figure 7.4 *A panelled set of rubrics*

When collaborating to write rubrics, the list below serves as a reminder of what good rubrics should be:

- clear and succinct (self-explanatory)
- free of jargon
- phrased in a positive way (what the person can do)
- devoid of all comparative terms and value judgements (poor, excellent, good, etc.)
- developed in consultation with subject experts
- a contribution to a description of an underlying developmental continuum of proficiency
- drawn from a pool of draft rubrics – write more than needed and then delete some
- based on a learning theory or taxonomy to help frame the criteria (Bloom, Dreyfus, etc.)
- developed from rough drafts without worrying about the language, then adjusted and edited
- written at first by people working individually, then developed through consultation
- written in a multiple-choice format
- exhaustively panelled by specialists in the subject area.

Extended example: The E5 model

The example of rubric-writing illustrated in Tables 7.9 to 7.13 shows the near-final stage of a framework with indicative behaviours and quality criteria. The changes and comments from a final panelling session have been left in the table in *italics* so you can see the issues that were still being discussed. You will see that, even at this stage, some rubrics do not follow all the rules for writing quality criteria. The rubrics are designed to examine and define teacher skill level in biological science and were developed for the Biological Sciences Curriculum Study E5 model, which consists of five phases: engage, explore, explain, elaborate and evaluate (DEECD 2009). The formal descriptions of the five phases are provided in the box below, and the figures that follow the descriptions illustrate how each of the phases is operationalised using the framework described in Chapter 6 and the guidelines provided in this chapter.

The E5 model

1 The teacher's intent in *engagement* is to draw out what is of value to the students, promote high mutual engagement and prepare students for future learning. The teacher builds on students' interests, backgrounds, experience, knowledge, skills and prior conceptions, supporting students to connect past and present learning experiences.

Connecting learning to real-world experiences, the teacher promotes high learner engagement by presenting activities that stimulate interest, curiosity and inquiry. The teacher involves students in framing up a purpose for learning new concepts, negotiating challenging learning goals and making assessment requirements clear to students. The teacher monitors and builds students' self-efficacy, developing their capacities and beliefs about themselves as learners. The teacher supports students to organise their thinking toward expected learning outcomes and to be self-managing learners.

2   The teacher's intent in *exploration* is to broaden students' experiences through designed exploration. The teacher presents intellectually stimulating activities for students to gather information and develop ideas. This common base of shared learning experiences expands students' perspectives, challenges their conceptions and supports them to question and generate new ideas and possibilities. The teacher provides tools and procedures for students to use prior knowledge and organise information for future reference. The teacher encourages students to reflect on their personal learning experiences, and intervenes to ensure students are appropriately challenged and motivated.

3   The teacher's intent in the *explanation* phase is to enrich students' shared experiences and ideas to promote improved and deeper individual and collective understanding of specific contexts. The teacher focuses on key ideas, demonstrating and eliciting multiple representations of understanding. The teacher orchestrates student involvement in substantial, sustained conversation that is both teacher and peer led, and listens to assess students' level of understanding. By providing students with a variety of collaborative opportunities, the teacher develops the social value of shared explanation. The teacher directly introduces concepts in response to student need, develops skills and provides tools, procedures and processes to assist students to make sense of their learning. The teacher supports students to organise and connect new knowledge into a conceptual framework.

4   The teacher's intent in the *elaboration* phase is to develop students' deep conceptual understanding and their ability to apply this to new situations and contexts. The teacher provides multiple representations and a range of learning experiences to challenge and consolidate students' knowledge and understanding. Students are supported to develop and demonstrate deep levels of thinking and to optimise their ability to retain and automatise their learning. Then the teacher selects a range of contrasting contexts, which progressively build the students' capacity to synthesise their learning and transfer and generalise from familiar contexts into unfamiliar contexts.

5   The teacher's intent in the *evaluation* phase is to support students' self-assessment and to formally evaluate student learning. The teacher assists students to reflect on their progress, achievements and learning processes. By providing opportunities for students to organise their knowledge, the teacher prepares students to demonstrate their learning across various assessment contexts. Assessment tasks are designed to enable students to demonstrate learning through diverse representations.

The teacher integrates assessment information from each phase to formally record students' progress against individual learning and curriculum goals.

E5 Instructional model – at a glance

Table 7.9 *Elaboration of the engage phase*

DOMAIN	CAPABILITIES	PERFORMANCE INDICATORS	QUALITY CRITERIA
Engage The teacher develops shared expectations for learning and interacting. The teacher stimulates interest and curiosity, promotes questioning, and connects learning to real-world experiences. Through the activities, the teacher elicits students' prior knowledge and supports them to make connections to past learning experiences. The teacher presents a purpose for learning, determines challenging learning goals and makes assessment and performance requirements clear. They assist students to consider and identify processes that will support the achievement of the learning goals.	Develops shared norms	1 Models expected behaviours	1 Treats individuals with courtesy 2 *Verbalises behavioural expectations* 3 *Changes behaviour to suit context* 4 Reinforces behavioural expectations for students *(does it fit with modelling?)* 5 Aligns own and student behaviour with *shared* norms
		2 Establishes protocols for interactions	1 Provides class rules 2 Determines *behavioural* expectations according to context 3 Negotiates protocols for *learning* interactions 4 Shares responsibility for reinforcing protocols
		3 Sets expectations for learning	1 Promotes effort and hard work 2 Conveys learning expectations for all students 3 Establishes *structures and* routines to support student learning 4 Promotes support for learning
	Determines readiness for learning	1 Assesses prior knowledge	1 Tests students to determine what they know 2 Uses stimuli to draw out what students know 3 Uses standardised tools and processes to capture student prior knowledge 4 Integrates previous data and elicited prior knowledge to determine the level of understanding
		2 Identifies a purpose for learning	1 Explains the reason for learning each topic or skill 2 Links the specific learning activity to the expected outcomes 3 Forecasts current and future learning based on a disciplinary continuum 4 Supports students to frame up their own purpose for learning based on a discipline-based continuum

	3 Connects to students' lives	1 Provides opportunities for students to link their experiences to a learning focus 2 Differentiates the learning focus according to context 3 Broadens the context in response to questions about the learning focus
Establishes learning goals	1 Uses evidence to inform learning goals	1 Focuses on learning goals based on learning level 2 Addresses learning goals based on student historical data *(concern about these first two occurring outside of the classroom)* 3 Adjusts learning methods based on student responses 4 Adjusts teaching approach to accommodate like needs (cohort/development stage) 5 Targets different learning goals for individual students
	2 Communicates assessment requirements	1 Informs students of assessment requirements 2 Provides assessment criteria 3 Provides examples of expected standards of work 4 Provides assessment rubrics to illustrate levels of performance based on standards
Develops metacognitive capacity	1 Models thinking processes	1 Demonstrates the use of tools and strategies to support thinking 2 Uses language of thinking 3 Verbalises own thinking processes 4 Challenges students to *verbalise their thinking*
	2 Provides strategies for students to monitor learning	1 Supports students to identify what they know and what they need to know 2 Provides tools and strategies for students to capture their learning 3 Develops processes for students to evaluate the effectiveness of their learning

Table 7.10 *Elaboration of the explore phase*

DOMAIN	CAPABILITIES	PERFORMANCE INDICATORS	QUALITY CRITERIA
Explore The teacher presents challenging activities to support students to generate and investigate questions, gather relevant information and develop ideas. Tools and procedures are provided by the teacher for students to organise information and ideas. The teacher identifies students' conceptions and challenges misconceptions. They assist students to expand their perspectives and reflect on their learning. Attentive to the nature of the activities and student responses, the teacher intervenes accordingly.	Prompts inquiry	1 Generates questions	1 Uses a repertoire of question types 2 Poses questions to stimulate investigation 3 Frames questions to challenge students' ideas 4 Selects questions to elicit expected level of thinking
		2 Challenges misconceptions	1 Asks students to demonstrate their *current* understanding of the learning focus 2 Selects experiences to draw out students' misconceptions 3 Provides evidence that challenges current understanding
		3 Broadens experiences	1 Encourages students to share their prior experiences 2 Makes links between learning focus and real-world application 3 Provides exposure to new contexts *(perspectives?)* related to the focus of inquiry
	Structures inquiry	1 Provides resources to support inquiry	1 Selects resources relevant to the inquiry 2 Presents alternative resources in response to student needs 3 Teaches students strategies to *select resources*
		2 Develops processes to select information	1 Provides guiding questions 2 Teaches strategies for identifying *information relevant to the inquiry* 3 Teaches students to evaluate the relevance of information

148

3 Presents tools and strategies to organise information	1 Provides examples of information in an organised format 2 Teaches tools and strategies to record information 3 Prompts students to select tools and strategies relevant to the information being collected
Maintains lesson momentum	
1 Manages time	1 Informs students of the time frame for the task 2 *Organises the overall use of time* 3 Adjusts time to the demands of the task *(is it student response to the task?)* 4 Provides strategies for students to manage their time
2 Provides a structure for the lesson	1 Presents an outline for the lesson 2 Establishes routines 3 Adapts routines to maximise learning opportunities
3 Responds to student behaviours	1 Uses rules to manage behaviour 2 Scans the classroom to intervene when required 3 Refers to shared norms to maintain expected behaviour 4 Uses cues to inform responses to individual students *(is it proactive enough?)*

Table 7.11 *Elaboration of the explain phase*

DOMAIN	CAPABILITIES	PERFORMANCE INDICATORS	QUALITY CRITERIA
Explain The teacher provides opportunities for students to explain their current understanding. The teacher explicitly teaches relevant knowledge, concepts and skills. This content is represented in multiple ways.	Presents new content	1 Selects content	1 *Introduces* content based on year-level standard 2 Presents content based on the level of understanding of the group 3 Differentiates content based on like needs
		2 Makes content accessible	1 Uses a variety of ways to present the content 2 Selects representations appropriate to content 3 Introduces different representations in response to student understanding 4 Creates representations that link content to the real world
The teacher provides strategies to enable students to connect and organise new and existing knowledge. To assist students in representing their ideas, the teacher uses language and images to engage them in reading, writing, speaking, listening and viewing. The teacher explicitly teaches the language of the discipline. They structure opportunities for students to practise and progressively assess students' understanding.	Develops language and literacy	1 Develops the language of the discipline	1 Models language of the discipline 2 Explicitly teaches vocabulary, symbol systems and genres *of the discipline* 3 Structures opportunities for students to use the language of the discipline 4 Reinforces *student* use of disciplinary language
		2 Teaches the conventions of English language	1 Models the use of English language conventions 2 Teaches spelling, grammar and punctuation rules 3 Structures teaching of the conventions of language as integral to the learning focus 4 Differentiates teaching according to English language proficiency

	3 Employs the modes of language	1 Uses different modes of *language* to communicate ideas
		2 Structures tasks that require students to use multiple modes of language
		3 Supports students to select the mode of *language* appropriate to the task
Connects new and existing content	1 Demonstrates connections	1 Verbalises connections between new content and past learning
		2 Provides tools and processes to make connections
		3 Uses analogies to explain the relationship between ideas
		4 Supports students to select strategies to make sense of the connections
	2 Utilises student explanation	1 Prompts students to clarify their understanding
		2 Structures collaborative opportunities for students to share their explanations
		3 Revisits misconceptions to clarify student understanding
Strengthens connections	1 Structures opportunities to practise	1 Provides strategies for students to reinforce their learning
		2 Varies practice contexts to strengthen learning
		3 Supports students to link practice context to the learning focus

Table 7.12 *Elaboration of the elaborate phase*

DOMAIN	CAPABILITIES	PERFORMANCE INDICATORS	QUALITY CRITERIA
Elaborate The teacher engages students in dialogue to continually extend and refine their understanding. The teacher supports students to identify and define relationships between concepts and to generate principles or rules. The teacher selects contexts from familiar to unfamiliar, which progressively build the students' ability to transfer and generalise their learning. In applying their understanding, students are supported to create and test hypotheses and to make and justify decisions. The teacher monitors student understanding, provides explicit feedback and adjusts instruction accordingly.	Facilitates substantive conversation	1 Promotes thinking	1 Selects topics that generate thinking 2 Provides wait time (*odd one?*) 3 Articulates own thinking processes throughout conversation (*too similar to PI in Engage*) 4 Asks questions to probe student thinking 5 Elicits student reasoning
		2 Maintains the flow of conversation	1 Uses strategies to involve all students in conversation 2 Develops protocols to facilitate conversation 3 Selects size of group appropriate to the purpose of conversation 4 Structures opportunities to sustain a conversation over time 5 Uses conversation as an integral part of the learning process
		3 Builds on participants' ideas	1 Asks students to share their ideas 2 Acknowledges the value of student ideas 3 Prompts students for further input 4 Encourages students to respond to others' contributions 5 Supports students to objectively critique ideas

Cultivates higher order thinking	1 Structures learning tasks	1 Explains the cognitive demand of the task 2 Demonstrates thinking tools and strategies relevant to the task 3 Provides open-ended tasks requiring different types of thinking 4 Provides a cognitive framework to scaffold students' thinking 5 Supports students to independently select thinking strategies relevant to the task
	2 Extends learning to new contexts	1 Provides opportunities for students to develop rules and principles across similar contexts 2 Models the application of rules and principles in unfamiliar contexts 3 *Structures opportunities for students to test their generalisations* 4 Supports students to challenge assumptions underpinning rules and principles
Monitors progress	1 Provides feedback	1 Provides feedback based on the task 2 Gives feedback at point of need 3 Structures opportunities for students to provide feedback to one another 4 Provides strategies for improvement
	2 Adjusts instruction	1 Modifies instruction based on observation 2 Adapts instruction based on group needs 3 Intervenes to address individual needs

Table 7.13 *Elaboration of the evaluate phase*

DOMAIN	CAPABILITIES	PERFORMANCE INDICATORS	QUALITY CRITERIA
Evaluate The teacher supports students to refine and improve their performance using assessment criteria in preparation for a culminating performance of understanding. Integrating evidence from each phase, the teacher formally records students' progress against learning goals. The teacher provides feedback and assists students to evaluate their progress and achievements and reflect on their learning processes. They support students to identify future learning goals.	Assesses performance against standards	1 Makes judgements based on evidence	1 Uses assessment criteria to inform judgements 2 Uses standard reference rubrics to make judgements of the culminating performance 3 Integrates multiple sources of evidence to inform judgements 4 Moderates judgements against standards
		2 Communicates progress	1 Articulates student achievement against learning goals 2 References the standards when communicating progress 3 Communicates progress at regular intervals 4 Collaborates with students to determine progress (*this is about communicating but not determining progress*)
	Facilitates student self-assessment	1 Supports reflection	1 Provides opportunity for student self-reflection 2 Models strategies for self-reflection 3 Supports students to self-reflect using evidence 4 Supports students to evaluate personal learning strategies
		2 Facilitates identification of future learning	1 Guides students to identify future learning goals 2 Negotiates students' future learning goals based on evidence 3 Supports students to determine future learning goals based on proficiency in the content area (*still a bit inaccessible for teachers*)

154

Apply to practice

Find a set of assessment rubrics that has been used either by you or by other teachers.

1 Examine the rubrics for those elements that either follow or do not follow the rules for writing quality criteria. Mark on the rubrics any parts that do not follow the rules.

2 Identify a developmental taxonomy or progression that best fits the area/s assessed. It may be that some rubrics assess one aspect (for example, knowledge) and others assess another aspect (such as skills). If this is the case, identify taxonomies that match each aspect. See Chapter 2 for more information on developmental taxonomies.

3 Write a set of rubrics for the same assessment that adhere to the rules for writing quality criteria. You may choose to use or modify any existing rubrics or write your own.

Check your progress

Below is a set of rubrics designed to help you reflect on your answers to the Apply to Practice questions and assess your understanding of this chapter. These can be used to help scaffold learning.

7.1 Your examination of the assessment rubrics with reference to the rules for writing quality criteria:

   a provided insufficient evidence that the rubrics were checked against the rules

   b checked the rubrics against the core rules provided in the chapter

   c determined the extent to which the rubrics followed the rules for writing quality criteria.

7.2 Your identification of the developmental taxonomy:

   a provided insufficient evidence that the skills, knowledge and/or attitudes were identified

   b identified where skills, knowledge and/or attitudes were assessed

   c matched a developmental taxonomy to the skills, knowledge and/or attitudes assessed.

7.3 Your assessment rubrics:

   a provided insufficient evidence of the application of the rules for writing quality criteria

   b described levels of increasing proficiency

   c were consistent with the rules.

Chapter 8

Test construction

Patrick Griffin and Esther Care

To identify students' progress, teachers rely on formal test data as well as informal information derived from classroom observations. Procedures for the development of formal assessment tasks are extensively outlined in the literature written specifically for teachers and educators (e.g. see Kubiszyn & Borich 2009; Lamprianou & Athanasou 2009; Payne 2003). In this chapter, we provide guidance to help teachers construct tests that are designed specifically to provide information about the learning of skills in a developmental context. The role of collaboration in test design is also addressed in detail.

Learning objectives

In this chapter you will learn to:

- understand the context in which large-scale educational testing occurs
- understand the processes used to design tests
- write a test blueprint
- draft test items matched to a test blueprint
- panel test items collaboratively.

The context and purpose of large-scale educational testing

In order to identify whether a student learns in some circumstances better, faster and deeper than generally would occur, many education systems use large-scale testing programs. The assessment instruments used in large-scale testing generally include brief and easy-to-score tasks. Standardised tests sample the key learning areas or subject content, such as reading, science and mathematics. This is fine for aggregate interpretation at a system level, but it allows only limited interpretation of individual student learning. Many reports derived from standardised tests tend to emphasise an 'effect size' – that is, how much improvement or growth has occurred over various periods of time. If the effect size is greater or less than those reported on the basis of meta-analyses (Hattie 2009), groups of students may be regarded as advantaged or disadvantaged by their schools or school systems. These conclusions are based on assumptions such as the following:

- Progressive improvement of academic achievement of students is possible (an assumption strongly endorsed in this book, and one that should be endorsed by every educator).
- Actual educational achievement is efficiently measured by objectively scored standardised tests.

Currently, large-scale assessment programs predominantly target literacy and numeracy. These two learning domains are prevalent in both international (e.g. PISA) and national (e.g. NAPLAN) assessments.

There is a reason for this emphasis on standardised tests. Measurement specialists have been developing these tests for over a century, and have become very good at this craft. Their work has convinced politicians and system leaders that these tests are measuring what is important. In any case, they are measuring what the decision-makers regard as important. There is always debate about whether these tests are useful to teachers, and those who work in the creative disciplines argue that their disciplines should also be assessed. There is an implied contradiction in this argument. On the one hand, the argument is to eradicate standardised tests because they don't measure disciplines such as the creative arts, but on the other hand, it is maintained that the creative subjects would be more important if they were tested in the same way.

Reflective questions

- What are your thoughts about the ways in which large-scale standardised tests are used?

- In what ways are they advantageous to schools? What are the disadvantages?

- How do they impact on the teaching of literacy and numeracy?

- How do they impact on those learning areas not assessed via large-scale standardised tests?

Critics of the predominant use of tests measuring literacy and numeracy, who complain that other disciplines are equally if not more important than reading and mathematics, may be correct, but they are yet to convince decision-makers of their argument and yet to secure the resources that would enable large-scale assessment of other disciplines to take place. They are also still to develop assessment measures that are cost-effective. When the critics have achieved these goals, we may see a different approach to large-scale assessment.

Despite this, change is imminent in large-scale standardised testing. In the Assessment and Teaching of 21st Century Skills project (ATC21S™) (Griffin, McGaw & Care 2012), skills such as collaborative problem-solving and learning through social networking are being assessed, and new techniques are being developed to do this. The exercises designed for this purpose are computer based and capable of providing large-scale data that reveal detailed information. For example, it is possible to monitor the skills of people working in collaborative teams by logging the following:

- actions
- time taken to respond to questions
- responses to feedback
- systematic approaches to problem resolution
- trial and error attempts.

This approach to assessment – which has as its focus an interest in the cognitive processes used by students to solve problems – generates information that describes the complexity of problem-solving procedures in a way that makes the processes amenable to teaching and learning. Similarly, logging the kinds of activities that students demonstrate as they work through multiple-choice questions can provide information about cognitive processes as well as problem solutions. It is possible to monitor students' thinking as they work through assessment tasks in such a way that their learning can be located on a developmental progression describing increasingly complex skills.

These approaches to assessment increase the value of test data beyond the mere indication of which alternatives students select and whether they give the 'correct' response. From such responses, we infer that the student has used the skill that the test writer identifies as being of interest. However, this may not always be the case. It is important to acknowledge that those who take such tests bring diverse perspectives and skills to their responses. Additionally, it is difficult to write test items that can generate 'correct' answers through using only a targeted skill.

The above notwithstanding, standardised large-scale objectively scored tests, such as NAPLAN, can generate data usable by teachers to inform their teaching of individuals and small groups of students. For example, tests can be designed to indicate student levels of skill across learning areas, such as literacy and numeracy, rather than indicating content mastery. Reports based on these tests focus on skill-based results within the context of developmental learning progressions, and provide information to guide teacher selection of strategies, activities and resources for appropriate interventions with students (Care et al. in press). This is the central question of this book: how do we best use test data within a developmental paradigm in order to interpret why a student chooses a particular answer and rejects others? This can also be expressed as the question of how a student arrives at one answer and not another. When we interpret test data to answer this question, we can move from this interpretation to an inference of how performance on a test indicates a level on a developmental progression. From that point, the judgement of the teacher can identify the best intervention to improve the student's position on a developmental continuum.

Reflective questions

- Do you have experience using the results from standardised tests to inform teaching?
- If you have, do the methods you use encourage you to take a developmental or a deficit approach (as described in Chapters 1 and 2)?

When addressing the question 'How do we best use test data?' we need to consider the tests themselves. In order to construct a test for your students, we recommend following the five steps outlined below.

1 The first step in creating a situation in which students will generate evidence of their understanding in a particular skills area is to define the construct of interest (see Chapters 2 and 6 for more information).

2 Once we have defined the construct, we need indicators that enable us to describe a person in terms of the amount of the construct being exhibited in behaviour patterns. Identifying these indicators is the second step.

3 The third step is to 'panel' the items – that is, check with a panel of experts that the items appear to target different levels of skill within the construct.

4 The fourth step in setting up a situation in which students will generate evidence of their skills is to pilot the test items with students – to see how they respond to them and identify whether in fact the targeted skills are the ones used by the students. The pilot data are then analysed to determine the extent to which the responses are clearly interpretable within the framework of the construct, with possible subsequent changes to the items.

5 The fifth step lies in having large numbers of students complete the test, in order to check its measurement properties.

In reality, when teachers are developing tests for classroom use, the fourth and fifth steps are rarely implemented.

We will focus on the second and third steps – that is, determining indicators and panelling test items – and ask how these might be managed within a PLT structure. Given the joint responsibility of the PLT for decisions concerning students, it is important that all members are involved in both assessment decisions and the development of assessment tasks.

Drafting assessment tasks

The drafting process is an integral part of the day-to-day assessment procedures of a teacher. It begins with describing the construct. As you know, the construct may be defined by an existing criterion-referenced framework or developmental assessment framework (see Chapter 6). The construct helps to formulate what is known as a test blueprint. A blueprint is a design document that illustrates the organisation of the development of the assessment tasks.

An example of a blueprint is provided in Table 8.1. In this assessment, students were asked to respond to test questions designed to assess their knowledge and understanding of Asia. Levels in Table 8.1 run from A to D, with A the simplest level and D the most complex. The assessment was used in the key learning areas of English, arts and social education (SOSE). Within each of the key learning areas, the hypothesised construct was established by meeting with teachers and reaching agreement regarding which student behaviours would be observed in the specific subject areas as students became more sophisticated in their knowledge and understanding of Asia. In this way, the content of the discipline became the context in which students would demonstrate their knowledge and understanding of Asia. This is an example of how cross-curriculum assessment can be conducted within the key learning content areas. This would apply equally well to assessment of the general capabilities of the Australian Curriculum across key learning areas.

Table 8.1 *Blueprint for a test of understanding Asia in arts, SOSE and English*

LEVEL	ENGLISH	ARTS	SOSE
D	Complex documents and advertisements: audience identification, purpose and persuasion of writer. Detailed exposition: conjecture and prediction based on extension beyond the data in the text. Extended and complex text: inference of writer's purpose, values and bias, comparisons of text and authors within an Asian context.	Links between music, art and culture. Reasons for presentation of art and change of art. Influences of external pressures on Asian art forms.	Able to deal with and identify different cultural elements in complex settings and to show the effects of cultural shifts.
C	Intersecting texts: locate cross-reference, inference, previous knowledge, interpretation, compare, locate multiple ideas and data, link ideas. Descriptive texts: locate, translate and/or interpret information directly from the text. Story-level texts: inferring from the text and predicting reasons and story endings.	Understands the influence of religion and politics on the presentation of art and how individual people respond to art forms.	Links the culture of the country to different patterns of behaviour, religions and customs.
B	Related lists: locate single-idea information in the text using specific prompts. Single-sentence prompt: locate information directly from the text, based on previous knowledge and inference. Short text: locate specific words, phrases, sentences and discrete information in the text.	Classifies artistic representations by region and country. Can recognise ways that common articles and people are represented through common art forms.	Understands effects of weather, national dress and some common customs in selected countries.
A	Simple lists: locate single-item information, single-sentence format; identify information in word arrangements, and use of simple lists. Sentence-level cues; applying cueing systems; word knowledge.	Recognition of simple art forms; using simple lists and commonly known examples.	Names locations and countries, places on maps, general simple knowledge.

The test blueprint in Table 8.2 describes the distribution of items in a reading test. In total in this test, 32 questions will be asked on narrative texts, 26 on expository texts and 25 on reading documents. The number of items targeting each level within the construct is also specified. The descriptions in the table provide item writers with details of the skills their items should aim to measure.

Table 8.2 *Blueprint for a reading test*

LEVEL	READING DOMAIN			
	NARRATIVE	EXPOSITORY	DOCUMENTS	
5	Linking ideas from different parts of text. Making inferences from text or beyond text, to infer author's values and beliefs.	Linking ideas from different parts of text. Making inferences from text or beyond text.	Use of embedded lists and even subtle advertisements where the message is not explicitly stated.	
	6	3	2	11
4	Seeking and confirming information when reading backwards through text.	Seeking and confirming information when reading backwards through text.	Linking more than one piece of information in different parts of a document.	
	9	5	4	18
3	Linking information portrayed in sequences of ideas and content when reading forward.	Linking information portrayed in sequences of ideas and content when reading forward.	Systematic search for information when reading forward.	
	8	10	8	26
2	Recognising the meaning of a single word and being able to express it as a synonym in order to answer the question.	Recognising the meaning of a single word and being able to express it as a synonym in order to answer the question.	Linking simple pieces of information to item or instruction.	
	7	6	9	22

LEVEL	READING DOMAIN			
	NARRATIVE	EXPOSITORY	DOCUMENTS	
1	Word/picture association involving positional or directional prepositions requiring the linkage of a picture to a position or a direction in order to answer the question.	Word/picture association involving positional or directional prepositions requiring the linkage of a picture to a position or a direction in order to answer the question.	Word/picture association involving positional or directional prepositions requiring the linkage of a picture to a position or a direction in order to answer the question.	
	2	2	2	6
Total items	32	26	25	83

The second step of the process is to identify indicators of behaviours that match each of the levels in the construct, as described in the test blueprint. To identify the indicators:

- Write down a summary of the kinds of things that students would do, say, make or write in order to demonstrate that they are learning at each of the levels.

- Identify the nature of the stimulus that would elicit the kinds of behaviours described at each level.

- Edit the items and link them to levels on the construct. This involves writing the items in the format in which they will appear on the test.

A developmental taxonomy can provide a starting point for a test blueprint when a detailed definition of the construct is not available. Table 8.3 shows examples of items that have been written to match the level descriptions from Anderson and Krathwohl's adaptation of Bloom's Taxonomy (Anderson et al. 2001). The items in the table are designed to assess content from a number of subject areas to show that this approach can be useful across a range of curriculum areas.

Table 8.3 contains items that can be assessed objectively (knowledge, comprehension, application and analysis) and by using judgement (evaluation, synthesis). When drafting objective items, the correct answer should always be included. Similarly, an assessment rubric or rubrics should accompany judgement-based items (see Chapter 7 for details).

Table 8.3 *Application of Bloom's Taxonomy to assessment items*

KNOWLEDGE	'REMEMBER OR RECOGNISE' TO DO WITH FACTS; KNOWLEDGE OF METHODS AND CATEGORIES; KNOWLEDGE OF PRINCIPLES AND THEORIES; ABILITY TO CARRY OUT ROUTINE OPERATIONS.
	This item has to do with periods of European history when certain implements, machines or processes were first used. For each period of history, choose a related implement, machine or process.
	Periods of history *Implements, machines, processes* 1 Early Civilisations A machine to spin cotton 2 Renaissance B the process of extracting copper 3 Industrial Revolution from its ore 4 Modern Times C the printing press
Comprehension	'understanding what is read' To do with reading a paragraph, poem, graph, etc. with understanding; changing from one language to another; putting things into order; drawing conclusions from data; predicting trends or courses of action; 'reading between the lines'; estimation; going from rule to example (but not from memory) and vice versa.
	Which one of the following formulae correctly represents a molecule of ammonium bicarbonate? A NH_4HCO_3 C NH_4CO_3 B $(NH_4)_2HCO_3$ D $(NH_4)_2CO_3$ *Note:* Translation for many higher level students; might even be knowledge recall if well known.
Application (use – transfer)	'genuine problem-solving in an unseen situation' Not only the solution, but also the method of obtaining it, must be unprompted. In other words, the pupil's first reaction to this type of item should be 'What is this all about?'
	Suppose an elevator is descending with a constant acceleration of gravity, 'g'. If a passenger attempts to throw a rubber ball upwards, what will be the motion of the ball with respect to the elevator? A It will remain fixed at the point at which the passenger releases it. B It will rise to the top of the elevator and remain there. C It will not rise at all, but will fall to the floor. D It will rise, bounce off the ceiling, then move towards the floor at a constant speed. E It will rise, bounce off the ceiling, then move towards the floor at an increasing speed. *Note:* Application items must be unseen to the student. Such items are not easy to set, and are often put into fictitious contexts to meet these conditions.

Analysis	'using analysis of relationships, organisational principles, bias' To do with unravelling complex situations; detecting errors; realising when a communication is biased; recognising style in art or literature; judging relevance in arguments.
	The arrest of Governor Bligh was carried out by officers of the New South Wales Corps under the command of Major Johnson. Which of the following statements about the arrest would most likely have been made by Bligh himself in his report to the British government? A 'On hearing the officers approaching, I hid myself in my quarters.' B 'Knowing the officers were in the hold below, I considered the best means of escape.' C 'As the officers climbed the stairs, I unbuckled my sword to prevent any injury to myself in the event of being challenged to fight.' D 'On being warned of the approaching officers, I immediately went to my quarters to secure all my papers and official reports.'
Evaluation	'making a reasoned judgement on a contentious matter' To do with justifying a decision; judging sheep; critically reviewing a book; marking an essay; assessing a student's 'character'; writing a school report or reference. For evaluation, the important factor is not the actual decision but the reasons given for that decision.
	Suppose you watch a teacher do the following things: A She measures the distance from one end of the school yard to the other. B She gives a large drum to a student at one end of the yard. C She gives a stopwatch to a student at the other end of the yard. D The student with the drum raises the beater and hits the drum soundly. E The student with the stopwatch starts it when the beater hits the drum. F The student stops the stopwatch when the sound from the drum is heard. What was the teacher trying to do? Write your answer as a short paragraph. *Note:* This item revolves around the derivation of a set of abstract relations, providing the situation is unseen. Clearly, a set of rubrics is needed, and you will be checking these in the 'Apply to Practice' section.
Synthesis	'doing something creative or original' To do with free expression; composing a poem; designing a house; planning a course of action; making an impromptu speech; setting an examination paper; making hypotheses; planning a teaching unit. Note that simply stringing facts together is not synthesis, but more likely at knowledge level.

> *Statement 1:* In the 1970s, Australia had military obligations overseas, particularly in South Vietnam.
>
> *Statement 2:* Conscription into the armed forces was the best way to meet these obligations.
>
> Directions:
>
> A   Take Statement 1 to be true, whether you agree with it or not.
> B   Decide whether you then agree with Statement 2.
> C   Write an essay which meets the following requirements:
>
> - Your first sentence should be a specific reply to (b).
> - The whole essay, including planning and re-reading, should not take longer than 30 minutes.
> - The essay should be a reasoned argument supporting your first sentence. You should consider at least the following points:
>   - Was conscription the only way to obtain enough personnel for the armed forces?
>   - What alternatives were there?
>   - Which alternatives were preferable?
> - Your essay will be marked on the success with which your arguments support your reply to (b). English expression will be considered only to the extent that your meaning must be clear.

Reflective question

How can using a test blueprint improve the usefulness for teaching purposes of the information collected by the test?

Using a blueprint

Considerations in drafting items

Although test development takes time, it needs to be seen as an intrinsic part of curriculum design and delivery, and should ensure that students are being assessed on the desired outcomes of the curriculum. A typical set of instructions given to item writers, with several specific to multiple-choice items or rubrics, is provided below. It is a long list but an important one. The instructions apply to the writing of rubrics as described in Chapter 7 as much as they apply to the writing of assessment items.

Item-writing guidelines

1   Items should be targeted at the range of student ability (use the level descriptions for guidance).

2 An appropriate range of content should be used in the items (use the test blueprint for guidance).

3 Item types should be selected to elicit the indicative behaviours.

4 Success in the items should be determined by the level of the student on the construct, not by other factors.

5 Ensure the item provides clear guidance about what is required to complete it.

6 Language complexity should be commensurate with the idea being tested.

7 Avoid over-use of negatives (if you need to use negatives, make sure they are clearly marked in bold or underlined).

8 Items should not be biased for gender, ethnicity, rurality, socio-economic status and so on.

9 Do not use 'trick' questions.

10 Avoid trivial factual questions.

When writing multiple-choice items, some additional factors must be taken into account:

11 Item stems should direct students' thinking (the student should not need to read the alternatives to understand what the question is asking).

12 Alternatives should be homogeneous with respect to sentence structure and grammar; clues should not be given by syntax or word associations.

13 Alternatives should be likely.

14 Present either one correct alternative or a series of alternatives to represent increasingly sophisticated approaches to the problem.

15 Do not use 'None of the above', 'All of the above' or 'I don't know'.

16 Incorrect alternatives should tap common student strategies.

17 Do not test opinions.

Using these guidelines to write items helps to ensure that a student's response on an item provides evidence from which an inference about the underlying construct can be made. You want to be sure that if a student gets an item wrong, it is because they lack the level of skill or knowledge necessary to answer the item correctly, not because they could not understand what they were meant to do or because they were tricked into an incorrect response by the nature of the question.

Item writing takes time and effort. One way to ease the burden of development is to use a stock of existing assessment tasks or items, and use or adapt them to your purpose. When selecting existing items, it is crucial to check whether or not each item fits into your test blueprint.

Skills auditing

One way to determine whether a test question is of use is to identify the cognitive skill that underpins the selection of the correct answer. This may sound easy, but it can be difficult. The process of identifying the skills demanded by each item is known as a skills audit. It is a skill in itself and, while it can be difficult at first, it becomes easier with practice. The process involves isolating the most advanced skill needed to answer the question. For example, let's consider an item in a reading comprehension test, where a person must have two skills to answer the item correctly. A person must first be able to decode the words in the question and the passage and then be able to make an inference from information presented across different parts of the passage. It is quite possible to have the skill of decoding the question and passage, but still not be able to answer the question correctly, so decoding is not the skill that would be listed against this item. The skill of decoding is necessary, but not sufficient to answer the question. Now consider the second skill: making an inference from information presented across different parts of the passage. It is not possible to answer this item correctly without this skill, and it is unlikely that someone would have this skill but not be able to decode, so this is the skill that is being assessed in this item. This is the most difficult skill required to answer the question. This argument is outlined in Table 8.4.

Table 8.4 *Example of decision-making when skills-auditing*

SKILL NEEDED TO ANSWER THE QUESTION	IS THIS SKILL NEEDED TO ANSWER THE QUESTION CORRECTLY?	IS IT LIKELY A PERSON COULD HAVE THIS SKILL AND STILL NOT ANSWER THE QUESTION CORRECTLY?	IS THIS SKILL LISTED IN THE SKILLS AUDIT?
Decode words in question and passage	Yes	Yes	No
Make an inference from information presented across different parts of the passage	Yes	No	Yes

Skills auditing is best undertaken collaboratively. Teachers working alone often operate with their own bias in their own particular discipline knowledge. Engaging in the activity as a group can counteract these biases, but a collaborative endeavour has multiple benefits. It develops the skills of all in identifying the quality and characteristics of test questions; it provides the PLT with a stockpile of usable questions; and it provides a basis for the PLT to generate assessment tasks with a common approach to the skills being assessed and the ways these can be targeted and reported. This latter outcome – reporting – is a critical aspect of formative assessment if students are to benefit directly from the process as well as through the teacher medium. It is important for students to understand the bases upon which they are being assessed. Having similar modes of reporting across areas can facilitate this outcome.

Reflective questions

Take a look at some test items from a test you have used, or one that has been recommended for use in an area you teach.

- Can you identify the skill underlying each item?
- Do the items follow the guidelines given above?
- How does this impact on your ability to use student results from this item to plan teaching?

Item information

Irrespective of the source of test items, some conventions should be followed when recording items. Each item should be accompanied by the following information:

- the author identity and an item number
- the draft item
- the scoring rules, which would be the nominated correct answer or alternatives for objective items, and scoring rubrics (see Chapter 7) for judgement-based items
- the cognitive skill required to supply the correct answer
- sufficient information about the level, topic and so on to determine how the item fits into the test blueprint
- acknowledgement of source materials obtained from the public domain
- copyright warnings or authors' permission to use sources.

Panelling

It is always difficult to write test items and/or rubrics alone. Reviewing and critiquing tests and rubrics collaboratively is a more effective and ultimately a more efficient process than independent review. This section sets out a successful way of reviewing tests. In Australia, it is referred to as 'panelling'. In Europe, test developers call it 'shredding' and in the United States it is part of the process called a 'cognitive laboratory'.

Panelling is a process through which a test is reviewed by a group of colleagues who have expertise in the area being assessed. Once the items are drafted, they should be panelled. This is conducted as a semi-formal process undertaken by a team of people who are responsible for the development of the assessment, with one person designated as the chair or panel leader. The members of the team use their specialist knowledge to review and critique the test items. There are strict rules that need to be adhered to by the team leader and by each member of the team. If the following instructions are not heeded the discussion can become chaotic and the time involved can expand to intolerable levels.

Panel leader's role

The panel leader should collect all the draft items and ensure that each item is accompanied by the required information (as listed above). As each item is to be written on a separate piece of paper, a coding system to identify the items is also necessary. This might include the initials of the author and the question number.

The panel leader distributes the draft items to the panel members with reminders:

- There should be a minimum of discussion during the review process.
- At the end of the review, the item sheets will be collected.
- There should be no comments or marks on the original items.
- The panel should focus on one item at a time.
- Each panel member is to recommend changes if required.
- If the author of the item is a member of the panel, the author must remain silent for the entire time that the item is being discussed (when this is ignored, it becomes clear that the personal opinions and views of the author are needed to explain the item, which nullifies the independence of the item).
- At the end of the individual review process, each recommended change will be discussed with a view to reaching agreement by the whole panel.
- At the end of the panel process, the changes to the draft item will be made.

The process is repeated for each item in the set. The item set is then checked for consistency with the test blueprint, and any gaps in the range and content of items as designated in the blueprint are identified. At this point, the team is directed to draft any additional items needed to complete the specifications in the test blueprint, if required.

Panel members' role

It is important that there is minimal discussion throughout the process in order for members to contribute independently. All comments should be written on a separate sheet of paper from the original items, and the identity of both author and reviewer should be clear. This optimises the clarity and objectivity of responses to the items.

No comments or marks should be made on the original copy of the items – this is the role of the panel chair: to mark up the original once all comments are collected. During the panelling process, each member should check that the draft item follows the guidelines for item-writing and that the information included with the item is correct and complete. Items should also be proofread to ensure correct grammar, spelling, labelling of diagrams and so on. The team member is responsible not just for critiquing the item, but also for improving it to address any issues identified during the checking process.

From the pool of panelled items, the final test can be constructed. Once it is in its final form, the whole test should also be proofread to check that it is ready to be used. In large-scale testing, a piloting phase would then take place, and finally the psychometric properties of the test items would be checked. While these steps are not practical for school-based assessments, some aspects of the performance of the test items can be checked using a Guttman analysis, as described in Chapter 10. Teachers using a test can also make notes regarding the administration and marking of the test, and these can be stored with the test or test items to provide information that will guide future use of the assessments.

Test construction in the PLT

Given the PLT's responsibility for monitoring student learning, members of the team are well placed to determine the parameters of test construction and to write tests themselves. The blueprint can establish the purpose of the test, the data to be collected and the reports and feedback to be generated. In some cases, feedback from assessment might only be verbal and directed primarily to students. However, some record of the assessment needs to be kept to contribute to a profile of overall achievement. This can be used to report development or growth to the PLT as well as to the student and parents. These reporting requirements should contribute to the design of the assessment.

To initiate the process of writing items, the writing instructions and the test blueprint containing the draft or hypothesised developmental progressions are distributed among the PLT members. There should be a discussion of the blueprint and the developmental progression that is to underpin not only the assessment but the teaching in the interim period between assessments. Teaching should always be linked directly to assessment. Although the focus in this chapter is on formal assessment, this in no way diminishes the importance of direct observation and monitoring of student performances.

Discussion in the PLT of assessment is important. PLT members need to discuss the range of skills to be elicited by the test, and identify the best questions to target particular groups of students. There is no point in allocating difficult tests to students who are struggling or very easy tests to students who are performing at high levels.

Targeted assessment is an essential aspect of gaining accurate information to identify the zone of proximal development and design intervention strategies. It makes no difference whether the test is standardised, computer based, commercial or constructed by a school or teacher. The questions should always be targeted to identify the ZPD.

The PLT is the best group to write test questions, whether they are multiple-choice or open-ended, performance tasks or extended writing tasks. In judgement-based assessments, the PLT can be used to write the rubrics. If the PLT is engaged in this process then all members take responsibility for what is to be learned by the students and for how it is to be assessed. Assessments designed by the PLT should supplement the use of online systems like ARCOTS or other commercial products.

Reflective questions

- Have you had experience of writing your own tests?
- Has this been undertaken individually or collaboratively?
- Writing tests collaboratively usually leads to better tests, but what are the disadvantages?
- How can any disadvantages (e.g. time limitations) be minimised?

Summary

The design and development of assessments is an essential pedagogic skill that sharpens the awareness of teachers regarding curriculum objectives and ensures that the information they derive is relevant to their teaching. Although the development of formal assessments may seem daunting, engaging in the activity collaboratively is an efficient process that not only increases the skills of the team members but can make the assessment activity more useful to students – those who have the most to gain from the process.

Apply to practice

Find an item from an existing test. If you do not have ready access to one, search online or use one of the items given as an example within this chapter. Pretend that you are a member of a group panelling this test item.

1 Conduct a skills audit on the item.
2 Identify the developmental taxonomy that best matches the item. If you have access to a construct matching the learning area, you may wish to use it instead of the developmental taxonomy. Use this as the test blueprint.
3 Which level of the taxonomy/construct would this item best assess?

4 Critique the item using the guidelines given in this chapter. If possible, adapt the item based on your critique.

Check your progress

Below is a set of rubrics designed to help you reflect on your answers to the Apply to Practice questions. The processes you have undertaken in this Apply to Practice are skills. For this reason, the Check Your Progress rubrics are based on Dreyfus's Model of Skill Acquisition. As with any skill, skills auditing and item reviewing become easier and more effective with practice!

8.1   Your skills audit was able to:

   a   name an area of the curriculum assessed by the item

   b   identify a skill or skills assessed by the item

   c   isolate the most advanced skill assessed by the item.

8.2   Your identification of the level of the taxonomy or construct:

   a   narrowed the levels that might be assessed by the item

   b   determined the level/s assessed by the item.

8.3   Your review of the item was able to:

   a   consider the item in light of the guidelines

   b   determine if the guidelines were followed

   c   adapt the item to follow the guidelines.

Chapter 9

Deriving a criterion-referenced framework

**Patrick Griffin and
Pam Robertson**

This chapter shows how criterion-referenced frameworks are derived. The first section describes the process of derivation using a list of ordered skills produced by item response theory (IRT). The second section shows how a similar list of ordered skills can be produced using Thurstone's (1927) method of pairwise comparison, which avoids the need for sophisticated computer analysis. When combined with the theories of Glaser, Rasch and Vygotsky, pairwise comparison enables teachers to produce criterion-referenced frameworks for use in decisions about teaching interventions within a developmental paradigm. This allows teachers to teach and assess with reference to a rigorously derived construct of their own making in any area of learning.

Learning objectives

In this chapter you will learn to:

- understand the theoretical basis on which criterion-referenced frameworks are built

- understand the theoretical basis on which students are located to levels on a criterion-referenced framework

- conduct a pairwise comparison of criteria

- build a criterion-referenced framework.

Introduction

One of the most crucial questions for teachers is 'What do I teach next?' To answer this question, teachers need to draw on their knowledge of their students and their understanding of the typical sequence of the skills being taught within their particular subject. This chapter describes methods that teachers can use to derive the typical order of development within a domain or strand of learning. The typical order of skills – otherwise known as a criterion-referenced framework or construct – provides a framework against which teachers can interpret evidence of student learning, identify student zones of proximal development and plan further teaching. The building of a criterion-referenced framework starts with a hypothesis about the range of skills that learners can demonstrate. Once this is established, the relative complexity of the skills identified can be considered either via judgement-based assessments (see Chapter 6) – in which teachers work collaboratively and draw on their knowledge and experience to construct a viable framework – or through objective assessments (see Chapter 8) – in which more technical and frequently large-scale methodologies drawing on actual results with greater levels of validity are employed. A combination of the two is also possible.

In building a criterion-referenced framework, skills are ordered from those that are easiest to demonstrate through to those that are hardest to demonstrate, with the range of skills normally matching the range of student abilities. Once the order is determined, the skills are then synthesised into a series of level descriptions that make up the criterion-referenced framework.

Earlier chapters have referred to item response theory (IRT), which is explained in Appendix A. IRT is the basis of many criterion-referenced frameworks. Here we look at how these are constructed using the ordering of items determined by IRT, before moving on to learn about how a similar process can be carried out without the need for sophisticated computer analysis such as IRT.

Ordering items

IRT produces a variable map, examples of which are shown in Figures 9.1 to 9.4. These maps provide a schematic representation of how item difficulties and student abilities relate to each other with respect to an underlying construct. The variable map illustrates how an analysis of this information can be used for interpretive purposes. This will be helpful in understanding how to organise judgement-based assessments.

In the left column of a variable map there is a series of Xs, each representing one student. The X that appears at the top of the distribution represents the most able student and the one at the bottom represents the least able student.

In the middle of the diagram is a double-headed arrow. This arrow is included to indicate that there is no top and no bottom level. Students can score higher or lower than indicated on the map.

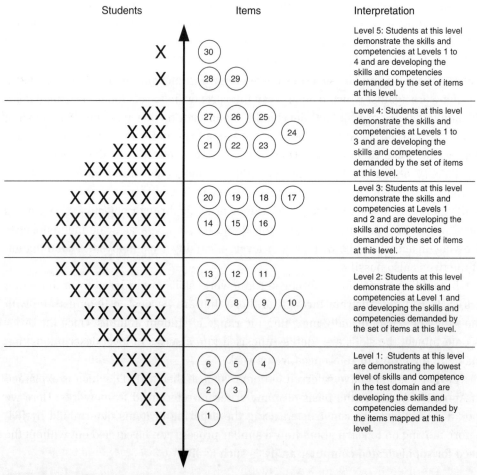

Figure 9.1 *Variable map*

To the right of the arrow in Figure 9.1 is a series of circles numbered 1 to 30. These represent 30 unique, objective test questions. Item number 30, which appears at the top of the second column, indicates the most difficult question. Items 1 to 6, which appear at the bottom of the column, indicate the easiest questions. Question 1 is the easiest of all. In the right column, levels of increasing competence have been described.

For our current purposes, this diagram shows that it is possible with IRT to order students and test items using the same scale. As each item is designed to assess whether or not a given skill has been demonstrated, this diagram also shows the relative difficulty of the tested skills.

Levels of competence

From this ordering of students and skills, levels of competence can be described. This is because it is possible to identify a student whose ability is approximately equal to

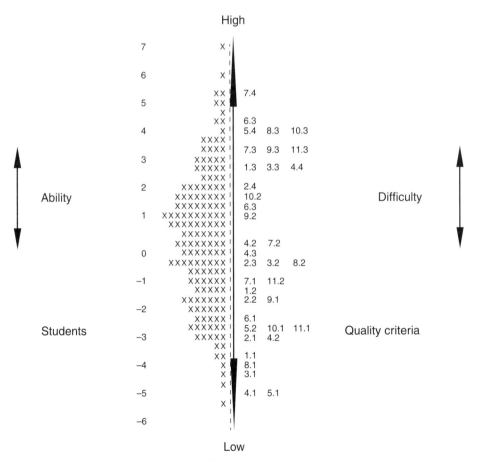

Figure 9.2 *Variable map identifying quality criteria*

the difficulty of a question. This enables the identification of the stages of increasing competence to which we have already referred. It is also possible to identify clusters of students whose abilities are approximately equal to the difficulty of the stage of competence. As we know, that stage of developing competence for each of the groups of students is what Vygotsky called the zone of proximal development (ZPD). By interpreting clusters of test items and developing generalised statements or descriptions of increasing competence, it is possible to identify the ZPD for groups of students identified in the diagram. Because of this, item response modelling enables us to identify the kinds of skills that students are ready to learn. This allows us to identify and plan teaching to move students from one level of competence to the next. This is called targeted intervention.

This approach can be generalised to focus on the analysis of rubric data. If, instead of plotting the numbers 1 to 30 representing 30 separate test questions, we plot the analysis of rubric data, we get a different type of chart, which we can use to determine a developmental progression. The steps to follow are demonstrated in Figures 9.2–9.7. In Figure 9.2, the Xs in the left column represent students in order of

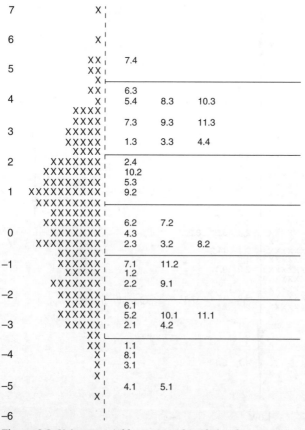

Figure 9.3 *Using a variable map to identify levels*

ability, from lowest at the bottom to highest at the top. In the right column, the codes represent quality criteria in rubrics, ordered according to their difficulty. The criterion code of 1.3 represents rubric number 1, quality criterion number 3. The criterion code 4.2 represents rubric number 4, quality criterion number 2. The most difficult criterion is 7.4 and the least difficult are 4.1 and 5.1.

As in Figure 9.1, where the test items were clustered, in Figure 9.2 we can see that the quality criteria are clustered in groups. If we look for separations in the clusters using natural breaks in the difficulty range, then the levels emerge. This is depicted in Figure 9.3. In this way, the stages of increasing competence for the levels on a developmental progression can be identified and interpreted.

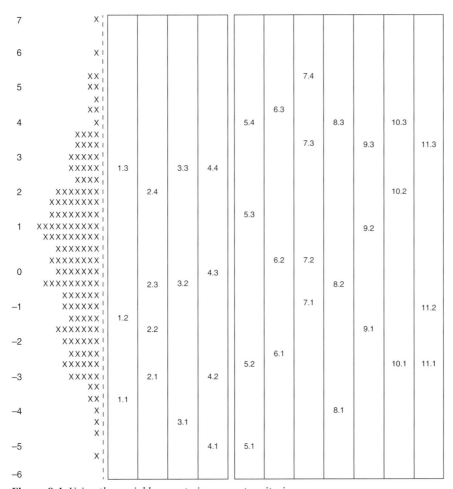

Figure 9.4 *Using the variable map to incorporate criteria*

The next step is to see how the criteria can be used to build a developmental progression. As explained in Chapter 7, a rubric is the combination of an indicator and a series of quality criteria. In Figure 9.4, each indicator is given its own column, so all the 1s (1.1, 1.2 and 1.3) line up vertically in a column, as do all the 2s, all the 3s and so on. As you can see, the criteria for some indicators cover a wider range of difficulty than others. The criteria for indicator 5, for example, range from the bottom of the chart to somewhere near the top, whereas the criteria for indicator 7 range from just below the halfway point to very near the top.

Now that the relative levels have been determined, it is no longer necessary to retain the distribution of students represented by Xs in the left column. At the same time, we can reintroduce the horizontal lines to represent the different levels of difficulty. This is reflected in the map shown in Figure 9.5, which is used to map levels of difficulty on the developmental progression.

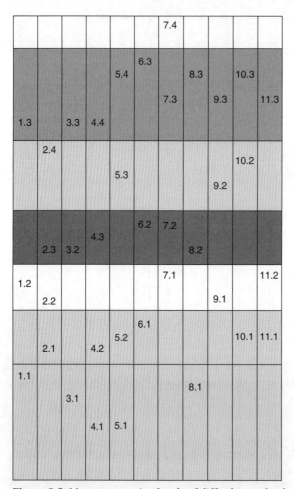

Figure 9.5 *Map representing levels of difficulty on the developmental progression*

This clearly establishes the levels of a developmental progression or criterion-referenced framework, but the use of criterion codes, such as 3.1 or 7.4, does not make clear which skills are being described. The next step is to insert the actual words that describe the skills in the criterion, as illustrated in Figure 9.6. This assists in interpreting the levels.

Now each of the levels can be interpreted more easily as a description of what students are ready to learn, as indicated in Figure 9.7.

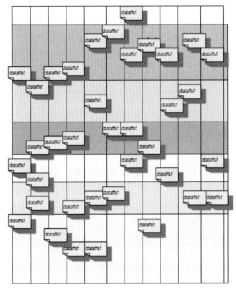

Figure 9.6 *Substitution of skills for criterion codes (the text is deliberately illegible)*

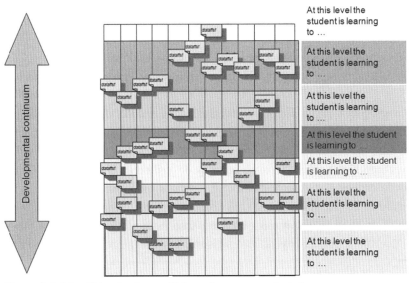

Figure 9.7 *Identifying levels at which students are ready to learn*

Pairwise comparison

We now turn our attention to how criterion-referenced frameworks can be constructed by teams of teachers or specialists working together without the use of large-scale data and without expensive computer software or knowledge of IRT.

Reflective questions

Traditionally, criterion-referenced frameworks are constructed by external bodies and given to teachers.

- What could be the consequences of enabling teams of teachers to make their own criterion-referenced frameworks?

- How could this change the nature of what is taught and what is learned in schools?

Teachers can construct a developmental framework, drawing on their professional experience and understanding. To begin, a developmental assessment framework is hypothesised, complete with indicative behaviours and criteria. This process is described in Chapters 6 and 7, and is often carried out by a small group of experienced teachers. The next task is to evaluate the difficulty of the criteria in relation to each other so the ordered criteria can be used to describe increasing levels of competence. This is done by a method called 'pairwise comparison', which was developed by Louis Leon Thurstone (1887–1955) and later formularised by Joy Paul Guilford (1897–1987), both of whom were psychometricians. It is a process that can be carried out by a group of experts or connoisseurs in a particular field or discipline, and that can produce a valid criterion-referenced framework. At school level, it is carried out by a group of teachers or experts in the subject-matter to be taught. Essentially, the process mirrors the steps that we have just looked at for objective assessments, but it works in reverse order, starting with criterion descriptions.

The work begins by writing out a set of assessment criteria on sticky notes – a single criterion on each note. Groups of participants then debate the difficulty of each criterion, relative to all the others. This involves comparing every criterion individually with every other. If the rubric-writing process described in Chapter 7 has been followed, then the criteria for each indicator in a strand or domain will already be ordered according to their difficulty, but this order should be checked by the group or panel. In addition, each criterion must be compared to the criteria of all the other indicators – hence the name 'pairwise comparison'. The panel must decide in each case which of the compared criteria represents the greater difficulty or higher level of skill.

The experts collaboratively order the criteria from the various indicators in a strand or domain. An actual example of a pairwise comparison is shown in Figure 9.8. The sticky notes must be positioned so that all members of the expert panel can see them. Often a section of wall is used for this purpose.

Figure 9.8 *Pairwise comparison*

Each criterion should be labelled using the numbering convention outlined in Chapter 7, and all the criteria relating to a particular indicator should form a column. The criteria in each column should be ordered from easiest at the bottom to hardest at the top. From the initial layout, the panel considers pairs of criteria in adjacent columns to determine which is the most difficult of the pair. The more difficult criterion is then moved higher than the easier one. After the first pair has been ordered, the process becomes more involved. The next criterion is placed relative to both criteria from the first pair. In doing this, two pairs are actually considered. Just as was found in the IRT analysis of difficulty earlier in this chapter, it is possible for multiple criteria to be judged as being of equal difficulty. In fact, it is common for clusters of items to appear at similar heights in the layout.

Sometimes pairwise comparison feeds back into the process of writing assessment rubrics for judgement-based assessments or the selection of items in an objective test. If there is not a spread of items across the levels, then it may be necessary to modify the assessment to make it more representative of the domain. Occasionally, two criteria for the same indicator end up in one level. This often means that the criteria are not describing sufficiently different levels of quality. This can lead to inaccurate marking, so if it occurs, one of the criteria should be removed.

Although pairwise comparison may seem tedious, it can happen quite quickly once all members of the panel become familiar with the process. Discussions, debates and challenges are welcomed as the panel collaborates to negotiate a final order. Once the pairwise comparison has taken place, cut-points between levels can be determined and the level descriptions written in the same manner as described earlier in this chapter.

Reflective question

Discussions, debates and challenges between colleagues during a pairwise comparison can make a positive contribution to establishing a culture of challenge within teams of teachers and schools as a whole. Imagine you are a student in a school where the staff have an established culture of challenge. What impact could this have on you and your learning?

Once the level-descriptions that form the criterion-referenced framework have been written, it is recommended that these be reviewed by others who have not been part of the process. The purpose of the review is to make sure that the terminology used is transparent and that the students who match the levels can be identified. This ensures the usability of the level descriptions.

Once constructed, the layout of the criterion-referenced framework indicates the relative difficulty of the criteria. If the assessment is being carried out within a standards-referenced environment, the standards (grades, pass/fail, etc.) aligned to each level can be included in the framework. This allows those being assessed to target their efforts.

Summary

This chapter has described how criterion-referenced frameworks are derived, using sets of criteria ordered by IRT and pairwise comparison. The process of pairwise comparison can be carried out by teachers in schools without the need for assessment data or specialised computer programs. The chapter thus outlines a method for empowering teachers to derive criterion-referenced frameworks themselves, ensuring that they can have at their fingertips a structure through which to make evidence-based decisions about student learning and teaching, irrespective of the domain being taught.

Apply to practice

Practise the process of deriving a criterion-referenced framework using a pairwise comparison. The collaborative problem-solving rubrics provided in Chapter 6 are one possible starting point, or you may use any other assessment rubrics or skills from any test. It is best to start small, with around 20 rubrics or skills, so it may be necessary to limit the task to criteria relating to one strand or even one capability. Answer the following questions to help you reflect on the process:

1   Based on your experience, what is necessary to make pairwise comparison an effective alternative to IRT?

2   How did the quality of the rubrics or skill descriptions impact on your ability to undertake the task?

3   How useful are the level descriptions you have derived? What has affected their usefulness?

Check your progress

Below is a set of rubrics designed to help you reflect on the process you undertook while completing the Apply to Practice task and assess your understanding of this chapter. These can be used to help scaffold learning.

9.1   Your description of the necessities for effective pairwise comparison:

    a   was general in nature

    b   considered factors necessary for the process

    c   generalised from the effectiveness of your experience to describe an ideal practice.

9.2   Your review of the impact of the quality of rubrics/skills:

    a   was general in nature

    b   discussed the impact of the rubrics/skills used in your experience

    c   hypothesised requirements for rubrics/skills based on your experience.

9.3 Your discussion of the usefulness of the level descriptions:

    a was general in nature

    b considered the pros and cons of the level descriptions you derived

    c evaluated the usefulness of the level descriptions you derived.

Chapter 10

Modified Guttman analysis

Patrick Griffin, Pam Robertson and Danielle Hutchinson

This chapter introduces a modification of an old approach to data analysis. We call it a Guttman analysis, in deference to Louis Guttman, who originally sorted data in ways that we use. It is not meant to be a Guttman space analysis. What we offer is an effective e-tool for grouping students on the basis of demonstrated skills. The chapter provides a step-by-step process through which teachers can organise data from either objective or judgement-based assessment tasks into a readily interpretable visual form. It shows teachers how to interpret data to evaluate the reliability of an assessment task, both at a general and an item level. The implications for this sort of analysis are considered, including the scenario where an assessment task does not capture skills within a student's ZPD. Finally, the chapter discusses the process of using data to target teaching through the formation of instructional groups based on student ZPD.

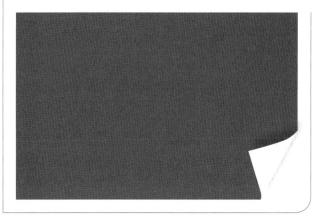

Learning objectives

In this chapter you will learn to:

- generate, analyse and interpret a Guttman analysis
- use both objective and judgement-based assessment data to identify zones of proximal development
- account for anomalies and sources of error
- interpret and use data to plan targeted teaching
- identify ways of improving assessment data through:
  - review of test administration
  - improvement of targeting
- use data systematically to formalise the evaluation of links between assessment data and student interventions
- examine the implications of data analysis for classroom organisation to enhance targeted teaching.

Using data to locate students' ZPDs

The developmental model of learning was introduced in Chapter 2. A central feature of this model is the process of interpreting student ZPD in relation to a progression of increasing complexity. Teachers can locate student ZPD using externally generated data, such as standardised test assessments, or they can use their own classroom data to generate a Guttman analysis. Either way, teachers are equipped with powerful information that can be used to target teaching in order to maximise student learning.

Analysing externally generated student data

As discussed in Chapter 2, an example of an externally generated student report is the Learning Readiness Report derived from the ARCOTS assessment. Learning Readiness Reports can be generated in real time to place students at levels or stages on progressions of competence.

The black bar on the report shown in Figure 10.1 shows the student's level on the progression. The associated stage description outlines the skills that a student at that level is ready to learn. One thing to note is that the student's estimated level on the report is not an achievement level, but rather an indication of their ZPD or point of readiness to learn. Their achievement level is below this point – it represents what they have already learned – but, as explained in Chapter 2, the ZPD is where teaching

Learning Readiness Report

Student name:
Student code: ALI0988
Student year: 1
Student class: PG
Subject: Literacy
Test Record: 23-01-13. Period 1 2013

THE UNIVERSITY OF
MELBOURNE

Pathway	Level	Pathway

Recognise methods used by author to influence and persuade the reader.

Interpret underlying themes, causes and points of view in the text. Interpret text in view of social context.

Identify fine nuances in text with unfamiliar contexts or styles.

Interpret text by linking information presented with relevant external knowledge. Use knowledge of text structure to evaluate the relevance of the information presented.

Infer author's perspective from what is written and what is implied. Identify how different texts are structured.

Infer characters' motives from descriptions of behaviour and actions. Interpret how word meaning changes when used in different context.

Combine separate pieces of data to infer the text's meaning. Identify and summarise evidence from the text to support hypothesis.

Make predictions based on understanding of ideas, sequence of events and characters. Identify purpose of the text.

Draw together ideas and information from across the whole text. Infer characters' feelings from narrative text.

Identify main ideas and characters in the story. Interpret paraphrased sentence at paragraph-level text.

Find information in the short text. Link paraphrased information within a single paragraph.

Locate and match adjacent words in text at word and phrase level.

▬▬▬ The student is estimated to be at this location

Figure 10.1 *Example of a Learning Readiness Report*

needs to be targeted in order to maximise student progress. Teachers can therefore draw on these reports to make decisions about a possible learning program for the student, and to set some goals and intentions for teaching and learning. Students can use this information as feedback on their performance, and to think about what they need to consolidate and what is the next focus for their learning.

Three levels are important:

1 *One level below the readiness level.* Teaching targeted at this level will consolidate the prior learning that underpins the readiness level. The student is likely to be able to perform most of these tasks independently.

2 *The readiness level.* Teaching targeted at this level will stretch and extend the student's emerging skills. The student is likely to be able to perform these tasks with the help of others.

3 *One level above the readiness level.* Teaching targeted at this level will be beyond the immediate level of student competence. The student is unlikely to be able to perform these tasks, even with the help of others.

These will be discussed further in the Using the data to target teaching section later in this chapter.

Analysing classroom-based student data

As discussed in Chapters 2, 3 and 9, the ARCOTS tests and instruments for students with additional needs (SWANs) have been calibrated using a form of statistical modelling called item response theory (IRT), but it is possible for teachers to do a similar form of analysis without the need for specialised software and statistical training. This type of analysis is called a Guttman analysis, and it can be done with the use of an Excel spreadsheet. This is a particularly effective tool for analysing assessment data and interpreting it to evaluate both student performance and the assessment tool itself. It is also another method of generating a progression or continuum but, unlike some others, it makes use of student results as a means of establishing the hierarchy of learning.

The Guttman analysis

In 1944 Louis Guttman (1916–87) published the steps to produce a *scalogram*, a simple method to gain a picture of qualitative data from questionnaires or tests without an understanding of statistics or time-consuming mathematical analyses. The Guttman analysis described in this chapter builds on Guttman's scalogram. The key feature of the Guttman analysis is its visual construction, providing an access point into data analysis for a broad range of users.

The Guttman chart synthesises a combination of approaches for analysing assessment data, allowing teachers to gain a picture of their class's current learning and their future learning needs from assessment data. It requires nothing more than some basic spreadsheet skills.

A Guttman chart orders actual student performances according to students' demonstrated proficiency, and orders assessment items (questions, observations, survey responses and so on) according to their difficulty. Students with similar skills can be identified and grouped together. The skills behind each assessment item can also be grouped to see the usual order of development of the skills assessed. Finally, groups of students can be matched to the group of skills they need to develop. In this way, the assessment data can be used to provide teachers with a clear picture of what each group of students is ready to learn. With this information to hand, teachers can select strategies and resources to meet the learning needs of each group.

As discussed in Chapter 2, the developmental model of learning combines the theories of Vygotsky, Rasch and Glaser, and focuses on locating each student's readiness to learn. A Guttman chart provides a visual representation of that point. In the chart, each correct response to an assessment is indicated by a 1 and each incorrect response by a 0. Using the chart, a teacher is able to isolate the zone in which a student's performance breaks down from mostly correct answers (ones) to mostly incorrect answers (zeros). This is the zone where teaching will be most effective. The Guttman chart also enables teachers to match this zone to the big ideas underlying the relevant skills. The big idea then becomes the next teaching target for the student.

Any assessment can check only a limited number of skills that the students within a subject area may have learnt. For each item that is included, there are many similar items that are not assessed. A Guttman analysis gives teachers the chance to generalise from the results on a specific assessment to see student progress on the broader ideas, or constructs, that underpin the subject area. Therefore, student progress can be tracked against the construct and teaching interventions can be planned with the aim of developing the student in the underlying construct, not simply remedying deficiencies shown on the skills included in one assessment.

A Guttman analysis can be performed on any assessment: NAPLAN results, a class test or assignment, an observational schedule or a behavioural checklist. The most important thing when planning to generate a Guttman chart is to determine whether the assessment task to be analysed is an objective assessment (for example, multiple choice, true/false) or a judgement-based assessment (for example, levels of quality described in a rubric, a score of 2 out of 3 for part of an assignment).

Reflective question

Look at the types of assessment tasks that you might routinely use to collect student data. Are they predominantly objective? Are they predominantly judgement-based? Are they a mixture of both? Do the items within the task provide opportunities for students to demonstrate skills at varying levels of difficulty?

Steps in constructing a Guttman chart using objective assessment

An objective assessment will generate results that permit each item (question, skill or task) to be recorded as achieved (1) or not achieved (0). The steps that need to be taken are as follows:

1 *Ones and zeros.* Break down the test, behaviour checklist or other form of objective assessment into *items* (or questions) in response to which students can be said to have demonstrated or not demonstrated a skill. Using a 1 to represent each demonstrated skill and a 0 to represent each undemonstrated skill, enter each student's data on a separate row in a spreadsheet, giving each item its own column. When using marking rubrics (partial credit), any level lower than that at which the student was marked is considered to include a skill which the student possesses and is therefore entered as a 1.

2 *Skills.* Each item must have an associated skill entered into the spreadsheet. Skills are written in the positive, outlining what the student has done, not described in the negative, as mistakes or omissions. For example 'adds two-digit numbers without trading', 'follows numbered steps to light a Bunsen burner' or 'identifies that "e" and "r" make the sound "er"'. A given assessment piece might assess the same skill in more than one item. Descriptions of skills are often long, and can be difficult to read in the spreadsheet cell. You can change the cell alignment, row height and/or column width to make the descriptions easier to read by wrapping the text and using a vertical writing orientation. See the spreadsheet tips on cell alignment and/or row height and column width in Figure 10.2 for help with this.

3 *Totals.* The totals for each student and each item are calculated and entered at the end of each row and each column. See the spreadsheet tips on summing and fill in Figure 10.2 for help with this.

4 *Colour or shade the ones.* Changing the colour or shading of the cells containing 1s allows patterns in the data to be seen more easily. See the spreadsheet tips on conditional formatting in Figure 10.2 for help with this.

5 *Student sort.* Sort the rows containing the student names according to their totals, from largest to smallest. Do not include the skills, item numbers or totals in the sort. The most able student (on that particular assessment), with the highest total, will end up at the top, and the least able student, with the lowest total, will end up at the bottom. See the Spreadsheet tips on custom sort in Figure 10.3 for help with this.

6 *Item sort.* Sort the columns containing the items from left to right according to their totals, from largest to smallest. Do not include the student names or totals in the sort. The easiest item, with the highest total, will end up at the left and the most difficult item, with the lowest total, will end up at the bottom. See the spreadsheet tip on left–right sort in Figure 10.3 for help with this.

The ZPD area marked on the Guttman chart in Figure 10.4 is an approximation for a group of 25 students who completed an assessment on fractions. It shows that different members of the student group had very different ZPDs. The students near the top of the chart answered many of the items correctly and had ZPDs which included some of the most difficult skills. The students near the bottom of the chart answered few items correctly and had ZPDs that encompassed the easiest skills. A Guttman chart is a very effective way to demonstrate the need for differentiated teaching. It is also a useful tool in evaluating the opportunities provided for students to demonstrate the scope of their skills. For example, this task was effective in locating the ZPD of the majority of this class. The pattern of the chart is typical in that most people occasionally make careless errors with items below their ZPD. With items above their ZPD, most people will guess the odd correct answer, or be able to correctly use a skill on one occasion.

However, this assessment was not useful in locating the ZPD for the top six students. That is because the task did not require the use of skills difficult enough to prompt a 50:50 zone for these students, who would need to be given the opportunity to undertake a task comprising more difficult skills before their ZPDs could be located. The same would hold true for the task if the chart revealed that a student did not demonstrate competence over the easiest skills. The task might have been beyond that student's capabilities, in which case the student would need to be provided with the opportunity to demonstrate skills at an easier level. Alternatively, the student might not have been engaged by the task. A lack of engagement can be due to the style of assessment, a student's attitude to assessment or distractions to the student at the time of assessment. It is important that, in such situations, teachers consider these options before making teaching decisions.

	A	B	C	D	E	F	G	H	I	J	K	L	M	N	O	P	Q	R	S	T	U	V	W	X	Y	Z	AA	AB	AC	AD	AE
1																			Skills												
2		identifies 3/4 - square	identifies 3/4 - diamond	circles 1/3 of group	shares 20 between 4	half from whole	shade 1/5 of rectangle	identifies 1/3 of choc bar	identifies 1/4 of choc bar	1/3 + 1/4 choc bar (number of pieces)	identifies fractional piece	shares 3 pizzas between 4	continues counting pattern (4s)	shades 3/4 of ribbon	mark fraction wall- fifths	mark fraction wall- tenths	marks 3/5 on number line	chooses number between 0 and 1/2 from list	Marks no. accurately on no. Line	Marks 1 given 1/3	Orders fractions with same denominator	Chooses equiv fractions (2/4 = 1/2)	Completes equiv fractions	Simplifies fractions	Matches decimals and fractions (1/2)	Matches decimals and fractions (1/4)	Matches decimals and fractions (1/10)	Matches decimals and fractions (2/5) with diagram	Chooses non-equiv fraction from list	Addition of fractions with same denominator	
3		1a	1b	2	3	4	5	6a	6b	6c	6d	7	8	9	10a	10b	11	12a	12b	13	14	15	16	17	18a	18b	18c	18d	19	20	
4	Baldr	1	1	1	1	1	1	1	1	1	1	0	1	1	1	0	1	1	1	1	1	1	1	1	1	1	1	1	1	0	26
5	Bragi	1	1	1	1	1	1	1	1	1	1	1	1	1	1	1	1	1	1	1	1	1	1	1	1	1	1	1	1	1	29
6	Dagr	1	1	1	1	1	1	1	1	1	0	0	1	0	1	0	0	1	1	1	1	1	0	1	1	1	1	1	1	0	22
7	Delling	1	1	1	1	1	1	1	1	1	1	1	1	1	1	1	1	1	1	1	1	1	0	0	1	1	1	1	1	1	27
8	Eir	1	0	1	0	0	1	1	0	1	0	0	1	1	1	1	1	0	0	1	1	1	0	0	1	0	0	0	0	0	14
9	Forseti	1	1	1	1	1	1	1	1	1	0	1	0	1	1	0	1	1	1	0	1	1	0	0	1	1	1	1	1	1	23
10	Freya	1	1	1	1	1	1	1	1	1	0	0	1	1	1	1	1	1	1	1	1	1	0	1	1	1	1	1	0	0	24
11	Fulla	1	1	1	1	1	1	0	1	1	0	0	1	1	1	0	0	1	1	0	1	1	0	0	0	0	1	0	0	0	16
12	Gefjun	1	1	1	1	1	1	1	1	1	1	1	1	1	1	1	0	1	1	1	1	1	1	1	1	1	1	1	1	1	28
13	Gmot	1	1	1	1	1	1	1	1	1	1	0	1	1	0	0	0	0	0	0	0	1	0	1	1	1	1	1	0	0	18
14	Iaunn	1	1	0	1	1	1	1	1	1	1	1	1	1	1	1	1	1	0	1	1	1	0	0	1	1	1	1	1	0	24
15	Jora	1	1	1	1	1	0	0	1	1	0	1	1	1	0	0	0	1	1	0	0	1	0	1	1	0	1	0	0	0	16
16	Kvasir	1	1	1	1	1	1	1	1	1	1	1	1	1	1	1	1	1	1	1	0	1	1	0	1	1	1	1	0	0	25
17	Loki	1	1	1	1	1	1	1	1	1	0	0	0	1	1	1	1	0	1	0	1	1	0	0	1	0	1	0	1	0	19
18	Mani	1	1	1	1	1	1	1	1	1	1	0	1	1	1	1	0	1	1	0	0	0	0	0	1	1	1	1	0	0	20
19	Mimir	1	1	1	1	1	1	1	1	1	0	0	1	1	1	1	0	1	1	0	0	1	0	1	0	0	1	0	0	0	18
20	Nanna	1	1	1	0	1	1	0	0	0	0	1	0	0	0	0	0	1	0	0	0	0	0	1	0	1	0	0	0	1	10
21	Nerphus	1	1	1	1	1	0	1	1	1	0	0	0	1	0	0	0	0	0	0	1	0	0	0	1	0	0	0	0	0	11
22	Odin	1	1	1	1	1	1	1	1	1	1	0	1	1	0	0	1	1	0	0	1	1	0	0	1	1	1	1	1	0	21
23	Sif	1	1	1	0	1	1	0	1	1	0	0	0	0	0	0	0	0	0	0	0	0	0	0	0	0	0	0	1	0	8
24	Sol	1	1	1	1	1	0	0	0	1	0	0	0	1	0	0	0	0	0	0	0	0	0	1	0	0	0	0	0	0	8
25	Thor	1	1	1	1	1	1	1	1	1	1	1	1	1	1	1	1	1	1	1	1	1	1	1	1	1	1	1	1	1	29
26	Tiki	1	1	1	1	1	1	1	1	1	1	1	1	1	1	1	1	1	1	1	1	1	1	0	1	1	1	1	1	0	27
27	Ulla	0	1	1	1	1	1	1	1	1	0	0	1	0	1	1	1	1	1	1	1	1	1	1	1	1	1	1	1	0	24
28	Vali	1	1	0	1	1	1	1	1	1	1	1	1	1	1	1	0	1	1	1	1	1	1	1	1	1	1	1	1	1	27
29	Total	24	24	23	22	24	22	20	22	24	12	11	19	21	18	14	13	19	17	13	17	20	8	13	20	17	20	16	14	7	

Figure 10.2 *Unsorted data*

Spreadsheet tips

Cell alignment
Use the cell alignment feature to wrap text so it fits in a cell, or to change the text direction.

Row height and column width
Change the height of a row or the width of a column by highlighting the row or column and then either dragging the boundary to the size you require or right-clicking and choosing Row Height or Column Width from the menu.

Summing
The spreadsheet can calculate the totals for you using a formula entered into the cell at the bottom of each column and the end of each row. Use the 'sum' formula or the 'autosum' feature.

Fill
There is no need to enter the same formula into repeated cells. The 'fill' feature will let you copy a formula from one cell into many cells within a row or column. It automatically adjusts the formula to take account of its new position.

Conditional formatting
Highlight all the cells containing ones and zeros. Use the 'conditional formatting' feature to use a rule to highlight the cells that contain a one. The cells containing zeros will be left white.

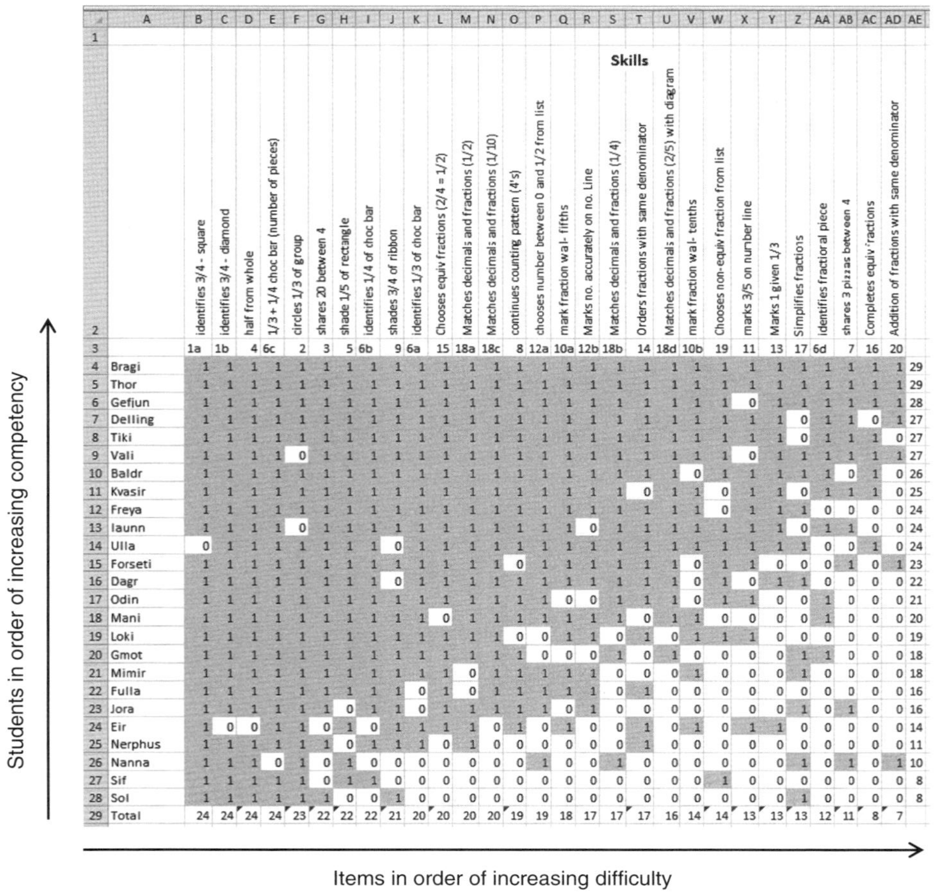
Students in order of increasing competency
Items in order of increasing difficulty

	A	B	C	D	E	F	G	H	I	J	K	L	M	N	O	P	Q	R	S	T	U	V	W	X	Y	Z	AA	AB	AC	AD	AE
1																			Skills												
2		identifies 3/4 - square	identifies 3/4 - diamond	half from whole	1/3 + 1/4 choc bar (number of pieces)	circles 1/3 of group	shares 20 between 4	shade 1/5 of rectangle	identifies 1/4 of choc bar	shades 3/4 of ribbon	identifies 1/3 of choc bar	Chooses equiv fractions (2/4 = 1/2)	Matches decimals and fractions (1/2)	Matches decimals and fractions (1/10)	continues counting pattern (4's)	chooses number between 0 and 1/2 from list	mark fraction wal- fifths	Marks no. accurately on no. Line	Matches decimals and fractions (1/4)	Orders fractions with same denominator	Matches decimals and fractions (2/5) with diagram	mark fraction wal- tenths	Chooses non-equiv fraction from list	marks 3/5 on number line	Marks 1 given 1/3	Simplifies fractions	identifies fractional piece	shares 3 pizzas between 4	Completes equiv fractions	Addition of fractions with same denominator	
3		1a	1b	4	6c	2	3	5	6b	9	6a	15	18a	18c	8	12a	10a	12b	18b	14	18d	10b	19	11	13	17	6d	7	16	20	
4	Bragi	1	1	1	1	1	1	1	1	1	1	1	1	1	1	1	1	1	1	1	1	1	1	1	1	1	1	1	1	1	29
5	Thor	1	1	1	1	1	1	1	1	1	1	1	1	1	1	1	1	1	1	1	1	1	1	1	1	1	1	1	1	1	29
6	Gefjun	1	1	1	1	1	1	1	1	1	1	1	1	1	1	1	1	1	1	1	1	1	1	0	1	1	1	1	1	1	28
7	Delling	1	1	1	1	1	1	1	1	1	1	1	1	1	1	1	1	1	1	1	1	1	1	1	1	0	1	1	0	1	27
8	Tiki	1	1	1	1	1	1	1	1	1	1	1	1	1	1	1	1	1	1	1	1	1	1	1	1	0	1	1	1	0	27
9	Vali	1	1	1	1	0	1	1	1	1	1	1	1	1	1	1	1	1	1	1	1	1	1	0	1	1	1	1	1	1	27
10	Baldr	1	1	1	1	1	1	1	1	1	1	1	1	1	1	1	1	1	1	1	1	0	1	1	1	1	1	0	1	0	26
11	Kvasir	1	1	1	1	1	1	1	1	1	1	1	1	1	1	1	1	1	1	0	1	1	0	1	1	0	1	1	1	0	25
12	Freya	1	1	1	1	1	1	1	1	1	1	1	1	1	1	1	1	1	1	1	1	1	0	1	1	1	0	0	0	0	24
13	Iaunn	1	1	1	1	0	1	1	1	1	1	1	1	1	1	1	1	0	1	1	1	1	1	1	1	0	1	1	0	0	24
14	Ulla	0	1	1	1	1	1	1	1	0	1	1	1	1	1	1	1	1	1	1	1	1	1	1	1	1	0	0	1	0	24
15	Forseti	1	1	1	1	1	1	1	1	1	1	1	1	1	0	1	1	1	1	1	1	0	1	1	0	0	0	1	0	1	23
16	Dagr	1	1	1	1	1	1	1	1	0	1	1	1	1	1	1	1	1	1	1	1	0	1	0	1	1	0	0	0	0	22
17	Odin	1	1	1	1	1	1	1	1	1	1	1	1	1	1	1	0	0	1	1	1	0	1	1	0	0	1	0	0	0	21
18	Mani	1	1	1	1	1	1	1	1	1	1	0	1	1	1	1	1	1	1	0	1	1	0	0	0	0	1	0	0	0	20
19	Loki	1	1	1	1	1	1	1	1	1	1	1	1	1	0	0	1	1	0	1	0	1	1	1	0	0	0	0	0	0	19
20	Gmot	1	1	1	1	1	1	1	1	1	1	1	1	1	1	0	0	0	1	0	1	0	0	0	0	1	1	0	0	0	18
21	Mimir	1	1	1	1	1	1	1	1	1	1	1	0	1	1	1	1	1	0	0	0	1	0	0	0	1	0	0	0	0	18
22	Fulla	1	1	1	1	1	1	1	1	1	0	1	0	1	1	1	1	1	0	1	0	0	0	0	0	0	0	0	0	0	16
23	Jora	1	1	1	1	1	1	0	1	1	0	1	1	1	1	1	0	1	0	0	0	0	0	0	0	1	0	1	0	0	16
24	Eir	1	0	0	1	1	0	1	0	1	1	1	1	0	1	0	1	0	0	1	0	1	0	1	1	0	0	0	0	0	14
25	Nerphus	1	1	1	1	1	1	0	1	1	1	0	1	0	0	0	0	0	0	1	0	0	0	0	0	0	0	0	0	0	11
26	Nanna	1	1	1	0	1	0	1	0	0	0	0	0	0	0	1	0	0	1	0	0	0	0	0	0	1	0	1	0	1	10
27	Sif	1	1	1	1	1	0	1	1	0	0	0	0	0	0	0	0	0	0	0	0	0	1	0	0	0	0	0	0	0	8
28	Sol	1	1	1	1	1	1	0	0	1	0	0	0	0	0	0	0	0	0	0	0	0	0	0	0	1	0	0	0	0	8
29	Total	24	24	24	24	23	22	22	22	21	20	20	20	20	19	19	18	17	17	17	16	14	14	13	13	13	12	11	8	7	

Figure 10.3 *Sorted data*

Spreadsheet tips

Custom sort

Highlight the cells you wish to sort and use the 'custom sort' feature to sort them. You can select which column you want the data sorted by and the order in which you want the rows arranged.

Left–right sort

Within the custom sort feature, there is an option to sort from left to right. Once the left–right option is selected, you can choose the row which you want the data sorted by and the order in which you want the columns arranged.

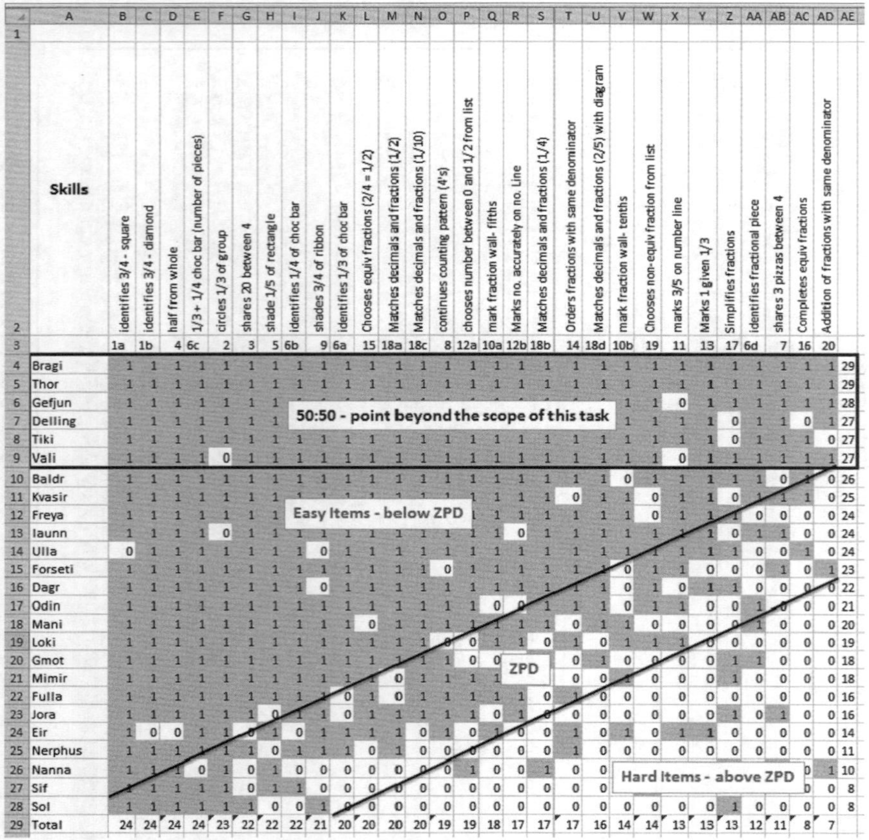

Locating ZPD

To locate the ZPD area on a chart, look for the area that shows a roughly 50:50 balance between correct and incorrect answers. It is identified on the chart in Figure 10.4 as the area between the two angled black lines. Note that the ZPD is student-dependent and varies from one student to another according to the skills they have demonstrated in the given task.

The width of the zone containing a mixture of ones and zeros is an indication of the reliability of the assessment. A very wide zone means that there is a lot of 'noise' in the measure of the students' abilities. A narrow zone indicates that the assessment is a reliable measure of the students' abilities in the underlying construct. 'Noise' might be due to a number of factors, including the following: that the students were not engaged in the task, that the assessment was not administered consistently, that the assessment is not of good quality, that the assessment measures more than one underlying construct.

Figure 10.4 *Interpreting a Guttman chart*

Labels within the chart: "50:50 – point beyond the scope of this task", "Easy Items – below ZPD", "ZPD", "Hard Items – above ZPD".

Column headers (skills):

Col	Item	Skill
B	1a	identifies 3/4 - square
C	1b	identifies 3/4 - diamond
D	4	half from whole
E	6c	1/3 + 1/4 choc bar (number of pieces)
F	2	circles 1/3 of group
G	3	shares 20 between 4
H	5	shade 1/5 of rectangle
I	6b	identifies 1/4 of choc bar
J	9	shades 3/4 of ribbon
K	6a	identifies 1/3 of choc bar
L	15	Chooses equiv fractions (2/4 = 1/2)
M	18a	Matches decimals and fractions (1/2)
N	18c	Matches decimals and fractions (1/10)
O	8	continues counting pattern (4's)
P	12a	chooses number between 0 and 1/2 from list
Q	10a	mark fraction wall- fifths
R	12b	Marks no. accurately on no. Line
S	18b	Matches decimals and fractions (1/4)
T	14	Orders fractions with same denominator
U	18d	Matches decimals and fractions (2/5) with diagram
V	10b	mark fraction wall- tenths
W	19	Chooses non-equiv fraction from list
X	11	marks 3/5 on number line
Y	13	Marks 1 given 1/3
Z	17	Simplifies fractions
AA	6d	identifies fractional piece
AB	7	shares 3 pizzas between 4
AC	16	Completes equiv fractions
AE	20	Addition of fractions with same denominator

Students (rows 4–28): Bragi, Thor, Gefjun, Delling, Tiki, Vali, Baldr, Kvasir, Freya, Iaunn, Ulla, Forseti, Dagr, Odin, Mani, Loki, Gmot, Mimir, Fulla, Jora, Eir, Nerphus, Nanna, Sif, Sol.

Row totals: 29, 29, 28, 27, 27, 26, 25, 24, 24, 24, 23, 22, 21, 20, 19, 18, 18, 16, 14, 11, 10, 8, 8, 7.

Column totals (row 29, Total): 24 24 24 23 22 22 22 21 21 20 20 20 19 19 18 17 17 17 16 14 13 13 13 12 11 11 8 8 7

Activity: Constructing a Guttman chart

Figures 10.2 to 10.4 took you through the construction of a Guttman chart using an objective assessment. It is now your turn to practise this skill.

Select a task for students. It is easiest to work with one with which you are familiar from your studies or teaching experience. Remember that the results must be scored as responses to items or questions on which the students have been successful (1) or not successful (0). To make it manageable in the first instance, select a task that has no more than 40 items or questions. A short topic pre-test is perfect. Choose a student sample of 40 or less. Enter the data.

Make the following checks:

1   Has the chart been sorted by:

- students from highest score (top) to lowest score (bottom)

- items from easiest (left) to hardest (right)?

2   Does it use conditional formatting to colour-code correct responses?

3   Does it provide a skills audit of each item? (Even if this is provided by the assessment, it should be checked to ensure the skills are described specifically and using terminology with which you are familiar.)

With reference to Figure 10.4, examine your chart and consider the following questions, discussing them with your colleagues or fellow students.

1   *Is there a discernible pattern of increasing skill difficulty in comparison to increasing student competence?* Note that if the chart looks like 'confetti', you might want to check that you have sorted it correctly. Otherwise, this might be a sign that you are trying to include unrelated constructs in the one analysis – for example, public speaking skills and historical reasoning skills. Alternatively, the task may have limited reliability. If you think you are trying to test different constructs, try dividing up the skills into two charts and see whether you achieve a more reliable result.

2   What do you think of the level of 'noise'? Can you account for it?

3   What skills can be identified as being below the ZPD of the majority of the students?

4   What skills can be identified as being above the ZPD of the majority of the students?

5   Are there any students for whom you were not able to determine a 50:50 point?

Identifying sources of error

Using a Guttman chart to investigate the performance of assessment items can provide information about how effectively an item is assessing a skill. It can also shed light on the legitimacy of the order of emergence of skills which is gained from the Guttman chart.

Item performance

Patterns are expected within the column for an item. It should start with a majority of ones, which is an indication that the item was easy for the more able students. It should finish with a majority of zeros, showing that the item was difficult for the less able students. In between, the pattern will break down into a mixture of ones and zeros.

Irregular item patterns

An irregular mixture of ones and zeros within a column shows that the item is not an indicator of a student's ability in the underlying construct. This may be due to ambiguity in the item or to inconsistent marking, or the item may not be matched to the underlying construct (e.g. if a maths question is written in difficult language, the question may measure reading ability, not maths ability). This pattern may also be an indication that the item is too difficult for the students undertaking the assessment. Items that perform in this way should be removed from the analysis. Teachers can use this information to improve their assessment tasks in the future.

Irregular student patterns

An irregular row of ones and zeros indicates that the student has not engaged fully in the assessment. The pattern is a reflection of the student's attention to the task, rather than their skills. Therefore, it is not possible from this assessment to identify the student's point of readiness to learn. Alternative means must be used.

Odd zeros

An unusual zero among a lot of ones is probably an indication of a lapse in concentration and not an indication that the student needs to be taught the skill again. We all occasionally make mistakes when doing things that we do well most of the time!

Odd ones

An unexpected one after the pattern has broken down should also be disregarded. It is an indication of lucky guessing or an unusual event, not a skill that the student has mastered. This outcome is much more likely if the assessment is a multiple-choice test, where the probability of guessing correctly is relatively high.

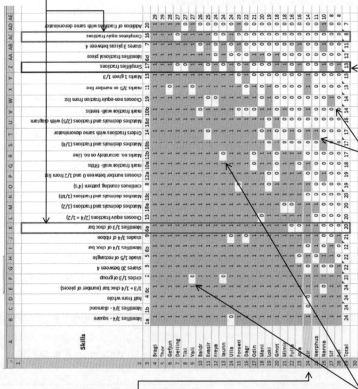

Figure 10.5 *Identifying sources of error in a Guttman chart*

Ideally, in a Guttman chart there should be a pattern showing that the more difficult items are those that are answered correctly by the more skilled students and incorrectly by the less skilled students. Also, the pattern should show that most of the students can answer the easier items.

To illustrate the information that can be gained about individual items, three items in Figure 10.5 have been singled out. Items 6a and 16 have been placed in grey boxes and Item 17 has been placed in a black box.

Item 6a is performing well. The more able students (at the top of the chart) have responded correctly, while the less able students (at the bottom) have not. In between is a mixed pattern of results, showing that the underlying skill for this item is in the ZPD for those students.

Item 16 is also performing well. This is an item at the 'top end' that very few students have been able to answer correctly (aside from the first six students – for whom, as we have observed, we do not have reliable data). It appears to be a 'problem-solving' question, which is consistent with the other questions above the majority of our students' ZPDs. These types of test items have performed reliably, however, and they show us where we are headed in terms of developing student skills.

Item 17 has a less consistent pattern. While the majority of students responded correctly, the students who did not respond correctly are spread across the ability groups, and many are from the more able group. This indicates that the item is affected by 'noise'. This could be caused by some students interpreting the item differently from the majority, in which case the item would not be a good predictor of the underlying skill. In this situation, it is worth going back to the assessment task or looking for patterns in the incorrect answers to uncover factors that may have contributed to the noise. For example, if this task was given as a written test, the layout might have influenced the way in which the students responded. If item 17 tested equivalent fractions but followed an item that required an answer in decimal form, you might discover that several of the students provided an equivalent decimal instead of an equivalent fraction, suggesting that they were distracted by the requirements of the previous question. Alternatively, you might realise that the item was ambiguous in its wording. If, after this type of investigation, it turns out that there was an alternative correct answer, you might consider reallocating marks and adjusting your scoring in the chart to see whether this generates a more reliable pattern. If this is not an option, item 17 should not be used to measure the underlying skill and the placement of the skill within the order of skill development should not be relied upon.

Using the data to target teaching

Teachers completing a Guttman analysis will regularly see a common set of skills emerging within a cluster of students. These patterns assist teachers to make generalisations about the sequence in which skills are typically learned. They also help teachers to maximise the opportunity for student progress by helping to identify which group of skills should be targeted for each student.

Generalising to levels of skill development

If data from a large number of students have been analysed using a Guttman chart, it is possible to generalise the order of skills to form a developmental progression that can be used independently of this group of students. From this, it may be possible to find commonalities between skills of similar difficulty and to generalise these to descriptions of different skill levels, just like the nutshell statements on the Learning Readiness Report.

One critical requirement in determining whether your progression is likely to be valid is to establish whether the task or test was built from a blueprint based on a developmental taxonomy, such as Biggs and Collis's SOLO taxonomy, or some other research base. This is because your progression will be built using the elements of the task or the tool used to collect the data. Due to this, your progression will be only as good as the task or tool that was used to generate it. For example, items not included in the task or test will not be captured as part of the progression, even though they may actually form part of the typical learning sequence for students.

For this reason, it is important to ensure that the purpose of the task or test is clear. A pre-test might be useful to capture data to plan teaching, but might not be as useful for generating a progression of learning. Also, if a skill emerges at a very different level than teaching experience would predict, or from items assessing similar skills, it is important that the item assessing that skill is examined to see whether it is a good measure of the skill. This involves examining the pattern of student responses and checking that the skill listed in the skill audit is really the skill that is being assessed. This is particularly important if the person interpreting the data is not the one who conducted the skill audit.

Finally, teachers should also take the opportunity to compare the Guttman results to the test blueprint, developmental taxonomy, pairwise comparison or other construct that was used to develop the assessment task. By doing this, teachers and PLT can work towards building a repertoire of robust, valid and reliable assessment tools.

Planning for teaching

In this approach, the developmental view of learning is intrinsic to the way assessment data are interpreted. The ZPD for a student or group of students can be identified from a Guttman chart. The skills within the ZPD are those that the student has a 50:50 chance of performing correctly. These skills are those at which teaching interventions for this student should be aimed. All skills within the zone should be addressed – even those represented by questions that the student answered correctly. This is the heart of the concept of 50:50 within the ZPD. The fact that a student demonstrates a skill correctly on one occasion does not mean that they will be able to do so on another occasion. The weekend golfer who achieves a fluke hole in one is not ready for the professional circuit. If I leave my keys on the desk, does it mean I am a forgetful person? We can't generalise from a single piece of evidence. It is always the case that we need multiple measures. The same applies to assessment in general. One good or bad performance on a test needs to be supplemented with evidence from other assessments in order to draw a conclusion about the student's readiness to learn. An incorrect response on one test does not necessarily indicate the absence of a particular skill. The driver who backs down a driveway and hits the mailbox for the first time in 20 years does not need driving lessons. If a student were to repeat a test, the set of items answered correctly and incorrectly might differ but the overall pattern visible in the Guttman chart could remain the same. Therefore, the teaching should address the skill level indicated by the overall pattern, not the individual items.

When teachers take a deficit approach to teaching, the interpretive use of data is managed differently. It may lead to direct teaching of only those skills tested by questions to which a student does not respond correctly, irrespective of what this says about the student's actual skills and how far above or below the student's ZPD the skills are. This is akin to someone who has backed their car into their mailbox once in 20 years of driving being required to take driving lessons in backing, or entering someone in the pro golf circuit because they got a hole in one. In a developmental approach, the taught skills are those that fall within a student's ZPD. Someone making an uncharacteristic mistake is not taught something far below their ZPD. Similarly, skills far above their ZPD are not addressed, even if they got the occasional answer correct, as it is inefficient to teach people skills above their ZPD, For example, the students in Figure 10.6 have been organised into five instructional clusters. The skills common to each of the groups are described in Table 10.1.

Figure 10.6 identifies the students in rows 21, 22 and 23 – Mimir, Fulla and Jora – as having a similar ZPD. Based on the data from this task, these students have similar emerging skills in relation to fractions. On this basis, the teacher would target teaching so that it consolidates skills in 'making fractions' (one level below) and scaffolds emerging skills in 'recognising equivalence of simple fractions and decimals' (the readiness level). Students are not expected to complete tasks that are beyond their level of competence, but it is important that teaching takes into account the direction in which learning is headed, to ensure that each level of learning provides a conceptually strong foundation on which the next level of learning can be built. This process of focusing teaching in this way should be completed for each of the groups of students with common ZPDs. To increase the reliability of the targeting process, decisions should be based on multiple sources of evidence and made in collaboration with others.

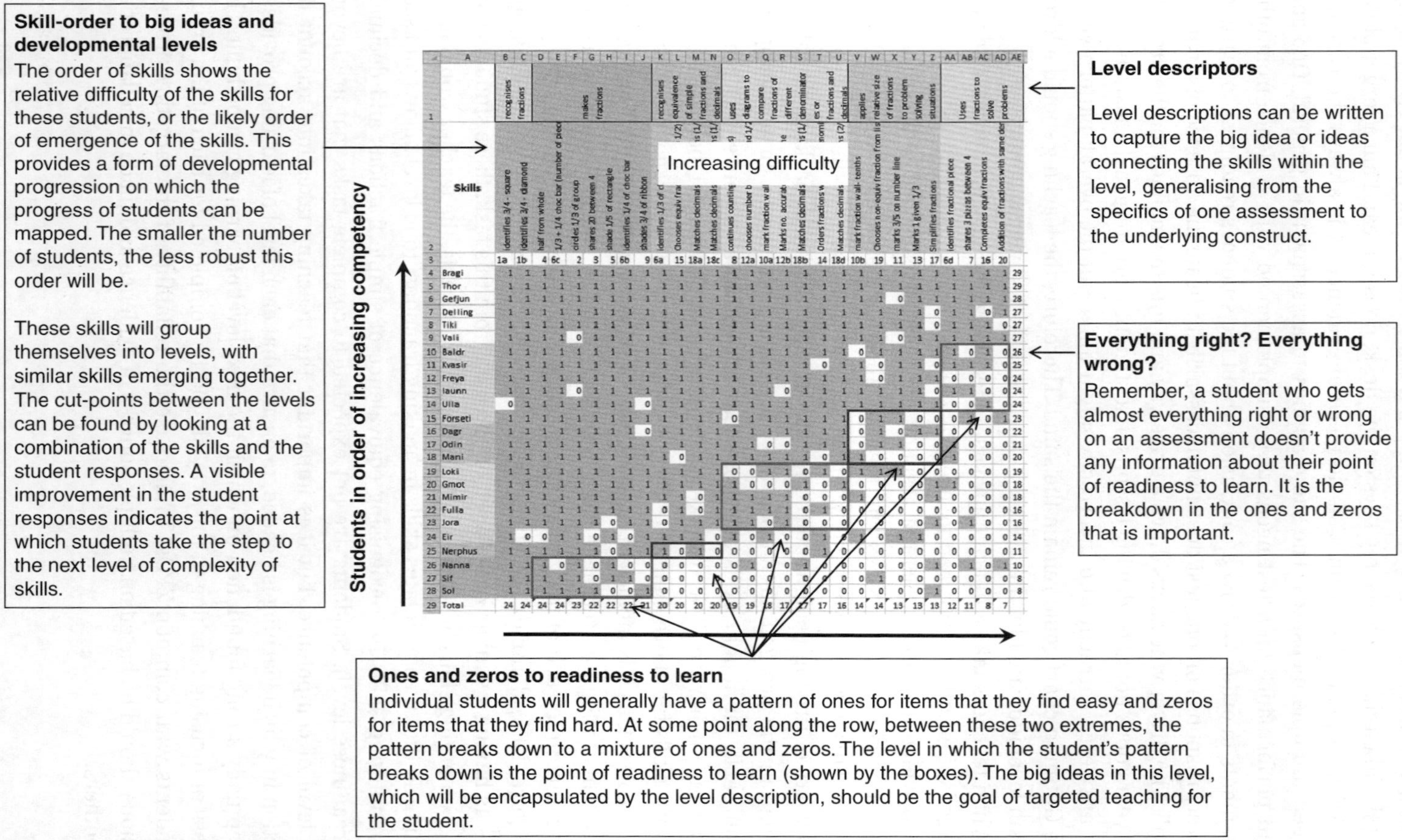
Skill-order to big ideas and developmental levels
The order of skills shows the relative difficulty of the skills for these students, or the likely order of emergence of the skills. This provides a form of developmental progression on which the progress of students can be mapped. The smaller the number of students, the less robust this order will be.
These skills will group themselves into levels, with similar skills emerging together. The cut-points between the levels can be found by looking at a combination of the skills and the student responses. A visible improvement in the student responses indicates the point at which students take the step to the next level of complexity of skills.
Students in order of increasing competency
Increasing difficulty
Skills
Level descriptors
Level descriptions can be written to capture the big idea or ideas connecting the skills within the level, generalising from the specifics of one assessment to the underlying construct.
Everything right? Everything wrong?
Remember, a student who gets almost everything right or wrong on an assessment doesn't provide any information about their point of readiness to learn. It is the breakdown in the ones and zeros that is important.
Ones and zeros to readiness to learn
Individual students will generally have a pattern of ones for items that they find easy and zeros for items that they find hard. At some point along the row, between these two extremes, the pattern breaks down to a mixture of ones and zeros. The level in which the student's pattern breaks down is the point of readiness to learn (shown by the boxes). The big ideas in this level, which will be encapsulated by the level description, should be the goal of targeted teaching for the student.

Figure 10.6 *Interpreting a Guttman chart*

Table 10.1 *Skills common to instructional groups identified in Figure 10.6*

	SKILLS	LEVEL STATEMENT (BIG IDEA)
INCREASING LEVEL OF DIFFICULTY	Identifies fractional piece	
	Shares three pizzas between four people	Uses fractions to solve problems
	Completes equivalent fractions $\left(\frac{3}{6} = \frac{1}{?}\right)$	
	Addition of fractions with same denominator	
	Simplifies fractions $\left(\frac{2}{8} = \frac{1}{4}\right)$	
	Chooses non-equivalent fraction from list	Applies relative size of fractions to problem-solving situations
	Marks $\frac{3}{5}$ on number line	
	Marks 1 given $\frac{1}{3}$	
	Marks fraction wall – fifths	
	Marks number accurately on number line	
	Orders fractions with same denominator	Uses diagrams to compare fractions of different denominators or fractions and decimals
	Matches decimals and fractions $\left(\frac{1}{4}\right)$	
	Matches decimals and fractions $\left(\frac{2}{5}\right)$ with diagram	
	Marks fraction wall – tenths	
	Chooses equivalent fractions $\left(\frac{2}{4} = \frac{1}{2}\right)$	
	Matches decimals and fractions $\left(\frac{1}{2}\right)$	
	Matches decimals and fractions $\left(\frac{1}{10}\right)$	Recognises equivalence of simple fractions and decimals
	Identifies $\frac{1}{3}$ of chocolate bar	
	Continues counting pattern (4s)	
	Chooses number between 0 and $\left(\frac{1}{2}\right)$ from list	

Table 10.1 *Continued*

SKILLS	LEVEL STATEMENT (BIG IDEA)
Shares 20 between 4	
Half from whole	
$\frac{1}{3} + \frac{1}{4}$ chocolate bar (number of pieces)	
Circles $\frac{1}{3}$ of group	Makes fractions
Shades $\frac{1}{5}$ of rectangle	
Identifies $\frac{1}{4}$ of chocolate bar	
Shades $\frac{3}{4}$ of ribbon	
Identifies $\frac{3}{4}$ – square	Recognises fractions
Identifies $\frac{3}{4}$ – diamond	

Reflective question

Reflect on how you might use data to inform teaching. In what ways might the use of a Guttman analysis support your practices? In what ways might it change your practices?

Steps in constructing a Guttman chart using judgement-based assessment

The process by which data are generated and interpreted for judgement-based assessments is very similar to the process for objective assessments. However, there are a few key differences. The main difference is that judgement-based assessment uses a partial-credit coding system to accommodate answers which have multiple 'credits' allocated to a single task. For example, a short-answer question forming part of a book report might be:

Q1. Write a short review of the book selected for the report (4 marks).

If the assessment task has been constructed using the principles set out in Chapters 6 and 7, there will be a marking rubric that describes the four levels of increasing complexity against which the student response will be evaluated. If SOLO is the tax-onomy used to develop the tasks, the levels might look something like this:

Reviews text

1.0 Insufficient evidence.

1.1 Review focuses on one element of the text, e.g. plot or characters.

1.2 Review discusses discrete elements of the text.

1.3 Review draws relationships between the different elements of the text to provide an over-arching evaluation.

1.4 Review synthesises elements of the text and evaluates it in the context of other literary works by the same author or within the same genre.

Entering the data

As discussed previously, when we put the data into a spreadsheet, the results need to be recorded as ones and zeros. In a partial-credit assessment like the one above, if a Guttman chart is constructed with one column for each test item, the numbers range from 0 to 4. This does not give us an indication of 'where our students are at' – that is, their readiness to learn. To avoid this problem, we need to separate out the 'credit'. The simplest way to do this is to create one column for each skill and allocate a 1 or 0 to each column. The coding for the single item above would then appear as shown in Figure 10.7.

The important thing to remember is that the scoring is cumulative, reflecting the increasing levels of complexity that need to be built into judgement-based items. This means that if a student demonstrates the skill at level 1.4, they have also dem-onstrated all of the skills preceding it and those preceding levels are also coded with a 1. If you find that you have a student with a 0 in between two ones, then the data have been entered incorrectly or the rubric structure is flawed.

To complete a Guttman chart for the whole task, continue to enter the remain-ing rubrics after 1.4, remembering that the 'total' column should remain the final column.

By organising the partial-credit Guttman analysis in this way, we are able to go on to sort and interpret the data in the same way as for an objective task. This means that we are able to collect data using tasks that allow students to interact with a given test item at a range of cognitive levels and we can retain the means of effectively analysing the data in order to inform our teaching.

Figure 10.8 shows a fully worked partial-credit example using the social skills rubrics of the Assessment and Teaching of 21st Century Skills project. For more detail on this project, see Chapters 6 and 8.

	Skills	Review focuses on one element of the text, e.g. plot or characters	Review discusses discrete elements of the text	Review draws relationships between the different elements of the text to provide an overarching evaluation	Review synthesises elements of the text and evaluates it in the context of other literary works by the same author or within	Total
		1.1	1.2	1.3	1.4	Total
4	Baldr	1	1	1	1	4
5	Bragi	1	1	1	0	3
6	Dagr	1	1	1	1	4
7	Delling	1	1	1	1	4
8	Eir	1	0	0	0	1
9	Forseti	1	1	1	1	4
10	Freya	1	1	1	1	4
11	Fulla	1	1	0	0	2
12	Gefjun	1	1	1	1	4
13	Gmot	1	1	1	1	4
14	Iaunn	1	1	0	0	2
15	Jora	1	1	1	1	4
16	Kvasir	1	1	1	1	4
17	Loki	1	0	0	0	1
18	Mani	1	1	1	1	4
19	Mimir	1	1	1	1	4
20	Nanna	1	1	0	0	2
21	Nerphus	1	1	1	1	4
22	Odin	1	1	1	1	4
23	Sif	1	1	1	0	3
24	Sol	1	1	1	1	4
25	Thor	1	1	1	1	4
26	Tiki	1	1	1	1	4
27	Ulla	0	0	0	0	0
28	Vali	1	1	0	0	2
29	Total	24	22	18	16	

Figure 10.7 *A partial-credit Guttman chart*

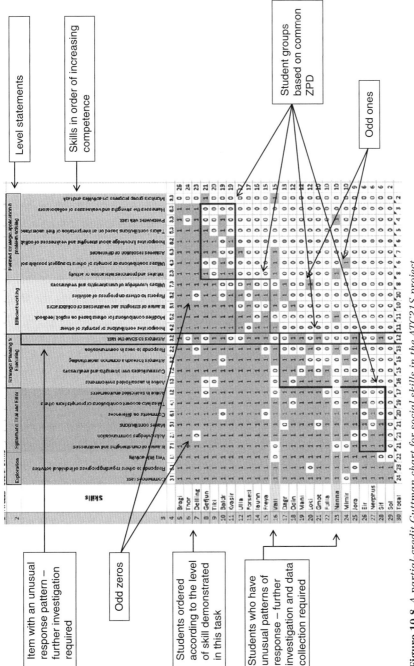

Figure 10.8 *A partial-credit Guttman chart for social skills in the ATC21S project*

Level statements

Skills in order of increasing competence

Student groups based on common ZPD

Odd ones

Item with an unusual response pattern – further investigation required

Odd zeros

Students ordered according to the level of skill demonstrated in this task

Students who have unusual patterns of response – further investigation and data collection required

Summary

When teachers have the tools to analyse student data, they are equipped to make evidence-based decisions. By analysing data, teachers can interrogate assessment tools to ensure that the data they provide allows valid inferences about student learning. Once it has been established that an assessment tool is able to provide meaningful data in relation to a learning area or construct, teachers can use the data to make decisions about how best to promote the learning of all students. This chapter has dealt with the part of this process involving the location of student ZPD at one time. The next chapter examines the considerations that teachers must take into account when evaluating student progress over time.

Apply to practice

In this book, we encourage teachers to look for ways to link data from assessment tasks to the skills that students are developing. Using a Guttman analysis facilitates this process. It can help teachers to produce developmental progressions based on student results of their own and to locate students on those progressions. Knowing the usual pattern of skill development can assist teachers to plan teaching sequences that will help students develop those skills. The Guttman analysis aids the teacher in locating the skills that each student is ready to learn and then grouping the students for targeted teaching interventions. It can also provide insight into the effectiveness of an assessment.

While not everyone needs to be able to make a Guttman chart, learning to interpret one empowers teachers.

Task

1 *Select a judgement-based assessment.* This task can be performed for any group of students who have done the same assessment (for example, a test containing the same items or questions). The exercise will be most useful if it can be completed in collaboration with others, and if it uses recent data on an area of learning that will be taught in the near future. A short topic pre-test is perfect. The assessment does not need to be a paper and pencil test. It can be a checklist, assessment rubric or survey.

   Remember that Guttman charts are easiest to interpret when the assessment has upper limits of:

   • about 40 items or questions (if you are using partial credit, each level is equivalent to an item – for example, 1.1, 1.2, 1.3 is equivalent to three items)

   • results from 40 students.

2 *Produce a Guttman analysis.* As the focus for this task is the interpretation of a Guttman chart, the chart you use may be one you produced yourself, or one

produced by another person. Before you begin to interpret your Guttman chart, check to see whether your Excel spreadsheet is arranged so that it:

- sorts students from highest score (top) to lowest score (bottom)
- sorts items from easiest (left) to hardest (right)
- uses conditional formatting to shade or colour-code correct items
- provides a skill audit of each item (even if this is provided by the assessment, it should be checked to ensure that the skills are described specifically, using terminology with which you are familiar).

3 *Discuss the Guttman analysis.* Discuss with your peers the use and interpretation of the Guttman analysis. Topics to discuss include:

- Skills in developmental progressions and constructs:
  - the order of the skills – does the order make sense in terms of increasing difficulty?
  - the possible grouping of skills into meaningful developmental levels (big ideas) using the Guttman chart – does the grouping indicate a series of big ideas that increase in sophistication?
  - the meaningfulness of the construct (big idea) underpinning the test – does the series of big ideas make sense as a developmental progression, and how can it help with establishing learning goals for students?
  - the relationship of the construct to your state or national curriculum.
- Teaching targets for groups of students:
  - the formation of instructional groups based on the Guttman chart
  - the use of the Guttman chart to identify teaching targets for groups of students according to the big idea each student is ready to learn
  - the use of the Guttman chart to identify students who require additional assessment in order to identify teaching targets
  - the implications of this data analysis for future teaching of these students.
- Review of the assessment and its administration:
  - the pattern of student responses on the Guttman chart that would indicate a problem with an assessment item
  - the reliability of the assessment as judged by the width of the region of transition from mostly right to mostly wrong responses
  - the pattern of student responses on the Guttman chart that would indicate that a student has not been engaged in the task
  - the sources of noise in the data and how these might be controlled in future assessment.

- Future use of Guttman analyses:
  - the implications of this Guttman analysis for the future teaching of students
  - the future use of this type of analysis within your professional activities.

Check your progress

Below is a set of rubrics designed to help you reflect on your answers to the Apply to Practice task and assess your understanding of this chapter. These can be used to help scaffold learning.

10.1   When grouping skills into developmental levels you:

   a   grouped skills based on the order of skills in the Guttman chart

   b   grouped skills based on the order of skills and the patterns of student responses on the Guttman chart.

10.2   When using the Guttman analysis to target teaching, you:

   a   used the order of students and big ideas in the Guttman analysis to identify teaching targets

   b   used the pattern of student responses and developmental levels in the Guttman chart to identify teaching targets.

10.3   When identifying students for whom you require additional data to set teaching targets, you:

   a   discussed how to use the Guttman chart to identify students for whom the assessments were too easy or too hard

   b   discussed how to use the Guttman chart patterns of response to identify students who were not engaged in the task.

10.4   When discussing the pattern of student responses on the Guttman chart that might indicate a problem with the assessment item, you:

   a   discussed the identification *or* possible causes of problems

   b   discussed the identification *and* possible causes of problems.

10.5   When discussing the implications of this data analysis for future teaching of these students, you:

   a   focused on individual classroom practices

   b   focused on the implications across the student cohort

   c   focused on the relationship between the classroom, the school and the broader educational context.

10.6   When discussing the possible future use of this form of analysis, you:

    a   discussed the ways in which individual teachers might make use of the Guttman analysis

    b   discussed the ways in which the data collected might inform future school policy directions

    c   discussed the ways in which the data might be used to contribute to the wider ongoing field of practitioner research or educational initiatives.

Chapter 11

Interpreting data to evaluate progress

Patrick Griffin, Pam Robertson and Danielle Hutchinson

This chapter promotes the development of knowledge and skills in data analysis for the monitoring of progress in teaching and learning. It draws attention to the importance of reliable data and the role of both direct and indirect evidence in the inference-making process. The chapter introduces teachers to the use of two-points-in-time data as a means of evaluating both student progress and the efficacy of teaching practice. It asks teachers to consider the implications flowing from the use of quartile comparison analyses, which often show that low-achieving students make progress while supposedly higher ability students stagnate. The chapter also encourages teachers to reflect on their own, often deeply held, theories of learning, particularly as the theories influence their teaching practice and conceptualisation of both learners and learning in relation to student progress.

Learning objectives

In this chapter you will learn how to:

- examine the elements of student profiles, class reports and quartile analyses, and account for anomalies and sources of error in the information they provide
- identify ways of improving assessment data through:
  - review of test administration
  - improvement of targeting
- interpret and use data to plan targeted teaching
- examine the implications for classroom organisation to enhance targeted teaching
- use data systematically to formalise the evaluation of links between assessment data and student interventions.

Measuring progress

Comparing data from two points in time allows a teacher to identify how much progress has been made within a given period. Not only does it provide evidence about the rate of progress of students; it can also be used to evaluate the efficacy of the teaching interventions implemented by the teacher. This type of analysis heightens the capacity for critical reflection, adding valuable information to the process by which records or logs of interventions are examined to identify effective (or ineffective) teaching strategies. Using this approach, the teacher is well placed to make professional judgements about where and how to intervene to improve teaching.

Student profile reports

One report that enables a two-points-in-time analysis is the student profile report generated by ARCOTS. This report maps an individual student's stage of learning and progress across a number of learning domains. These might be reading, mathematics and problem-solving, if the student has taken all three ARCOTS tests. An example of a profile report featuring these three domains is provided in Figure 11.1.

The profile report is designed to help the teacher take a student's overall pattern or profile of abilities and readiness to learn into account. The black bars on the report show the student's point of readiness to learn, within their zone of proximal development as determined at the time of the most recent assessment. Note that this time does not need to be identical for all learning domains; the date of the most recent assessment for a particular domain is shown above the black bar on the report. If the student was assessed in a previous test period, a grey bar and date will indicate the level and time of that test.

Using two points in time on the profile report, the teacher can identify how much progress has been made over the elapsed time between the two assessments. The

Student Profile Report

Student name :
Student code: NNN9999
Student year: 5
Student class: PG
Student code: 9999
Print date: 25 March 2013

THE UNIVERSITY OF
MELBOURNE

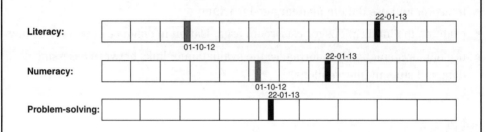

Literacy: 22-01-13
                          01-10-12

Numeracy: 22-01-13
                          01-10-12
                          22-01-13

Problem-solving:

Current level descriptions for student

Literacy: Level J – Identify fine nuances in text with unfamiliar context or styles.

Numeracy: Level H – Analyse problem and apply strategies to solve problem. Calculate area
                         and volume of 3D objects. Equivalent fractions.

Problem-solving: Level E – Select appropriate multi-step strategy to solve problems. Translate
                         problem into a rule.

▌ Most recent record for student   ▌ Second most recent record for student

Figure 11.1 *Example of a student profile report*

teacher can use these data to help identify why interventions were made and how effective they have been, bearing in mind that each point in time on the profile report is only one source of evidence. As discussed in earlier chapters, additional sources need to be considered when determining a student's ZPD.

Reviewing student progress

Useful questions to ask while reviewing profile reports include:

- What does this student know how to do? What does the student do well and with confidence?
- What does the profile report tell us about the student's particular pattern of strengths and abilities?
- What is the student on the verge of learning? What might the student do with scaffolding, modelling or the support of the teacher or a more capable peer?
- How can other information about the student's learning – such as work samples or observation of their classroom behaviour – be used to develop a richer understanding of their developing competence and readiness to learn?
- What sorts of learning goals might challenge this student but at the same time promote progress and success?
- What kinds of experiences and instruction would be most useful in helping the student make progress?
- Are there other students in this class with similar patterns of skill and understanding who can be grouped with this one for instruction?

Reflective questions

Think about the ways in which you have been taught to review student progress.

- What types of evidence do you use?
- Is the evidence drawn from multiple sources?
- Is it also used to reflect on the efficacy of the implemented teaching practices? If so, what is done with these reflections?

Planning for teaching and learning

In determining learning goals for the student, teachers should consider both long- and short-term goals in the context of the developmental progression. Learning goals should be clear and achievable so that students understand what they need to do or demonstrate in order to make progress and experience success within a developmental framework. Developmental learning progressions are very useful in this process, as they describe the skills and abilities at the student's previous, current and next level. The previous level is important for consolidation, the current level is important for intervention, and the next level is important for setting aspirational goals. The key question to ask at this point is:

> What teaching strategies and learning experiences will help students who are at this level of competence to make progress?

Over time, teachers will build up a bank of successful strategies and learning experiences for students at each developmental stage.

Stipulating evidence of progress

In order to evaluate whether or not students are responding positively to an intervention program, teachers can stipulate evidence of progress. One of the important factors in stipulating evidence is to ensure that multiple sources are used and that the balance between direct and indirect evidence is planned consciously. Direct evidence is captured when the teacher is able to directly observe student performance. The teacher is an eyewitness to the event. An example of this type of evidence is data collected via an observational checklist. Indirect evidence involves tasks in which student performance is not directly observed. In this situation, the teacher must infer that the performance is representative of student capacity. Examples of indirect evidence include group-work tasks or take-home assignments. Using multiple sources of evidence is important, as it ensures that the chances of a student 'slipping through the cracks' are minimised. In attempting to strike the right balance, it is important to consider both pedagogical imperatives as well as the reliability of the inferences that can be drawn about a student's learning. For example, where a teacher uses tasks that provide indirect evidence, such as a take-home assignment, it is important that they consider whether or not any rational conclusions can be drawn, other than that the student has progressed in their learning. The image of the enthusiastic parent eagerly asking, 'So how did "we" go on "our" assignment?' will be familiar to many teachers. This is not to say that opportunities for collaboration are to be avoided. Rather it is about strengthening teacher dialogue to include a conscious consideration of the weight that should be given to a particular task as evidence of student learning.

Put simply, if the assessment data are flawed, then teaching approaches based on that assessment may also be flawed. Once the assessment has been repaired and the data can be trusted, much can be achieved.

The process of stipulating evidence can be assisted by answering the following questions:

- What do you expect to observe in the students' behaviour? What will they do, say, make or write?
- Will this evidence of learning be directly observable, as it would be in an observational checklist, or will the evidence be indirect, as it would be in an assignment or take-home task?

- If the evidence is indirect, can any rational conclusion be drawn other than that it is evidence of student learning?
- What will you be able to infer that the students know or understand that they did not know or understand before?
- Have they moved to a new level in the developmental framework?
- Are they ready to take on new challenges in their learning? Are they ready to consolidate, learn and aspire to higher-order goals?
- Are there other sources of evidence that support or challenge the inferences that are being drawn?

Intervention and targeted instruction: Class reports

Often the same or similar learning intentions can be used for groups of students who are working at the same generalised level of proficiency. In many classrooms, students will be working at two, three, four or even five different levels of learning readiness (but rarely more). One way to visually determine groups of students operating at the same stage or level is to use a class report, another of the ARCOTS reports. An example is shown in Figure 11.2.

The class report can help to group students according to their learning readiness. This forms the basis of organising the class into groups for differentiated learning opportunities that best meet the needs of students who are working at different stages of understanding or proficiency. The practice of targeted instruction, introduced in previous chapters, is discussed in more detail later in this chapter. The class report can also be used to foster opportunities for mentoring and scaffolding of new knowledge with more capable peers, and to allow students at a similar stage of learning to work together to support each other in coping with a common problem or challenge.

In addition, a class report can display student learning assessed at different points in time. This is indicated on the report by differently shaded bars for each student. Teachers may choose to monitor student learning over time by comparing each student's most recent assessment (shown as a black bar in Figure 11.2) with their earlier assessment outcome (shown as a grey bar). To help plan and implement differentiated teaching, the following questions should be asked:

- How many students are working at each level of proficiency?
- How can teaching activities be modified and differentiated to suit the skills and knowledge that students at each level need to develop and consolidate?
- Did all students who started at the same learning stage make similar progress over the period between assessments? If not, why did the teaching program lead to better outcomes for some students than for others?
- What can be improved or adjusted to make sure that all students benefit from instruction?

Assessment for Teaching

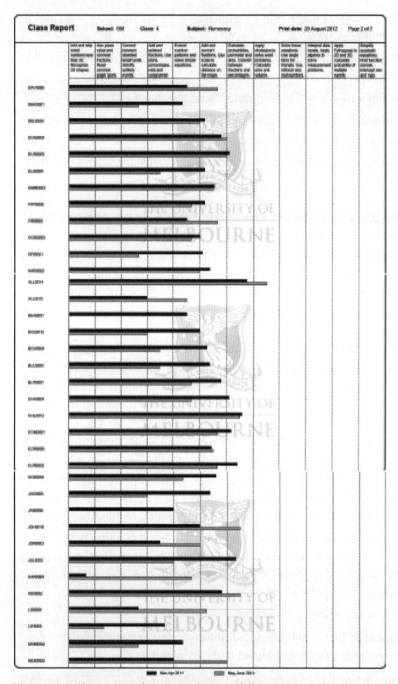

Figure 11.2 *Class report showing students at different stages of skill and understanding at two points in time*

The challenges of assessment

The challenge of linking assessment to teaching arises when teachers see change in the student results and there is a need to explain why a student appears to have developed or not developed – or, in some cases, regressed. Before any conclusions about teaching can be drawn from changes in assessment data, it is essential that teachers understand the quality of the data. Previous chapters of this book have emphasised the importance of targeting assessment, controlling sources of error (noise) and making sure that the quality of assessment data is sufficient to enable proper decisions to be made.

The first thing to do when unexplained changes in results occur is identify the sources of error in the assessment data. These may include the following (discussed in detail in Chapters 3 and 4):

- the assessment task or test
- the student characteristics and disposition
- the context of the assessment
- the administration procedures
- the person administering the assessment
- the group interpreting the evidence.

If errors are controlled or minimised, teachers can have some confidence in making decisions on the basis of the data. When there are anomalies in the data (results that don't match expectations), it is necessary to examine why they have arisen. For this purpose, it is advisable for teachers to create a log file such as the one provided in Figure 11.3, which records a teacher's analysis of test targeting. This creates a record for future reference and provides an opportunity for teachers to reflect on the validity of unexpected results. For example, it is obvious that if a student has completed a 40- to 50-item test in five minutes, then the results will be meaningless. If it is fairly clear that a test has been mistargeted – that is, it was too easy or too difficult for the student – then the score will not be as useful as when the test is more accurately targeted. Note the comments in the log file in Figure 11.3. Mistargeting of tests often leads to unstable results.

Year 2010	Test	Time	Level 2010	Targeting 2010 comment	Test 2011	Time 2011	Level 2011	Targeting 2011 comment
3	LL	11	D	Looking at the results, it should have been yellow test if teacher felt student is really good. Also this student sat test for 11 minutes therefore the estimated level at time 1 can't be correct.	LL	49	F	Correct choice
3	NR	14	E	Student level is incorrectly determined as student sat test for only 14 minutes.	NL	2785	C	Totally wrong. From the last round results and taking into account the short time in the first round best choice would be Numeracy orange.
3	LR	28	E	Correct choice of test	LP	41	F	Totally wrong and there must have been suggestion.
3	NR	29	C	Correct choice of test	NR	28	C	Correct choice
3	LR	18	B	Correct choice of test but short time (18 min), which reflects in the result.	LR	47	D	Correct choice and good time. Test is now 40 items long
5	LL	44	J	Student should have sat Green test. There would be recommendations in the ARCOTS for that.	LG	45	I	Correct choice
5	NG	44	F	Wrong choice. Test is way too hard for student. Results only appear reasonable because test is so high on the scale. That is why we have increased number of items in the test from 2010 to 2011.	NL	61	G	Correct choice
5	NL	42	H	Correct choice	NA	44	G	Wrong choice. There was no reason from students.
5	LA	38	I	Better choice would be green test. Consequently this result was inflated. However it is not too bad.	LA	52	I	Green maybe looking from last year's results but this time aqua was definitely a more appropriate choice.
3	LG	21	J	This is a year 3 student. Literacy lime would be better choice. Result is inflated because of administering the test that is high on scale.	LL	89	H	Correct choice
3	NY	14	A	No result here. There was a recommendation in ARCOTS to sit lower test. This student was in year 3 so he/she could not have been fully exposed to the content of yellow test.	NL	175	F	Correct choice
5	LY	22	G	Correct choice of test	LL	34	F	Should have stayed with yellow test.
5	NY	25	E	Possibly better choice would be orange test, but yellow test is still acceptable.	NL	34	F	Should have stayed with yellow test.
4	LY	31	H	Correct choice of test	LL	36	F	Should have stayed with yellow test.
4	NY	42	H	Correct choice of test	NR	57	F	Should have stayed with Numeracy yellow. Red test does not go high enough for this student.

Figure 11.3 *A sample log file discussing a teacher's analysis of test targeting*

Reflective questions

Examine the class report in Figure 11.2 and note the relative length of the grey and black lines. The grey is the pre-test. The black is the post-test.

- Which students are likely to have taken a pre-test that was too easy?
- Which students might have taken a post-test that was too difficult?
- It is not possible to be certain, but the instability of the data suggests a range of error sources or noise. How might this be corrected?

Read the teacher's analysis in Figure 11.3 for further information.

When mistargeting of a test is combined with mistargeting of instruction, the risks of worsening outcomes for students are compounded. But when we are confident that the data show that gains have been made, the next step is to link the change to teaching practices.

What reasons can you think of that might explain why some students appear to develop while others do not?

The opportunities and challenges of teaching

It is important to see what happens when instruction or opportunities to learn are not provided to each of the instructional groups. Suppose we identify only three groups – upper, middle and lower. An examination of the upper and lower groups in each class can be instructive. Consider the chart shown in Figure 11.4.

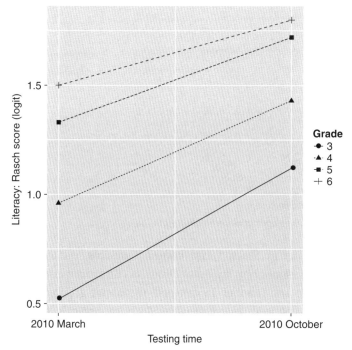

Figure 11.4 *Student growth between testing times 1 and 2*

Figure 11.4 shows the results of two testing occasions for Years 3 to 6. If the line rises from left to right, it indicates an improved performance. The values on the vertical axis are used to map students on to a developmental level. They indicate relative readiness to learn. The higher the number on that axis, the higher the skill level. When looking at the overall pattern of growth across the year, it seems probable that all students are progressing. However, if we drill down into the data, separating out the growth patterns for the upper and lower quartiles, we can see that the growth patterns shown in the figure are in fact misleading.

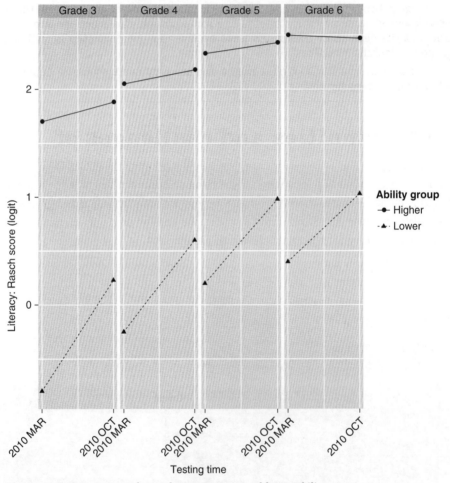

Figure 11.5 *Comparison of growth across upper and lower ability groups*

By separating out the students in the top and bottom quartiles, Figure 11.5 reveals that the lower group, represented by the dotted line, has improved considerably in the period between March and October. In contrast, the upper group, represented by the solid line, shows a reduced rate of growth. More importantly, in Year

6 the students in the upper quartile appear to be regressing. Research has revealed that this is a very common result in Australia across all year levels in both government and non-government schools, and it appears in mathematics as well as literacy (Griffin et al. 2012).

Reflective questions

* What do the results in Figure 11.5 indicate about teaching and class organisation?
* Consider the impact of focusing on skills, not scores. How might this change the patterns of student progress?

Using data to plan for targeted instruction

The charts in Figure 11.6 show how student performances change from one test period to the next. The light grey line indicates the performance of the upper 25 per cent of a class and the dark grey line indicates the performance of the lower 25 per cent. As in the previous figures, if the line rises from left to right, it indicates an improved performance. If it falls, it indicates a deteriorating performance. If it is level, it indicates no change.

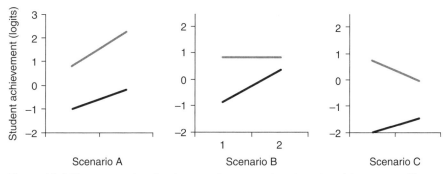

Figure 11.6 *Three scenarios showing two classes, testing times 1 and 2, upper and lower 25 per cent of each class*

Reflective questions

What is the nature of the progress for each group represented in Figure 11.6?

SCENARIO	IMPROVING	REGRESSING	STATIC
1.1 The upper group in scenario A?			
1.2 The lower group in scenario A?			
1.3 The upper group in scenario B?			
1.4 The lower group in scenario B?			
1.5 The upper group in scenario C?			
1.6 The lower group in scenario C?			

- Which is the ideal scenario and why? Discuss and explain your reasoning.
- What are the implications for teaching? Discuss and explain your reasoning. In your answer, be sure to touch on whole-class and targeted teaching.

The role of learning theories in informing considerations on student progress

Teachers usually hold implicit theories about teaching and learning that inform their planning and day-to-day decision-making. Yet the theories typically are applied intuitively. This chapter is designed to help you use data to inform your application of learning theories. The following information about different learning theories may help you and your peers to discuss implicit theories in order to make them explicit, relate them to data and develop a shared language for applying them in your teaching practice. By having a shared language, teachers become better equipped to begin to unpack the ways in which they conceptualise learning and learners in relation to progress. This informs the dialogue of teachers in relation to classroom organisation, resource allocation, 'closing the gap', expectations of progress and so on.

Options for teacher planning – working backwards or forwards?

Scardamalia and colleagues (2010) propose two general and complementary strategies for teaching and learning: one based on the approach of working backwards from goals, and the other described as an 'emergence' approach. The latter strategy allows for the identification of new goals based on the capabilities of learners and their location within a developmental progression. When teachers declare that they want students to understand a certain set of facts, or master a procedure or strategy that can be identified clearly within a developmental progression or framework, it links to the ZPD and establishes a goal for instruction. Usually there is a well-defined set of steps towards that goal or level on the progression. This links well with a view of learning as a constructivist activity, in a Piagetian sense, in which new ways of knowing are developed through the accommodation or assimilation of information and experiences.

Teaching and learning as intentional, goal-directed activities

John Dewey (1938) described teaching and learning as intentional and goal-directed activities. He also emphasised child-centred education and the special role of the teacher in making sense of the world for students. Dewey argued that teachers should become expert observers of their students, and use their observations and knowledge of expected patterns of development to determine the kinds of instructional activities and experiences for which their students are ready, and that are likely to interest and motivate them.

Further, Dewey maintained that a classroom activity could not be described as a learning activity unless it had been planned with a clear instructional purpose in mind. He recommended that when teachers plan classroom activities for their students, they ask themselves how a particular activity will build on what the students can already do and what sorts of skills or abilities it will help them to develop or improve. They should ask why it is important for their students to develop these skills and abilities, and consider how this will help them to lead richer and more satisfying lives.

Building on Dewey's insights, we believe teachers need to invest time and effort to:

- carefully observe their students, and get to know them well in terms of their abilities and interests
- plan activities and instruction tailored to the current level of understanding and the interests of students
- purposefully and explicitly target their students' acquisition of new skills and the broadening or extension of existing ones
- link the new skills to a ZPD and a target level on a continuum
- organise and document their observations, plans, strategies and activities.

Teaching and learning as a social transaction

The theme of social relationships for teaching and learning can be drawn from Vygotsky's (1978) understanding of learning as a fundamentally social process in which children and young people learn to use the tools and materials of their social group – tools such as language, numbers, texts, technologies and cultural modes of reasoning, discussion and argument, to name but a few – within the context of supportive relationships with more able others. Indeed, Vygotsky argued that everything is learned first through interaction with others and then internalised by the individual.

In earlier chapters, we discussed assessment framed by Vygotsky's definition of a student's ZPD. Fundamental to this idea is a belief that in order to best support a student's learning, we should think about the skills that are 'budding' or showing the first signs of development, and work with the student to scaffold that burgeoning understanding and knowledge by providing models, mentors, feedback, encouragement, supported opportunities for practice and so on.

Scaffolding and the shared responsibility for learning

As envisioned by Vygotsky, learning is effective when teachers model the use of strategies and construction of knowledge in the process of completing a task. This contrasts with a model in which the teacher instructs and the students listen, and then relate their understanding so the teacher can evaluate what has been learnt. In that scenario, knowledge is neither personally constructed nor applied. When using the Vygotskian model of scaffolding, teachers perform complex tasks with students helping. Over time, and with repeated modelling of the task, students take on more and more of the responsibility, while the teacher helps only as needed. Eventually, students perform the task on their own. Support, in the form of explicit teaching, occurs over time until the students master the new strategies, learning how and when to use them.

The Vygotskian scaffolding-based model is different from a deficit-based teacher- or student-centred approach. It requires mutual effort and responsibility on the part of students and teachers. Other approaches, sometimes embedded in the assessment-for-learning paradigm, place almost all responsibility for learning with the student. The scaffolding of ZPDs leads to a different definition of teaching and requires a different kind of classroom – one that may not look at all like a traditional classroom. A teaching model based on Vygotsky's ideas is presented in Figure 11.7.

The knowledge base for teaching

The developmental model of learning advocated in this book also recognises the professional knowledge base fundamental to the craft of teaching. The use of data to target teaching in a developmental framework in no way conflicts with the professional knowledge base of teachers. Shulman (1987) describes this knowledge base as including:

- knowledge of students
- knowledge of the subject to be taught
- general knowledge of teaching processes, management and organisation that 'transcends the subject-matter'

Student responsibility->	Adult-then-joint-responsibility->			Self-responsibility
Zone of actual development	Zone of proximal development			
What the student can do unassisted	Assistance provided by more capable others: teacher or peer or environment: classroom structures and activities	Transition from other's assistance to self-assistance	Assistance provided by self	Internalisation, automatisation
				Inner speech The student's silent, abbreviated dialogue carried on with self that is the essence of conscious mental activity
	Social speech Adult uses language to model process Adult and student share language and activity			
		Private speech Student uses language that adults use to regulate behaviour (self-control)		
				Private speech internalised and transformed to inner verbal thought (self-regulation)

Figure 11.7 *A teaching model based on Vygotsky*
Source: Adapted from Wilhelm, Baker and Dube (2001).

- 'pedagogical content knowledge', which includes curricular knowledge of 'materials and programs'; knowledge of how to teach particular kinds of content; knowledge of educational contexts and situations; and knowledge of educational ends, purposes and values.

All of this knowledge can be used to support evidence-based teaching within a developmental model.

Differentiated instruction as targeted teaching

It can be challenging to work out how the individual learning needs of each and every student in the classroom can be met. In the last two chapters, we have suggested a pedagogical approach that Tomlinson (2008) describes as 'student-aware teaching'. In this approach, teachers acknowledge the different starting points, readiness for learning, targets and requirements for support of the students in their classes. They can, for example, use information provided by their class reports (see above) to help them group students appropriately so they can better target and differentiate learning activities and experiences.

Tomlinson points out that a precondition for differentiation is that teachers must know what students can do, and must monitor student progress towards their learning objectives within a developmental framework. In Tomlinson's view, the critical elements of differentiated instruction relate to the building of trust between teachers and students, ensuring a good fit between learning experiences and students' abilities and interests, honouring and encouraging the 'voice' of students or their self-determination as learners, and developing student awareness of their own learning.

While we believe all these factors are important, we prioritise ensuring a good fit between learning experiences and students' abilities as determined by their ZPD. This is what we define as targeted teaching.

Planning for targeted teaching

An example of a tool that might be used to plan targeted teaching is shown in Figure 11.8. The format was developed by one school involved in the Assessment Learning Partnerships (ALP) professional development program offered by the Assessment Research Centre.

As can be seen, the targeted teaching sessions utilise an understanding of the developmental model of learning to plan teaching in order to consolidate the ZAD and stretch emerging skills within the ZPD. This is just one example of the way in which teachers might cater for a range of student abilities in the classroom. This planning template would ideally be completed as part of a collaborative process in a

	Group 1				Group 2				Group 3				Group 4			
Student	Name	PM	Neale	ARC	Name	PM	Neale	ARC	Name	PM	Neale	ARC	Name	Al	Neale	ARC
	Sif	14	1	B	Fulla	20	2	C	Odin	25	2	D	Freya		3	E
	Sol	14	1	B	Jora	21	2		Mani	26	2	D	Iaunn		3	E
	Delling	14	1	B	Fir	22	2	C	Loki	27	3	D	Ulla		3	E
	Thor			B	Nerphus	22		C	Gmot		3	D	Forseti		3	E
	Bragi	16	2	B	Nana	23	2	C	Mimir	28	3	D	Dgar		3	E
	Baldr	16	2	B					Vali	28	3	D	Gefiun		3	E
	Kvasir	16	2	B									Tiki			E

Target levels 1: ZAD 2: ZPD 3: Next	Group 1	Group 2	Group 3	Group 4
	1. A: Locate and match adjacent words in text at word and phrase level.	1. B: Find information in the short text. Link paraphrased information within a single paragraph.	1. C: Identify main ideas and characters in the story. Interpret paraphrased sentence within a paragraph.	1. D: Draw together ideas and information from across the whole text. Infer character's feelings from narrative text.
	2. B: Find information in the short text. Link paraphrased information within a single paragraph.	2. C: Identify main ideas and characters in the story. Interpret paraphrased sentence at paragraph-level text.	2. D: Draw together ideas and information from across the whole text. Infer characters' feelings from narrative text.	2. E: Make predictions based on understanding of ideas, sequence of events and characters. Identify purpose of the text.
	3. C: Identify main ideas and characters in the story. Interpret paraphrased sentence at paragraph-level text.	3. D: Draw together ideas and information from across the whole text. Infer characters' feelings from narrative text.	3. E: Make predictions based on understanding of ideas, sequence of events and characters. Identify purpose of text.	3. F: Combine separate pieces of data to infer the text meaning. Identify and summarise evidence from the text to support your hypothesis.

Figure 11.8 *Example of weekly targeted teaching plan for reading comprehension adapted from Lilydale Primary School*

(Continued)

Day 1	GR: My House – locate and discuss words within a page or paragraph.	Silent Reading 'Tilly Tompkins'	Silent Reading 'Book Bonanza Week'	Silent Reading 'Melissa's Bunyip'
	Worksheet – matching words and phrases to diagrams from text	GR: What was the main idea of the story? List the main characters.	Cloze Activity (Worksheet)	What were the bad actions of Jason? Why did Jason act this way?
Day 2	Retell the paragraph in your own words (paraphrase)	Computer – Soundway	GR: Discuss: Bringing the ideas and characters together (write a synopsis of the story focusing on the relationships between the characters)	How did the actions make Melanie feel? How do you know this?
	Main Idea Cards (paragraph/page level)	Describe Tilly's party	Write the sentences in your own words	Describe and draw the bunyip
Day 3	Cloze Activity (worksheet)	Cloze Activity	Comprehension Cards	Computer
	Draw a picture of one of the houses – write four adjectives to describe it	Draw the different hats Tilly made	Create a story map with the main ideas and characters	Predict the meaning of the following words: notice, dwell, respect, impress, scoff, stagger, comment, attempt, drift, complain. Compare and contrast with dictionary meanings.
Day 4	Word Search	Small cards – Main Idea	Computer	GR: Discuss: What is the purpose of the text? How do we know this? How would this affect the writing of a sequel? (Write a storyboard for a sequel.)
	Paraphrase (write story in your own words)		How do you think Dale and Kim felt when they met each other? Write a conversation between them using speech bubbles.	

Figure 11.8 Continued

PLT, as discussed in Chapter 4. It would also be supported by PLT logs, which would provide specific detail about the teaching strategies that would be used and the evidence that would be collected to evaluate student progress.

Summary

When we make use of a two-points-in-time analysis, we are not only examining student progress, but also looking for evidence of the quality of our teaching. Within the context of the developmental model of learning, we would argue that, based on student progress, teachers can draw inferences about the efficacy with which they planned the learning opportunities for their students in order to consolidate the skills in the ZAD and scaffold the budding skills emerging at the ZPD, all within the context of the learning that is yet to come. Armed with the capacity for this kind of evidence-based, reflective practice, teachers are equipped to build a bank of knowledge that will inform their decision-making around future teaching practices, policy directions and resource allocation for all learners.

Apply to practice

Task 1

This task is about the use of data to plan targeted teaching and examine implications for classroom organisation.

Refer to Figure 11.9. Create a teaching plan based on the results generated at the first point in time (the grey line). You might use the example provided in Figure 11.8 or you might develop your own template.

1 How many instructional groups would have been recommended after the first assessment? Which students would be in each group?

2 In what ways is developing a plan like this similar to or different from the teaching practices with which you are familiar?

3 What are the implications for implementing targeted teaching in relation to:

  a classroom organisation

  b school resources/facilities

  c teacher knowledge, skills and beliefs

  d student knowledge, skills and beliefs

  e community expectations?

Task 2

This task is about interpreting data to monitor student progress and evaluate the effectiveness of teaching interventions.

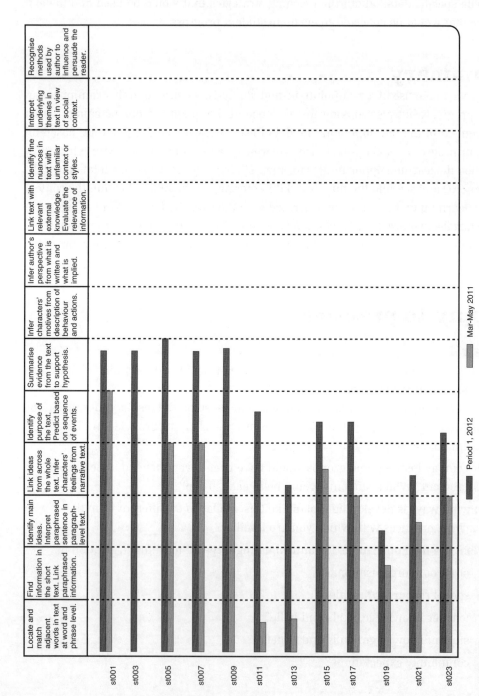

Figure 11.9 *De-identified section of a class report*

Suppose that the results shown in Figure 11.9 are to be discussed by a group of teachers or students. What are the main points that need to be considered? Which group improved the most – the upper or the lower? Examine the change in performance of the top three students on the pre-test (students 001, 005 and 007) and the bottom three on the pre-test (011, 013 and 019).

1 Refer again to Figure 11.6. Which scenario (A, B or C) does this class report best represent?

2 How might the student grouping change after the second assessment?

3 What other advice would a PLT have for the class teacher?

Check your progress

Below is a set of rubrics designed to help you reflect on your answers to the Apply to Practice tasks and assess your understanding of this chapter. These can be used to help scaffold learning.

11.1 When analysing data to generate a teaching plan, you made choices based on:

   a personal opinion

   b the use of targeted teaching.

11.2 When considering the implications for teaching, you:

   a considered implications in isolation

   b considered implications in relation to one another

   c synthesised implications to make generalisations that can inform school policy.

11.3 When analysing the data to determine student growth, you:

   a described patterns of growth

   b evaluated patterns of growth in terms of expected outcomes of targeted teaching.

11.4 When analysing data to make recommendations to maximise student progress, you:

   a made recommendations based on opinion

   b utilised data to make recommendations

   c integrated your understanding from student results that showed growth, stagnation and/or regression to propose improvements across student groups.

Chapter 12

Developmental assessment for students with additional needs

Kerry Woods and Roz Mountain

This chapter describes how the approach to assessment for teaching covered in this book has been applied to support the teaching of students with additional needs (SWANs). It provides detail of a process of assessing students, interpreting results, setting goals and developing individualised learning plans. Developmental progressions are central to this process, and their importance is emphasised in inclusive school contexts where teachers may or may not have experience of or training in supporting the learning of students with additional needs.

Learning objectives

In this chapter you will learn:

- what is expected of you as a teacher of students with additional needs
- what it means, and why it is important, to take a developmental rather than a deficit approach to teaching students with additional needs
- how to use a developmental progression to set learning goals and targets for students with additional needs, and to plan a program of tasks and activities to achieve these.

Introduction

The approach taken to assessment and teaching throughout this book is grounded in the philosophy that all students can learn, and that teaching and learning are optimal when correctly targeted for students or for groups of students working at similar levels. This chapter applies that approach to the question of how teachers can draw on information presented in the form of a learning progression to design and implement tailored learning programs for students with additional needs (SWANs).

Those students in this group are characterised by very specific and often complex educational needs. The aim of the chapter is to empower teachers of students with additional needs through the use of resources to guide students' progress as they build the foundations of learning. The themes and ideas that underpin the chapter were introduced in Chapters 2 and 4. This chapter shows how those themes and ideas apply to the education of students with additional needs, as they do to all students.

Background: Inclusive education

In 1994, representatives of 92 governments and 25 international organisations met in Salamanca, Spain, at a conference jointly hosted by the government of Spain and the United Nations Educational, Scientific and Cultural Organization (UNESCO), the purpose of which was to articulate a shared philosophy of inclusive education (UNESCO 1994). This was described as 'recognition of the need to work towards "schools for all" – institutions which include everybody, celebrate differences, support learning, and respond to individual needs' (1994, p. iii). The proclamation issued at the completion of the conference established the tone for subsequent debate around the education of students with additional needs. It stated that:

- Every child has a fundamental right to education, and must be given the opportunity to achieve and maintain an acceptable level of learning.
- Every child has unique characteristics, interests, abilities and learning needs.

- Education systems should be designed and educational programs implemented to take into account the wide diversity of these characteristics and needs.

- Those with special educational needs must have access to regular schools, which should accommodate them within a child-centred pedagogy capable of meeting these needs.

- Regular schools with this inclusive orientation are the most effective means of combating discriminatory attitudes, creating welcoming communities, building an inclusive society and achieving education for all; moreover, they provide an effective education to the majority of children and improve the efficiency and ultimately the cost-effectiveness of the entire education system. (pp. viii–xi)

Inclusive education practices have been widely supported, in principle, since the *Individuals with Disabilities Education Act 1975* and the *Warnock Report* (1978) outlined the US and UK governments' respective policies for special education provision. They have been advocated over many years by government systems and human rights organisations such as the United Nations, which published its Convention on the Rights of Persons with Disabilities in 2006. In Australia, for example, the Disability Standards for Education (2005) protect the rights of all students to access and participate in education without experiencing discrimination.

Yet the practice of inclusion remains incompletely realised. Many schools and teachers lack information about how best to support the learning of their students with additional needs. Both in Australia and internationally, many teachers lack the training and professional expertise to design and implement programs of instruction for these students, and to make appropriate and sensitive adjustments to the learning environment to support their full participation in education. The successful implementation of inclusive education policies is challenged by a dearth of practical advice and support for schools and teachers.

This chapter describes research that was conducted to address this challenge. It refers to examples drawn from the students with additional needs (SWANs) learning progressions, which were designed at the University of Melbourne to describe proficiency for students in their development of literacy and communication (Woods 2010; Woods & Griffin 2013), social understanding (Coles-Janess & Griffin 2009), emotional self-management and personal learning skills (Roberts & Griffin 2009). It refers to a specific example that relates to students' capacity to make meaning from written and produced symbols and text as the foundations of their development of early literacy skills (Woods & Griffin 2013). The chapter provides an example of the application of ideas and practices described elsewhere in this book to the purpose of teaching students who, for a variety of reasons, may learn in ways that differ from their classmates and whose starting point for instruction may be at a lower level of skill and understanding. These are students who are often overlooked by large-scale testing

learning progressions can guide teachers' recognition of each student's current level of understanding, and provide a picture of the likely way ahead for the student.

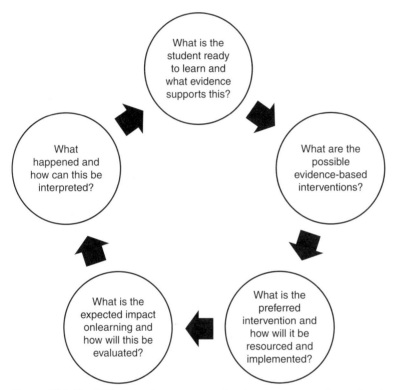

Figure 12.1 *The PLT cycle of assessment, planning, implementation and review*

The SWANs learning progressions were developed by a team of researchers at the University of Melbourne's Assessment Research Centre (ARC), working with the support of the Victorian Department of Education and Early Childhood. They drew on research conducted in both special and mainstream schools that engaged more than 2300 school-aged children and young people with a diverse range of disabilities and additional needs. In addition to the development of learning progressions in foundational skills related to communication, social understanding, emotional self-management, personal learning and literacy (the last of these shown in Table 12.1), the SWANs research led to the design of an online assessment and reporting program to guide teachers' observations and understanding of their students.

The learning progression shown in Table 12.1 describes a pathway of increasing skill and understanding as a student develops the capacity to use and interpret symbols and text. The first level describes examples of evidence a teacher might reasonably expect to observe in the classroom for a student who is exploring and

Table 12.1 *Literacy learning progression: Making meaning from symbols and text*

Level Seven Learning to apply and extend understanding of written material	The student is learning to use strategies to confirm or modify understanding of written text. They may decode or predict unfamiliar words using knowledge of spelling patterns and other words in a sentence, or use partial reading and knowledge of similar materials to support comprehension. They may seek out the meaning of unfamiliar words (for example, by looking in a word list or dictionary). The student may adapt different materials for drawing or writing to suit different tasks, seek ways to improve attempts at drawing or writing, and be starting to plan and order ideas in written work to express and explain meaning and ideas. They may combine information from reading with their own ideas and reflections when re-telling stories, thus showing understanding and identification with the plot or characters.
Level Six Learning to use conventions of print	The student is learning to break words into components (blends, clusters of letters), and to recognise spelling patterns that are common in English. They may predict the meaning of a word using all or most of the letter information in the word, and are beginning to use and respond to information obtained through reading. The student may write and draw with confidence and control, and may know how and when to use upper and lower case forms of letters in written work.
Level Five Learning to use relationships between letters and sounds	The student is learning to use letter–sound relationships, and may be starting to understand some basic rules of grammar, punctuation and spelling. They may use partial reading supported by pictures to predict the meaning of a sentence. The student may be able to break simple words into sounds, identify words that rhyme, suggest words that have the same first sound, or use the sounds of letters and symbols in attempts at spelling. They may copy words and sentences, present writing from the top of a page to the bottom and from left to right across a page, and experiment with different materials and media for drawing and writing.
Level Four Learning to use letters, numbers and pictures to communicate with others	The student is learning to recognise letter–sound relationships. They may name individual letters and identify their most common sounds, and name the sounds at the start and end of one-syllable words. They may seek clarification of word meaning and the correct forms of words. The student is beginning to understand how writing should look, and that it has a consistent meaning. They may be able to identify spaces, letters and words in text, and recognise letters in their upper and lower case forms. They may be learning to predict the meaning of familiar words using partial cues (such as beginning letter and the shape of the word). The student may re-tell a familiar or favourite story in their own words.
Level Three Learning to recognise letters and numbers	The student is becoming aware of print in the environment and may sort, match or identify letters and numbers. They may recognise some very familiar words by sight, and link these to basic needs or familiar people and activities. They may show interest in reading and writing, and be making choices about materials. The student may follow or point to a line of text as it is being read. The student is learning to recognise the start and end of reading materials, may make linear scribbles that include repeated forms, or 'write' from left to right across a page. They may copy letters or simple words from models, and use pictures or symbols to re-tell a familiar story or message. The student may comment upon or point to illustrations in reading materials, or use these to predict the topic of reading materials.

Level Two Exploring pictures, shapes and sounds	The student is learning to identify pictures, shapes and sounds. They may role-play reading and writing, label images, draw non-linear forms or trace over some letter shapes and forms. The student may recognise their own name in print, perhaps using visual cues such as beginning letter or shape of the word. They may be learning to press keys on a computer keyboard and move a computer mouse.
Level One Engaging with the environment	The student is exploring objects within a familiar environment, and may show interest in photographs of familiar objects or people. They may accept different materials for drawing, and be learning about books and stories. The student may make choices between objects (or photographs of objects) or hold and use large crayons or pencils. They may show enjoyment of literacy activities (for example, being read to, drawing) perhaps by looking, smiling, relaxing or remaining present.

Source: Woods (2010).

engaging with objects, and possibly also realistic photographs of objects, in the immediate sensory environment. This summary does not describe all possible skills that such a student could demonstrate, but rather some likely indicators that the student is working at this general level of skill.

The second level describes behaviours that a teacher might expect to observe if a student is learning to identify pictures, shapes and sounds. Such a student might demonstrate some early awareness of books and print. The third level describes a student who is building on that early awareness, to show an increasing knowledge about letters and numbers, recognition of some familiar words and a beginning ability to connect text and pictures to a consistent and interpretable meaning. A student at the fourth level on the progression has developed a beginning understanding of the relationship between letters and sounds, and may use pictures, letters and numbers as tools of communication, while a student at the fifth level uses letter–sound relationships to support their attempts to read and spell new words and may, for example, use partial reading, pictures and background knowledge to predict the meaning of a short sentence. At the sixth level on the progression, a student shows increasing understanding of the conventions of print and is starting to use and respond to information obtained through reading. At the seventh level, a student may use a range of strategies to confirm understanding of the meaning of text, unlock the meaning of new words, and be starting to plan and order the presentation of written work. From this point onwards, a student has demonstrated their capacity to use and interpret written material at a level of sophistication that enables access to the regular curriculum. Depending on the age of the student, some additional support and adjustments may be required to foster full participation in schooling; however, in general, the student's broad level of literacy skills should support rather than impede future learning.

As discussed in Chapter 2, when we take a developmental learning approach, the aim is to move our students forward along a progression of increasingly complex knowledge and skill, regardless of where they start on that progression. This approach helps us to focus on our students' readiness to learn, and to build on their current level of understanding. It can be viewed in opposition to a deficit approach to assessment, which focuses on describing, and then attempting to remediate, the things that a student does not understand or do well – an approach that draws attention to how far behind a student lags or how poorly a student performs. Also described in Chapter 2 was Vygotsky's seminal concept of the zone of proximal development (ZPD). Vygotsky pointed out that learners differ not only in terms of their actual developmental level (in other words, the things that they can do independently), but also in their ZPD (the distance between their actual developmental level and the level of potential development as determined by action under adult guidance or in collaboration with more capable peers). As Vygotsky (1978, p. 86) argued:

> The zone of proximal development defines those functions that have not yet matured but are in the process of maturation … These functions could be termed the 'buds' or 'flowers' of development rather than the 'fruits' of development. The actual developmental level characterises mental development retrospectively, while the zone of proximal development characterises mental development prospectively.

To improve teaching and learning for all students – and certainly for those who have difficulties with their learning – it is clearly more useful to look at the things a student is just beginning to be able to do and understand.

Planning a personalised program of instruction

The SWANs learning progressions can be used as a framework for the sorts of decisions that schools and teachers routinely make when planning a program of instruction for students with additional needs (see Figure 12.1 for examples of these). While they can be used by a teacher working in isolation, the optimal use of the learning progressions takes the form of collaborative decision-making and moderation by a team of teachers and other professionals and, where appropriate, the student and their parents or carers. The process of planning a program of personalised instruction for an individual student – or, indeed, for a group of students working at the same general proficiency level – can be broken down into a series of steps and questions for reflection, as described below.

Locating the student's level of proficiency on a learning progression

For each student, the question that should be asked at the outset is 'Where is this student currently working in terms of their learning?' To answer this question, teachers need to draw on their observations of the student and defend their judgement using direct evidence. They may refer to the student's responses to activities, tasks or, where appropriate, tests, and to examples of the student's classroom participation and work. Teachers may begin by scanning through the information provided by a learning progression to decide on the general level at which they think their student is working. For example, based on their observations of the student, review of the student's classroom work and discussion with the student, the student's family members and other teachers or specialists, the teacher may place the student at the third level on a learning progression such as the one shown in Table 12.1. The teacher may judge that the student is currently learning to recognise letters and numbers, and may base this judgement on observations that the student recognises some familiar words by sight, sorts and matches letters, shapes and numbers, and shows interest in reading and writing activities. Working with the student, the teacher may note that they can follow a line of text as it is being read aloud, and that their scribbling shows repeated forms or shapes, and progresses from left to right across a page. The student may not yet demonstrate all the skills described at this proficiency level, and may not have attained mastery of those skills they do demonstrate. The student's level on a learning progression is designed to point towards the 'buds' of learning rather than its 'fruits' (Vygotsky 1978, p. 86) and, as such, to provide information to guide decisions about the student's readiness for future instruction.

This form of assessment draws its meaning and interpretation from the observations and judgement of a teacher, which – as discussed in Chapter 6 – may be open to challenge due to concerns over lack of objectivity (McCloskey 1990). While this is an area of potential weakness, it can be addressed by teachers' use of a well-defined framework to guide and record their observations (Gentile 1992). In addition, improved quality of judgements made in the context of special education and early intervention has been linked to moderation between teachers (Bagnato et al. 2006). This brings to our notice the importance of formal procedures that direct and organise teachers' observations, and thereby enhance both the reliability of judgement-based assessments and their efficacy for improving teaching and learning. As described in Chapter 4, a team-based approach to assessment, interpretation and planning can provide the supportive context in which such moderation of teacher judgement can take place. A learning progression such as the one described in this chapter can be used to structure teachers' collection and interpretation of data based on classroom observation.

Setting goals for teaching and learning

In order to plan instruction, it is important to have a sense not only of the student's general level of skill and understanding but also of where the student is likely to go next in their learning. To formulate some learning goals, teachers may ask themselves whether a student – or a group of students – seems ready to make a transition to a new level of proficiency along the learning progression. For example, teachers may consider whether students who are currently working at the first level on the learning progression shown in Table 12.1 seem ready to extend their exploration to include pictures of familiar objects as well as realistic photographs and concrete examples. For students working through the second level, teachers may set learning targets such as identifying, sorting and matching simple shapes followed by letters and numbers, or recognising some familiar everyday words. For those working at the third level, teachers may set targets of naming letters and linking them to their most common sounds, identifying words and spaces in text, and recognising letters in their upper and lower case forms.

Regardless of the proficiency level at which students are working, teachers can aim to provide a broad range of enriching activities targeted to the students' current proficiency levels, and introduce some activities designed to expand their understanding to the next level. Learning targets should also recognise each student's current knowledge and skills and the most probable next step forward, and use that information to devise a personalised program of instruction.

Devising a tailored teaching program

Once targets have been established for student learning, teachers need to decide how to structure the school and classroom environment, and provide activities and experiences to help the students reach those targets. The SWANs researchers worked with experienced special education teachers in 12 schools to document examples of the sorts of teaching strategies and resources used to promote learning for students working at different levels on the learning progression shown in Table 12.1. For example, teachers reported that they routinely personalised materials to suit an individual student's interests, and to include representations of the student and favourite or familiar items, food, people and activities. This was particularly the case for students at the lower levels of proficiency (Woods & Griffin 2013). Other teaching strategies and resources widely used for students at lower proficiency levels included multi-sensory activities, music and songs, games and puzzles, ICT resources such as interactive whiteboards and interactive computer programs, choice-making activities, augmentative communication systems and pictorial-aided language displays, a print-rich environment, daily individual and small-group reading sessions, and pre-writing activities to build strength and coordination. Some of these are illustrated in Table 12.2. Most teachers also recorded the importance they placed on the establishment of structured and predictable classroom routines for their students, in many cases presented in the form of visual timetables (Woods & Griffin 2013).

Many teachers who contributed to the SWANs study noted the challenge of sourcing materials that were well matched to a student's proficiency level in reading but not intended for use by very young children (Woods & Griffin 2013). They commented that the internet provided them with options to personalise literacy materials for

Table 12.2 *An example of a PLT log for a student working at the second level on the literacy progression*

STUDENT/STUDENT GROUP						
Date:						
Developmental domain	SWANs literacy					
Where are the students? **Developmental level and nutshell statement – Level 2:** The student is learning to identify pictures, shapes and sounds. They may role-play reading and writing, label images, draw non-linear forms or trace over some letter shapes and forms. The student may recognise their own name in print, perhaps using visual cues such as beginning letter or shape of the word. They may be learning to press keys on a computer keyboard and move a computer mouse.						
1 Evidence for this level? (What makes you say this?)	This student enjoys looking at pictures in books. He points to pictures of objects and familiar people when they are named. He likes to turn the pages in favourite picture books, and he also likes to listen to short stories on an iPad. He can locate these independently. He recognises the first letter of his name in print.						

Where do they need to go?		*How will they get there?*			*What is needed to get them there?*	*What worked? What did not work?*
2 Learning intention/s (Specific skill or concept or part thereof to be learned)	**3. Evidence** (What the students will be able to do, say, make or write)	**4. Teaching strategy** (What the *teacher* says, does, makes or writes)	**5. Learning activity** (What the students are actually going to do)		**6. Resources** (People, place or things used in the activity to realise the learning strategy)	**7. Review and reflection**
2.1 To recognise his name in print	Given the full set of names for the class, he correctly identifies and selects his name.	Offer a smaller number of names to choose from. Offer two completely different names. Cut around the names, to give them their own unique shape.	He matches letters of his name with and without a model. He completes a jigsaw puzzle of his name. Given several names written on cards of different shapes, he matches the shape with his name to the card given to him.		Cards Access to a laminator A jigsaw with the student's name and photo	**Review date:** Reflection:

Table 12.2 *Continued*

2 Learning intention/s	3. Evidence	4. Teaching strategy	5. Learning activity	6. Resources	7. Review and reflection
2.2 To trace over the letters of his name, and to copy the letters of his name from a modelled example	He traces over a dotted template of his name following the form closely. He copies his name letter by letter on the line below his name printed in large letters.	Print out outlines of his name and letters in the name. Trace the student's name within the letters. Present his name in different textures (sandpaper, bubble wrap). Laminate his name and work with him to trace over his name with a whiteboard marker.	He copies the teacher tracing over outlines of the letters in his name, and then his name as a whole. He explores the textures of the different materials by tracing his fingers over his name.	Access to a laminator Various textured materials – sandpaper, bubble wrap, velvet Whiteboard marker	**Review date:** Reflection:

their students; and, for students at all levels of proficiency, resources such as interactive whiteboards, tablet computers and other ICT tools were widely used.

For students at higher levels of proficiency, teachers used strategies such as guided reading and writing activities and shared drafting and editing (Woods & Griffin 2013). The use of skills in authentic, commonplace and practical situations was strongly emphasised by experienced special education teachers. Many planned programs of instruction around excursions, cooking activities, shopping trips and sporting events, as well as internet research, emailing and social network use, to emphasise reading and writing as skills with personal relevance for students. In addition, more proficient students were introduced to thinking and planning tools that combined written and visual presentation of information, such as graphic organisers, task cards, timetables and personal schedules, and were encouraged to make and use personal word banks or dictionaries.

Significance of the SWANs research in supporting inclusive education

The SWANs research linked strategies for teaching, and adjustments to materials and the learning environment, to levels on a learning progression for students with additional needs, and then validated and extended that research in

68 schools to include other progressions and more detailed advice (Griffin, Woods & Awwal 2012; Victorian DEECD 2012). The research drew attention to the flexibility and variety of learning experiences that teachers provide to their students, while pursuing the same broad educational objectives for them. This placed the concept of inclusive education in a new light, and gave substance to Vygotsky's avowal that:

> Children with a defect do not constitute 'a special breed of people' … Instead, we discover that all developmental uniqueness tends to approximate determined, normal, social types. And the school must play a decisive role in this 'approximation'. The special school can set a general goal for itself; after all, its pupils will live and function not as a 'special breed of people' but as workers, craftspeople, and so forth, that is, as specific social units. *The greatest difficulty and profoundest uniqueness of the special schools … is precisely to achieve these common goals, while using unusual means to reach them.* (Vygotsky 1993, p. 48, emphasis in original)

Vygotsky's words remind us that the child with a disability is, quite simply, a child like any other. These children and young adults do not belong to a special or different breed of people. The aspirations we have for them – that they learn to communicate, to interact with other people in positive ways, to take their place in our community – are the same aspirations that we have for all students. By focusing only on the unique or particular development of these students – in other words, on their difference – we risk missing how very like other students they are. However, in order to reach their full potential, some students may need additional support, and sensitive and thoughtful adjustments to their learning programs and environment. Teachers and schools may need to use unusual means, as Vygotsky puts it, to help students with additional needs progress towards those shared and inclusive goals of education.

Summary

This chapter has shown how teachers can take the ideas of assessment for teaching, firmly based on developmental progressions that are described in this book, and apply them to monitor and support the learning of students with additional needs. It has described ways of using evidence to determine the learning readiness level for students, set specific learning targets and design personalised learning programs for students to succeed in moving to higher levels of skill. If instruction is appropriately and sensitively targeted, students can expect to experience success as learners. This offers a practical way to realise the educational rights of students with additional needs by supporting their learning and development on the same basis as for all other students.

Apply to practice

To apply the principles of this chapter to the practice of teaching students with additional needs, you will need to use evidence of students' developing skills to set both long-term goals and shorter-term targets for their learning, and to plan programs of classroom instruction. To do this, you will need to observe your students' current levels of skill and understanding, and be able to predict the way ahead for them. You may have students working across several proficiency levels in your classroom. How, then, can you draw on classroom evidence to locate your students on a learning progression such as the example provided in Table 12.1? How can you use the information in the learning progression to set learning goals for your students?

Task

Refer to the SWANs literacy learning progression (Table 12.1) and read each of the level descriptions. Collect information about your students' skills and understanding, using only direct evidence of the things that students do, say, make or write. This evidence may take the form of samples of their classroom work, a brief checklist of relevant behaviours, video footage of their responses to learning activities, observations of students' interactions with others and so on. Use these sources of evidence to locate each student on the learning progression and reflect on this process for one of your students by answering the questions set out below. If you work with others – such as classroom aides or professional therapists – who are involved in the teaching and support of your students, they could provide valuable additional information.

To establish learning goals, you need to think about the likely way ahead for the student as well as the student's current level of skill and understanding. Read the extended description for each level on the learning progression. Has your student just started to demonstrate some of the behaviours described at the relevant level? If so, you may wish to set goals that broaden the student's repertoire of skill and understanding at the current level. Can your student demonstrate at least half of the behaviours described at the relevant level? If so, you should look ahead to the next level to identify learning goals that will challenge and extend your student.

1 List the skills that are observable in the evidence you have collected.

2 How have you used your observations to locate the student on the learning progression? Was the evidence sufficient for you to make a judgement? Do you need to gather more information?

3 Based on your observations and your judgement of the student's location on the learning progression, list two or three short-term learning targets for the student.

Check your progress

Below is a set of rubrics to help you reflect on your answers to the Apply to Practice task and assess your understanding of this chapter. These can be used to help scaffold learning.

12.1 Identification of student skills:

   a I identified student skills from work samples.

   b I differentiated between the skills in evidence.

   c I critiqued the validity of the evidence of student skills.

12.2 Using a learning progression to set goals:

   a I nominated goals for learning based on the student's broad developmental level on a progression.

   b I defended the selection of learning goals based on the student's location within a developmental level.

   c I combined information about a student's current level on a learning progression and other sources of evidence to plan instruction for the student.

Chapter 13

Case study: Warragul Regional College

Esther Care

This chapter provides a case study of a large rural secondary school in Victoria, Australia, where the assessment and teaching methods described in this book have been implemented successfully. The chapter describes the policy planning, implementation and sustainability initiatives undertaken by the school. It explains how the school, headed by a strong leadership team, has embarked in a deliberate and coordinated manner on a professional development program involving the organisation of professional learning teams and the use of developmental assessment. Beyond the management and scheduling of professional learning teams, the school has implemented strategies at both teacher and student levels, ensuring a common approach to teaching and learning. The school provides an invaluable example of the use of assessment for teaching.

Learning objectives

In this chapter you will learn how one school:

- translated the approaches and theories of this book into practice
- identified links between needs and strategic responses
- differentiated between part- and whole-system approaches to change management.

Introduction

Warragul Regional College (WRC) is a rural secondary school located 104 kilometres east-south-east of Melbourne, founded in 1911. The school has an enrolment of about 700 students in the Victorian state school system. The town of Warragul is home to three secondary schools funded by the state, Catholic and independent sectors respectively. Warragul is a noted farming area, primarily for dairy products. The school identifies as having low to medium socio-economic status, based on the Family Occupation Index, and has a low proportion of students with non-English-speaking backgrounds. Overall, for 2012, the school scored similarly to comparable schools in the national assessments (NAPLAN) and the Victorian Certificate of Education (VCE).

Like many Australian schools, WRC promotes the message of enhancing students' skills for success in the twenty-first century, both at school and in life beyond, through a focus on student learning, student engagement and well-being, and student pathways and transitions.

Strongly echoing the 'assessment for teaching' approach, the school's Annual Implementation Plan 2012 identified the following targets to raise student learning outcomes:

- Develop data literacy of all Key Learning Domain (KLD) Leaders.
- Strive for greater accuracy in teacher judgements via moderation and the PLT process.
- Review assessment data regularly to build baseline data on student performance and to measure student growth.
- Monitor student growth towards listed four-year targets.

Eight strategies were identified to reach these targets, and the targets associated with student engagement and well-being, and pathways and transitions. Table 13.1 presents a summary of the strategic approaches to the targets.

The focus on professional learning, the learning culture, accountability, explicit teaching and differentiated curriculum, and evidence-based assessment practices is testament to the whole-school approach to change, as described in Chapter 5. The will to implement this change has stimulated multiple strategic plans and consequent initiatives at WRC.

Assessment for Teaching

Table 13.1 *Warragul Regional College Strategic Plan 2012*

FOCUS	STRATEGY	OUTCOMES
1 Teachers	Build teacher capacity to consistently implement pedagogy that reflects high expectations for all students. Provide explicit teaching and differentiated curriculum approaches to cater for individual learning needs.	• Teachers will: – have a clear understanding of each student's current ability – understand how the student fits on the learning continuum for each subject – utilise strategies to ensure that all students learn – collaboratively reflect on and review student learning progress
2 Students	Develop a student-centred learning culture that embeds active student participation in learning.	• Students will be empowered to take a more active role in: – their learning – the school community
3 Curriculum	Embed evidence-based assessment practices.	• The curriculum will be: – differentiated for all students – responsive to students' starting points and performance (evidence-based practice) – shared and collaborative
4 Leadership	Strengthen the college's performance and learning culture through the continuous improvement of internal accountability processes.	• Leaders will: – support the building of teacher capacity – empower students in their learning – support differentiating the curriculum – actively develop future leaders
5 Attendance	Implement strategies and programs to achieve improvement in the areas of student attendance, engagement and participation.	• Improve attendance for students in Years 7–10 by tackling areas of: – student safety – parent complicity – mental illness – students with major attendance issues
6 Student culture	Implement strategies and programs to achieve improvement in the areas of students' attitude to school.	• Student culture will be enhanced by developing strategies to improve: – peer-to-peer relationships – anti-bullying programs – number of students performing leadership roles – compliance with college values feedback loops
7 Pathways (plans)	Improve the tracking of individual student progress.	• Deliver: – high-quality learning – Individual Learning Plans (Managed Individual Pathways, or MIPS) – intervention and support as required – Pathways appropriate to students' needs
8 Transition	Strengthen community partnerships.	• Promote: – a broadening of options for student choice – appropriate student pathways – shared ownership of student pathways – broader/deeper family engagement

Leadership

Led by the principal, key staff at WRC participated in professional development seminars and, as a group, engaged in assessment activities related to their learning. These activities were implemented concomitantly with planning for the following academic year to ensure that PLT would be in place to steer the evidence-based approach to teaching. This technical leadership (Sergiovanni 1992) provided an enabling platform for staff to be involved and engaged in the cultural change. The assessment tasks embedded in the professional learning series themselves acted as vehicles for whole-school planning for logistical and educational commitment by staff.

Late in 2009, the feedback from the Staff, Student and Parent Opinion Surveys had indicated problems around student engagement. In response, the school was concerned to increase student motivation and sought strategies to engage students through teacher enthusiasm and connecting with students. From its research, the school took the view that student engagement is affected by three linked factors, which previously had been viewed in isolation: relationships, pedagogy and curriculum:

> The final 'Eureka' moment occurred in our professional learning about the 'zone of proximal development' and the understanding that students switch off, not necessarily because of poor practice or tenuous relationships, but often because the curriculum is too easy/hard. This idea is very challenging in a secondary school as we have traditionally tried to mould the student to fit the curriculum we offer. This worked when we lived in an industrial age – however in the information age this model no longer works, so new ways of thinking are required. (Juratowich 2009)

Accordingly, the school planned to move on the three fronts at the same time: relationships, pedagogy and curriculum. First, year-level teacher teams discussed and modelled desirable classroom behaviours in order to teach students explicitly the social skills needed for them to become effective classmates and learners. Second, year-level teacher teams had previously devised a set of 10 agreed Principles of Effective Learning. Teachers surveyed their classes using a questionnaire based on these principles, and then worked with peers to assess and act on the feedback. These activities were supplemented by leadership team Learning Walks through the classroom, and in 2010 participation in Instructional Rounds activities (Fowler-Finn 2013) to inform the process and bring external resources to the discussions. Third, as a result of a review of curriculum delivery, teachers were called upon to:

- work collaboratively
- be data-driven
- create developmental frameworks based on VELS progression points
- create differentiated curricula for individual students
- be democratic in allowing student voices and sharing the learning process with students.

The focus on the well-being and engagement of students as enablers for successful learning outcomes brought the capacity of the school structure to host these changes into stark relief. A marked difference between primary and secondary schools traditionally has been the grade-based structure of primary schools and the move away from a focus on the grade and towards a discipline structure in secondary schools. This has been a natural consequence of the need for specialist input in key discipline areas as students encounter increasingly complex and sophisticated knowledge and skills. The structural differences between the sectors has brought about major transition issues, and in many schools these remain unresolved as the students move through their secondary education. The three-front approach of WRC highlighted the natural consequence of this secondary structure: isolation of information about students to within curriculum areas, and at times to within class. WRC adopted a structure of year-level teams, which were responsible for the total student experience, integrating well-being, curriculum and pedagogy. The limitation of this structure was a lack of clear links across year levels.

The PLT model implemented across curriculum teams was then introduced, with a mandate to implement differentiated curricula for all students in all subjects. Staff were to belong both to year-level teams and curriculum teams, which would meet weekly as PLT.

Guidelines for the PLT included:

- identification of purpose to enable small groups to collaborate, with a specific focus for each year of operation
- specification of size to maximise participation
- allocation of teachers to one team for the year in the domain of the majority of their teaching
- scheduling of regular meetings
- designation of leaders who were allocated a time allowance for management of the team, leadership of the team and involvement in continuing professional development.

In 2013, nearly five years after the events outlined above had been initiated, WRC remained in the implementation and evaluation cycles, embedding evidence-based practices with a staff of some 60 teachers. School leadership acts to facilitate 'buy-in' to the process, with two strands of activity in mind: the teachers and the students. WRC takes a self-conscious approach to engagement, expecting feedback both from teachers and students about implementation of an evidence-based approach to teaching and the use of assessments. In terms of the eight levels of involvement for school leadership described in Chapter 5, there is the same expectation of all staff as of the leadership team, and that expectation is firmly fixed at Level 5 and upwards: involved, engaged, committed and ownership.

The teachers

Organisational structure for the management of change is tiered, with two curriculum, assessment and reporting leaders (CARLs) working with curriculum (or domain)
leaders, and the domain leaders working with their PLT.

Measurement of engagement occurs through collection of staff and student data.
These data also act as benchmarks for respondents to plan performance targets. This
strategy is in place from the students through to the principal. For example, for the
CARLs, the goals in 2012 were:

- to facilitate teams to become self-sustaining and accountable, including effectively
  monitoring norms
- to facilitate teams' use of the inquiry cycle as a framework for their decisions about
  student learning.

Data brought to bear in addressing these goals were measures of teacher attitudes
over two time-points. Figure 13.1 depicts levels of understanding of the approach
and its implementation (self-assessed) at mid-year in 2012. The numbers of teachers are grouped within domains – mathematics, technology, languages other than
English (LOTE), English/humanities, arts, science and health/physical education. The
English/humanities and mathematics teachers are spread across junior and senior

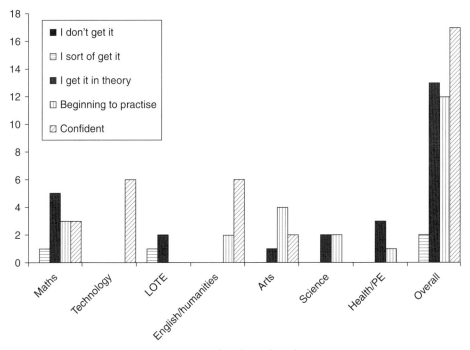

Figure 13.1 *Curriculum team evaluation of evidence-based practices*

levels, ensuring effective numbers of teachers in teams and the capacity to address different levels within the curriculum.

Data such as these are used by the CARLs in their work with domain leaders. Building the capacity of the domain leaders through activities and readings provides them with the resources with which to work within their PLT. Readings are drawn from literature on professional learning teams, evidence-based pedagogy and formative assessment. Such reading helps to formalise concepts and tends to change the tenor and level of discussion. The data on attitudes provide an accountability mechanism and drive change at the CARL level through mentoring with the principal, at the domain leaders level through team discussions, and at individual PLT level. The critical and constructive discussions at domain leaders level ensure the existence of a critical mass of teachers able to provide challenging but safe environments for analysis of well-being, pedagogical and curriculum data within the PLT. This epitomises a cultural shift from individualised to collaborative practice.

PLT are guided by four critical questions, as outlined by, DuFour, Eaker and Many (2010):

1   What is it we expect students to learn?

2   How will we know if they have learned it?

3   How will we respond when they don't learn?

4   How will we respond when they already know it?

The inquiry cycle used at Warragul Regional College reflects the PLT cycle introduced in Chapter 1 and expounded in Chapter 4, and is shown at Figure 13.2.

At WRC, PLT review student progress and engage in professional development activities designed to focus attention on effective pedagogical and assessment strategies. For example, 'Teach the Team' is an activity in which a teacher models a strategy they think is effective, and PLT members review this for relevance in their own teaching. They consider the extent to which the strategy is appropriate in different curriculum areas and for different ages.

At WRC, there are several non-negotiable assumptions underpinning the PLT activities. These include:

- evidence-based practice
- use of assessment data
- use of common assessment tasks (CATs)
- agreed essential learnings within curricular areas
- evidence from multiple sources
- links of evidence to learning continua.

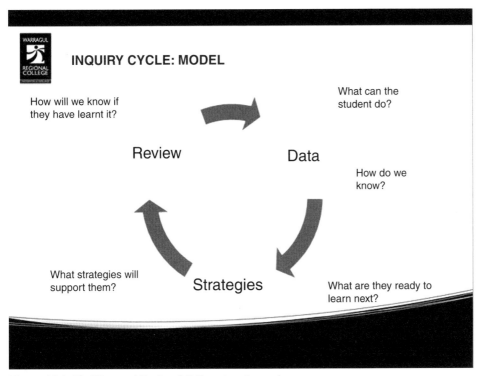

Figure 13.2 *The Warragul Regional College inquiry cycle*

The CARLs drafted a Curriculum Teams' Curriculum (Table 13.2) to help them monitor their progress and plan for continued improvement. In drafting the document, they relied on multiple resources (e.g. Fullan, Cuttress & Kilcher 2005; Griffin 2009; Halverson et al. 2005), combined with in-school experience, again mirroring the process of collection and use of assessment data. The document was a response to concerns that planning might not be followed by review – that the cycle might not be completed.

Although engagement in the process can be measured to a reasonable extent through self-report mechanisms such as questionnaires, and through observation of PLT meetings, teaching plans based on evidence need to be evaluated for their effectiveness. The daily, weekly and term pressures on the curriculum can impede this process. Where a curriculum is presented across a sequence of topics, there is great pressure for the teachers and students to move on to scheduled topics, which runs the risk of not deriving the full richness of information from the previous evaluation cycle. The 'Use of Data' section of the curriculum in Table 13.2 makes explicit the need to complete the cycle, and this is complemented by strategies such as the use of CATs.

Table 13.2 *The Curriculum Teams' Curriculum*

	LEVEL 1: BEGINNING	LEVEL 2: CONSOLIDATING	LEVEL 3: EXPERIENCED	LEVEL 4: SUSTAINABLE
PLT features	• Novice leader • Developing a culture of support for each member of the group • Establishing a new team	• Leader with some experience, using wider range of protocols and processes • Collective responsibility for student learning • Move from sharing practice to questioning practice • Professional readings used for understanding and discussion prompts • PLT process is recognised as the core work • Development of a sense of ownership and momentum • Accountability is evident to school community	• Experienced leader • Cohesive team • Teaching and learning is the core business of the school • Meeting schedules arranged to accommodate teaching and learning opportunities • Team leader takes on a coaching role • Classroom visits and feedback to teachers are enabled • Team's work is guided by a goal that is linked to school priorities	• Deeply embedded PLT practices in the school culture and priorities • Teams can survive a change in key personnel • Collaborative practice is the driving force behind student learning growth
Collaboration and team work	• A focus on learning and building trust using behavioural norms and protocols • A common language is developing and there is evidence of sharing of resources and strategies • Decision-making rests with the team leader, who sets the agenda, leads the meeting and uses the PLT log	• Focus moves to greater collaboration based on trust and use of a common language • Decision-making occurs as a result of consensus, facilitated by team leader • Leader able to reflect on team progress • Team achievements celebrated and the team can identify areas for growth	• With a high level of trust, members are able to take risks in a supportive environment • The team is cohesive with some respectful challenge occurring • Shared responsibility for decision-making and planning and regular formative reflection on progress	• Collaborative planning of learning and teaching is common practice • Team displays openness, honesty, mutual trust, respect, support and care for each other, which are evident in their collaborative practice • Problems solved jointly with sharing of evidence-based ideas and strategies

		• Team achievements are celebrated and shared with the school community • PLT leader begins to reflect on the PLT process	• Team members can recognise strengths and weaknesses and work towards improvements • Team members have a high level of responsibility and accountability to the group and understand, support and promote the PLT philosophy	• Reflection is continuous and informs professional learning • Roles and responsibilities are established and easily transferred to others
Use of data	• Common understandings of how to implement assessment tools are developed • Common assessment tasks (CATs) are set to establish evidence of student learning. Identifies skills, knowledge and processes required to complete CATs • Agrees on the use of which assessment tools, student work samples and class reports for differentiation • Team is encouraged to analyse more than one data source	• Comprehensive rubrics are developed and used in the moderation of CATs • There is common understanding of prior and content knowledge and skills students need to acquire • A clear process is established for how the information collated from assessment tools will be used to plan for a differentiated curriculum • Three sources of data are collected and analysed across the cohort • A secure system is established for storage of data	• There is collective responsibility for the development and implementation of CATs as well as a common understanding of assessment tools and how they impact on explicit teaching and learning • Teachers are proficient in analysing and using multiple sources of data to inform student learning • There is a published assessment schedule • A team member is appointed to ensure the systematic collection of data which is stored centrally and presented in an accessible form for teachers • Student learning is tracked in the school and is passed on from year to year	• The use of common assessment tasks is embedded into teacher practice • There is a shared understanding of the implications of data for planning and improving teaching and learning • Evidence of learning is collected, analysed and used to support the PLT process • There is collective responsibility for the use of data across the school

Table 13.2 *Continued*

	LEVEL 1: BEGINNING	LEVEL 2: CONSOLIDATING	LEVEL 3: EXPERIENCED	LEVEL 4: SUSTAINABLE
Sharing and reflecting on classroom practice	• Student learning is aligned to VELS/AUSVELS outcomes. Teachers use protocols to moderate student work samples and share anecdotal evidence • Team members reflect on and describe student learning after explicit teaching of learning goals. There are common understandings about content to be implemented • Student learning needs are catered for by adjusting tasks • Various forms of evidence are used to begin discussion on student learning and teacher practice	• There is a shift in culture from sharing to respectful challenge. Professional learning impacts on team discussions and classroom practices • Curriculum is differentiated with regular reflection and refining • Evidence-based data on student learning is collected through peer observation and/or video footage using agreed protocols	• The learner is the focus of planning and teacher practice with teachers modelling and practising effective teaching • There are opportunities to observe each other's lessons regularly • The team leader starts to do some coaching using agreed processes • Learning is shared across the school	• Team leader takes on the role of a teaching and learning coach. Staff look beyond the school for new ideas and strategies, which strengthen teaching and learning • New learning is transferred into practice. Whole-school discussion takes place on learning, progress, development and the success of individual students • Staff are confident with the use of a wide range of methods to investigate learning and teaching, using a range of data (primary and secondary) to inform and develop their practice

School organisation, leadership and culture	• The leadership team begins to develop and share a learning vision and focus for curriculum teams • Team members participate in discussion about their own and the school's vision and values about student learning • Structures are put into place to support the curriculum teams, including meeting time, spaces and communication methods • Principal and leadership team members participate in teams	• Structures and systems are in place to support ongoing PLT development • The principal and leadership team work to build trust and actively engage in team meetings • There is regular reporting back to other staff members and team leaders and links made to school performance documents • Principal's performance plan is aligned with the PLT priorities and school improvement is viewed as a collective responsibility • There is a developing cohesive and consistent approach towards student learning and instructional change • Team leaders utilise the learning of the teams to engage staff in formal and informal discussion on student learning and effective teaching • New initiatives are implemented only if they are aligned with the improvement of student growth	• Curriculum teams are central to school organisation and structure of other teams within the school • The vision and policies of the school are reflected in the PLT processes and goals with regular evaluation of the team's progress • Decision-making of the team is guided by the shared vision for student learning. • Principal promotes learning growth rather than teaching as the core purpose of the school and their actions reinforce this focus • The leadership structures, including building teacher capacity, are evident • Curriculum teams contribute to school-wide improvement strategies	• Senior leaders are deeply committed to the development and sustainability of the school's PLT and prioritise this as a major leadership and management task • Distributive leadership is an accepted practice and enables sustainability of the school's PLT • Teams adapt to reflect the changing school environment and priorities • A shared vision and values for student and teacher learning are embedded in the school culture and are demonstrated through collaborative and classroom practice • Student learning growth is the basis for adopting and/or assessing school improvement strategies

Source: Adapted from the Wellington Network (Frost & Ridsdale 2012a).

The students

The second strand of the WRC change in culture concerns the students. Identification of the well-being needs of students, together with the teacher focus on the use of assessment data, stimulated awareness by the school that students frequently do not understand the purpose or function of assessment. This lack of comprehension can actually increase student disengagement, and can limit the usefulness of assessment data to a mere benchmarking tool.

An initial concern to address was the perception that formative assessment is essentially a backward-looking tool, an estimate of what a student has achieved. As one strategy, the CARLs developed a *Formative Assessment Strategies Booklet* (Frost & Ridsdale 2012b) for use within the school. It promotes a set of activities to be undertaken at four levels: the self; peer-to-peer; the classroom; and the whole school. With recognition of Wiliam's (e.g. 2012) work on activating students as learning resources for one another and as owners of their own learning, the guide combines the PLT log approach with explicit involvement of students in the formative activity. As another strategy, and to address related concerns about idiosyncratic delivery of the curriculum, CATs were developed for all subjects by the domain teams.

Formative assessment strategies

The school's official *Formative Assessment Strategies Booklet* provides sets of strategies designed to elicit diagnostic information from the student, for both student and teacher use. The strategies have direct impact on students and have the potential to clarify their learning, as well as the teaching process and its rationale. Examples are the use of questioning, providing wait time for students to think through their responses, and using one student's responses to feed others in a formal manner. Strategies for students to self-assess in procedural ways, and methods for students to design tests that can act as diagnostic tools for themselves and for others, are provided.

An 'Exit Pass' tool provides for students to offer feedback or ask questions of their teacher at the end of a class. The information is then fed back into the teaching at the next session – 'from what I collected yesterday, this is what we need to look at today'. This demonstrates to students their own accountability in the process. The guidance for self-assessment, in particular, helps students to understand how teachers use rubrics for assessment and makes the process more transparent.

The implementation of formative assessment in the classrooms can be confusing for students initially. It implies that a 'correct and incorrect' approach to assessment is no longer adequate, and requires students to justify their positions, to articulate their learning and to refine it. In so doing, they come to an informed position on how and why their performance is assessed, and are introduced to ways to improve this performance. By the end of the 2012 year, students were no longer asking why they were being assessed. Not only did they know why, but they were explicitly and overtly a part of the process.

The outcomes of these strategies are measured in two ways. One source is student opinion survey data, collected in the second and fourth terms of the academic year. A second source of evidence is student progress data, which are disseminated to students and parents six times each year.

Student survey

The student survey lists statements for agreement or disagreement across a variety of classroom experiences, including the variety of assessment methods, teacher encouragement, teacher knowledge about the student and expectations. The survey drew on items from the Student Attitudes to School Survey (DEECD 2012) and the selection of items for inclusion was based on their capacity to reflect student motivation. The class results provide useful information to guide classroom practices and address student misconceptions. The survey also provides information about change over the two-term period. Where teachers have implemented changed practices on the basis of the Time 1 data, the impact of these practices can be evaluated at Time 2.

Student progress report

Student progress data reflect student behaviour, effort, self-management, class work and homework across seven levels of performance or activity. Teachers complete the progress report grid for each student in each subject. This provides the opportunity for comparing progress by the student across subjects for subsequent analysis so that the data are used for monitoring and supporting the student. In the move toward team teaching and shared responsibility for student outcomes, these reports act as a mechanism for PLT discussions of student needs. Changes in the patterns of data act as diagnostic signals for teachers to intervene with students and to discuss with parents. The progress report ensures that there are few surprises for parents or students at the end of the year or at other milestones. Student progress is celebrated in the school both implicitly through the involvement of teachers and students, and explicitly through congratulations and tokens of esteem.

Summary

At Warragul Regional College, individual and cohort student data are collected to inform instruction and provide intervention using the inquiry cycle. Student data are also tracked to measure learning growth. Staff data are collected and analysed to ascertain the levels that staff feel they have reached in their confidence about and understanding of evidence-based practice, and also to inform their future learning. These activities combine to form a culture of evaluation, which relies on its ownership by the school leadership and the school staff. It depends on logistical support, and seeks external input to ensure a culture of challenge and change. Warragul Regional College epitomises a whole-school approach to implementation of a culture of evidence-based practice.

Acknowledgements

This chapter owes much to Kay Frost and Robyn Ridsdale, Curriculum, Assessment and Reporting Leaders, to Robert Juratowich, Principal of Warragul Regional College, Victoria, Australia, and to the teaching staff of the college. The author is also grateful for the contribution of the Wellington Network.

Appendix A
Using the online tests and reports

Masa Pavlovic and Nafisa Awwal

This appendix guides you through a sample of the ARCOTS assessment and reporting system that you can access online at www.cambridge.edu.au/academic/arcots. Detailed instructions are given here to step you through the assessment process. This will allow you to try out the use of online developmental assessment to plan teaching strategies for implementation in your classroom. When using the tests, we encourage you to follow the PLT cycle discussed in Chapter 4, including planning, implementing and evaluating your teaching strategies.

ARCOTS overview

The ARCOTS tests were developed as part of the Assessment and Learning Partnerships project (see the Introduction for more detail on the project). They are intended to be used by teachers as one of many sources of evidence that reflect student learning. They provide teachers with a means to track student progress for the purpose of informing and evaluating teaching. The test results are used to identify the point of learning readiness or ZPD, and they are reported as a level on the corresponding developmental progression. The progressions were developed for three learning domains: numeracy, reading comprehension and problem-solving, and each domain has a corresponding test. The reports are available instantaneously, through the ARCOTS reporting system, upon completion of an assessment. The corresponding progressions are provided in Chapter 2.

Technical requirements

Table A.1 lists the minimum technical requirements to successfully conduct ARCOTS tests. ARCOTS can also be run on iPads using a Flash-compatible browser such as Puffin, iSwifter or similar. If you are considering testing with iPads, we advise a trial run prior to commencing student testing to check compatibility and speed.

Note: In addition, please check whether you need an IT technician to whitelist (allow access to) the ARCOTS site in your school.

Table A.1 *Recommended minimum requirements for accessing the tests*

Internet Explorer 6 or later Mozilla Firefox 3 or later *Other browsers are also compatible.*
Internet connection (minimum 56 bit/s)
A recent Adobe Flash Player plug-in The latest version can be downloaded from www.adobe.com/products/flashplayer.
Minimum screen display: 1024 × 768
Keyboard and mouse
It is recommended that you clear the browser cache of each student's computer before administering the tests.
We recommend that students close all other applications and web pages while taking the tests so that only an internet browser with a single window or tab is open.
We also recommend that schools contact their internet service provider (ISP) in advance of heavy testing periods to ensure that there are no scheduled service interruptions and that allowances are adequate to deal with the anticipated number of concurrent users.

Test access

Samples of ARCOTS developmental assessments and the reporting system are provided on the website. The purpose of the sample tests is to give teachers an experience of using developmental progressions to inform teaching and implement the processes described in this book.

Before the testing and reporting systems can be accessed, you will need to register. To register, you will need to have a valid email address. During the registration process, you may be asked to provide some additional details, but those details are optional (see Figure A.1). Please note that registration is limited to one user for each copy of the book. The class size is limited to 40 students.

Once registration has been successful, you will be notified automatically of the login details for the system via the email address you have provided during registration. The email will also contain details (test URL, test access code, etc.) to access the tests and the reports. Using the link and password provided in the email, you will have access to both the teacher and the student view of the system as shown in Figure A.2.

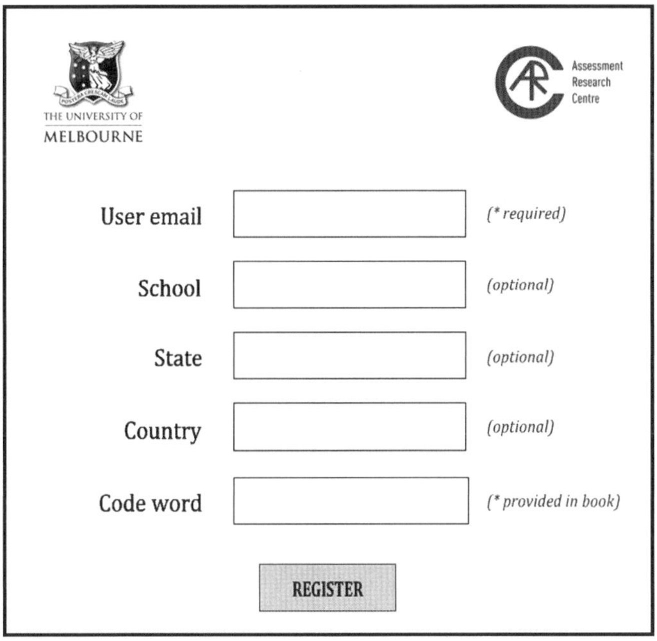

Figure A.1 *User registration for test access*

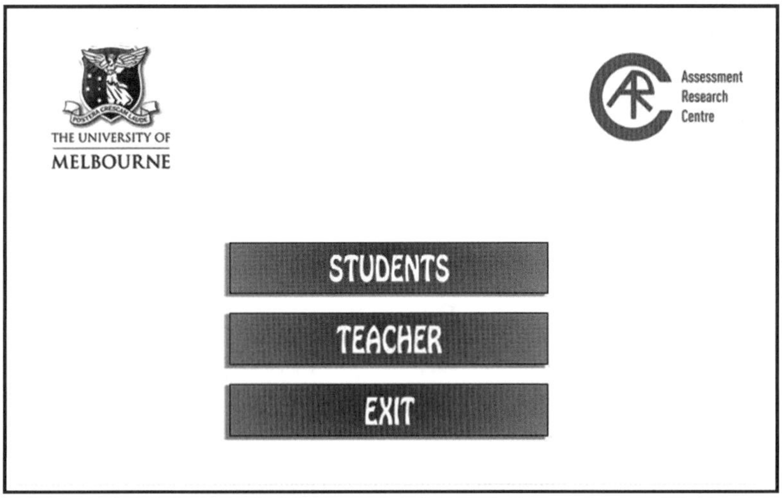

Figure A.2 *Testing and reporting system main page*

As a teacher, you can access the tests through the teacher section of the system. During the login procedure, you will be asked to provide your username, password and test access code (as shown in Figure A.3), all of which can be found in the email you receive when you register. Once logged in, you will have access to all the tests for the three domains, while reports will be available as soon as students have completed any of the tests. Teachers can also explore any of the tests from the teacher section of the site.

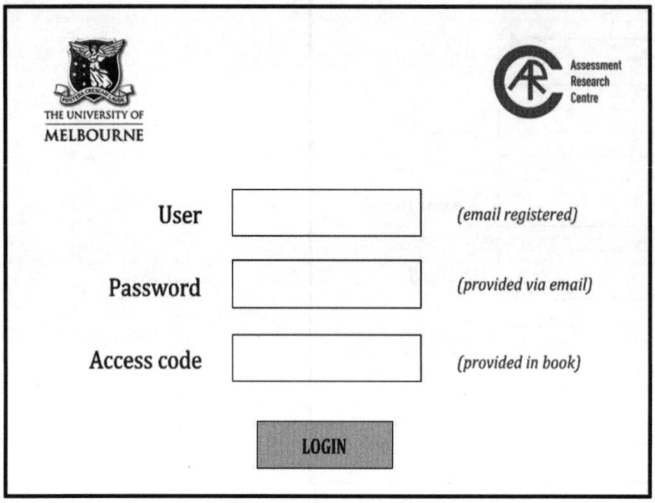

Figure A.3 *Teacher login page*

As part of the test administration process, you will need to guide students through the login procedures. The login page, as shown in Figure A.4, can be accessed from the student section of the site. You will need to supply your students with the test access code provided in the email. They can then log in with their first name and date of birth (DOB). The DOB will need to be entered in the format *DDMMYY* without any

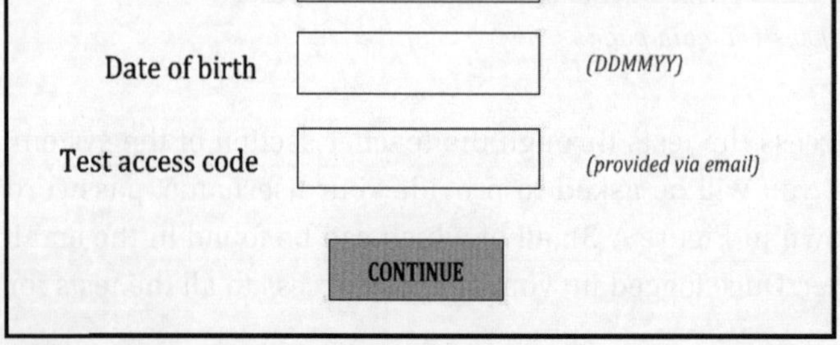

Figure A.4 *Student login page*

spaces or special characters such as hyphen (-) or forward slash (/). The system also requires the student to enter only their first name. Please note, if there are two students with exactly the same first name and DOB, it is recommended to add a digit to the student name without any spacing, so that students' responses are not overwritten. Once the details entered by the students go through the authentication protocol, they will have access to all the tests. The test administration can then be overseen by you as described below. If the internet connection is lost during testing, it can be resumed, when the connection is available again, by using the same login details.

How to target tests

There are eight different ARCOTS tests for determining a student's position on each of the numeracy and reading comprehension progressions, and three different tests for the problem-solving progression. Each test points to a group of levels on the relevant progression. The levels on the numeracy and reading comprehension progressions are labelled from A (lowest) to L (highest). The levels on the problem-solving progression are labelled from A to F.

Each test covers a few levels, some of which are also covered by adjacent tests in the series (see Figures A.5 to A.7), but it is important to select the right test to get the most accurate results. This means it is essential to select a test at the appropriate level of difficulty for the student. Remember that an appropriate level of difficulty is one at which the student will answer around 50 per cent of the items correctly. (See the end of this appendix for an explanation of IRT, which is used to match item difficulty with student ability.) While tests of numeracy and reading comprehension are broadly intended for students attending eight different year levels, it is not recommended to simply align each test with a student year level. That is because the tests vary both in the complexity of the skills needed to answer the questions correctly and in their content. The process by which the teacher selects the test for the individual or group of students is called test targeting.

Test targeting is a three-step process:

1 Explore the content of the tests.
2 Identify tests with content appropriate for the specific student or group of students.
3 Select a test of appropriate complexity.

The order of tests is related to the order of colours in the rainbow (see Figure A.5). The red tests are the simplest, followed by orange, yellow, lime, green, aqua, blue and purple (for the problem-solving domain, only yellow, green and blue tests are available). Each test is linked to the next test through a set of common items. When the tests were designed, the common items were selected with respect to the skills and knowledge appropriate for adjacent test levels. That is, the selection of common items was based on the rule that items should not be too difficult or too easy for the students taking either of the adjacent tests, and that students taking either test should be familiar with the content. Student performance on the common item set was then used to determine relative test difficulties.

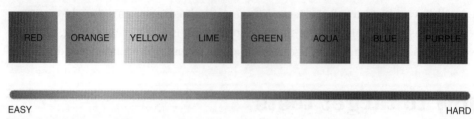

| RED | ORANGE | YELLOW | LIME | GREEN | AQUA | BLUE | PURPLE |

EASY   HARD

Figure A.5 *Order of tests*

While all of the tests in a learning domain are mapped to the same underlying continuum, each test is designed to provide maximum accuracy at a small range of levels on the continuum. This is represented in Figures A.6, A.7 and A.8.

	READING COMPREHENSION								
LEVEL	**RED**	**ORANGE**	**YELLOW**	**LIME**	**GREEN**	**AQUA**	**BLUE**	**PURPLE**	↓
A									
B									
C									
D									
E									
F									
G									
H									
I									
J									
K									↓
L									

Increasing skill complexity

Figure A.6 *Test targeting for reading comprehension*

The tests are most accurate for the dark shaded levels. The area that is lighter indicates results that are less accurate but can still be used to make inferences about students as long as the teacher is aware of the greater risk of error. For example, if a student is determined by the orange test to be at level G, it is possible that the student is actually at either a higher level (H) or a lower level (F), as there are not enough items in the orange test (at those levels) to provide accurate separation of the levels.

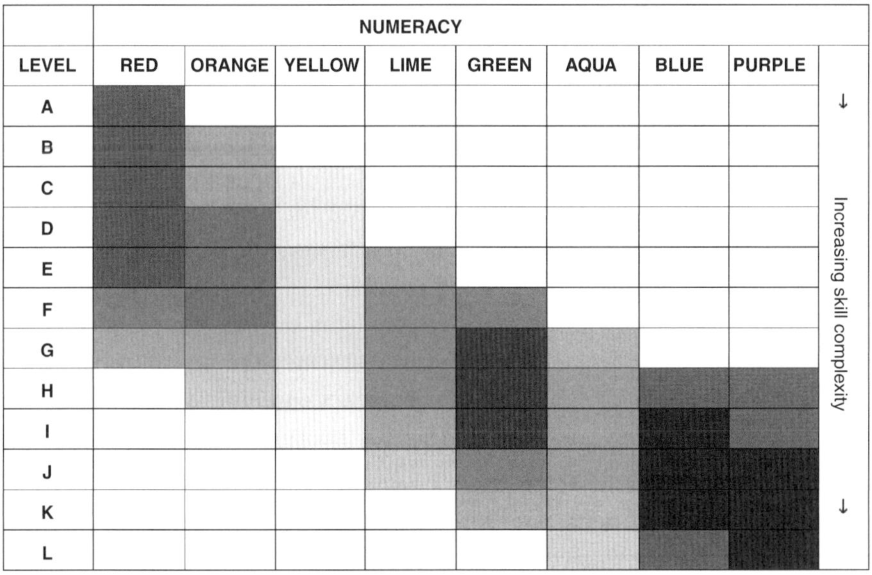

NUMERACY									
LEVEL	RED	ORANGE	YELLOW	LIME	GREEN	AQUA	BLUE	PURPLE	
A									↓
B									
C									
D									Increasing skill complexity
E									
F									
G									
H									
I									
J									
K									↓
L									

Figure A.7 *Test targeting for numeracy*

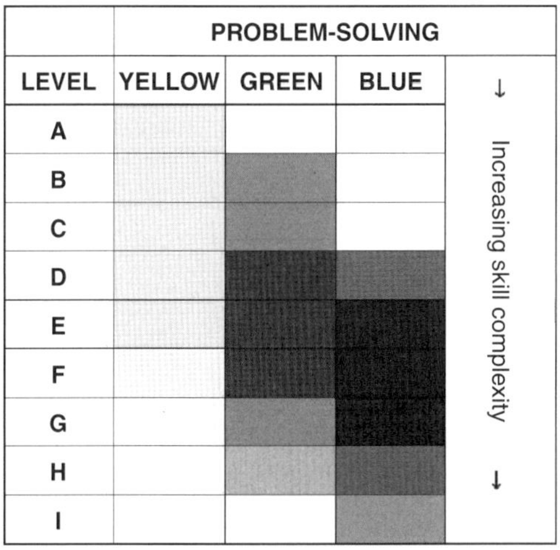

PROBLEM-SOLVING			
LEVEL	YELLOW	GREEN	BLUE	↓
A				
B				
C				Increasing skill complexity
D				
E				
F				
G				
H				↓
I				

Figure A.8 *Test targeting for problem-solving*

The student may have guessed correctly a few items in the test, leading to a result of G instead of F. Conversely, the student may have made a few careless mistakes, leading to a result of G instead of H. ARCOTS is designed to be quasi-adaptive to address this issue, so students who are reaching higher scores on a test will receive 10 additional items specifically targeted to a higher level. The teacher may check if the student was given additional items by checking the reported number of items completed.

Test administration

Before the tests are conducted, teachers need to plan where and when to schedule the tests, giving careful consideration to all factors that can influence the validity of inferences made from the test results (see Chapter 3).

Each test consists of 40 multiple-choice items, with an additional 10 items provided automatically if the student answers most of the 40 items correctly. The recommended administration time for a test is 40 minutes, but students should not be put under pressure to complete the test in this time.

The test menu page is shown in Figure A.9. Students select a test by clicking on the domain and colour as instructed by their teacher. Once the appropriate test is selected, the student is taken to the test page. Teachers can quickly check whether students are taking the correct test by checking the background colour of the test page, as illustrated in Figures A.10 and A.11.

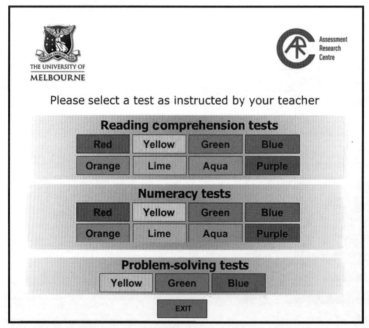

Figure A.9 *ARCOTS test menu page*

Note the different organisation of reading comprehension items in Figure A.11 when compared with numeracy items in Figure A.10. Reading comprehension items are grouped according to the common text passages to which the items refer. For example, items Q1–Q5 in Figure A.11 refer to the same text passage.

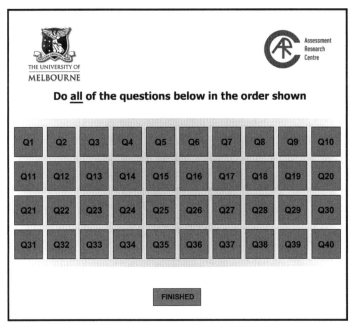

Figure A.10 *Test page for the yellow numeracy test (background colour is yellow)*

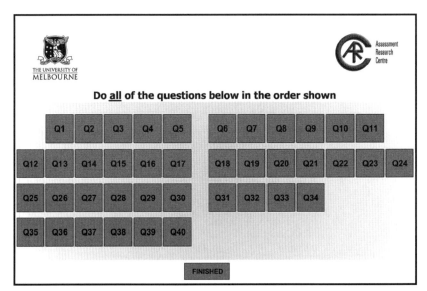

Figure A.11 *Test page for the aqua reading comprehension test (background colour is aqua)*

Once the student selects an answer to an item, the shading on the button for that item changes so the student can monitor which items have already been completed, as shown in Figure A.12. However, the student can go back to any item and change the answer. When an item is reopened, the previous answer is displayed in the upper right corner of the page, as shown in Figure A.13.

Appendix A

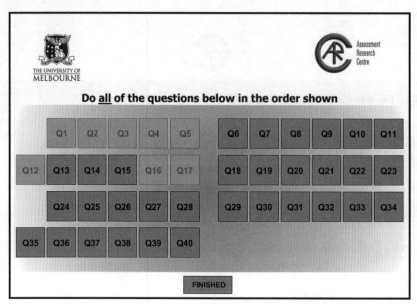

Figure A.12 *Distinction between completed and uncompleted items*

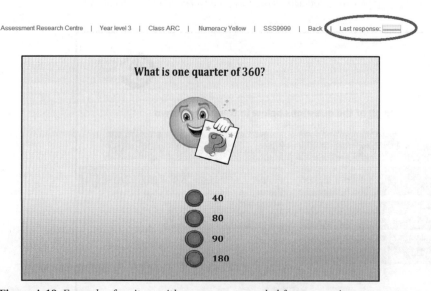

Figure A.13 *Example of an item with an answer recorded from a previous attempt*

When all students have reached the test page showing the question buttons but testing has not commenced, the teacher should read the following instructions:

You now see three or four rows of grey buttons numbered 1 to 40 (or 30 in the case of problem-solving). These buttons take you to the questions on the test. When you click on a number, the test question appears. When you have answered that question, you will come back to the screen with the numbers. You will notice that the boxes for the questions you have completed will be a lighter shade than the other questions. You can return to any question to change the answer if you wish. You will notice that when you do this, the answer you first gave will appear at the top right of the screen.

Please answer all questions. When you have completed the test you should click the FINISHED button at the bottom of the screen. Check your details and click FINISH to end the test.

You may use a pen and paper while doing the test. You may not use a calculator or enter any other computer programs or internet sites.

If your internet connection fails or your screen freezes, don't worry. None of your answers will be lost. In order to resume the test, you log in again, starting by typing the URL for the tests in the address bar of your internet browser.

Once all students have started the test, the supervising teacher must check each student's identification details and record them for later use. Student details are shown in grey at the top of each page of the test, so students can continue to work through the tests while the teacher is checking the details. These details are the only way that test results can be matched to particular students. If a student finishes a test using another student's ID, then the original student's results will be overwritten.

Teachers should actively supervise the students at all points during the testing.

Item response theory

When assessment data are used to define a developmental progression, the assumption is made that there is an inherent underlying order in which students generally acquire skills and knowledge, and this typical order is calibrated using item response theory (IRT). The approach involves analysing a large number of responses to test questions and determining how well items are able to distinguish the different ability levels of students. The result of this analysis is that items can be ranked in order of difficulty, and then grouped and mapped to a range on an associated developmental progression through an interpretation of the cognitive skills required to answer each question correctly.

Test scores can be used to rank students, but on their own test scores cannot provide information on students' abilities, and performance cannot be compared from one test to another without a measure of the relative difficulty of the tests. Conversely, the level of relative difficulty of a test cannot be determined without knowing the ability of the students who took the test.

Item response theory is based on two assumptions: first, that students' performance on a test item can be predicted by their abilities; and second, that student performance on a test item can be described by a mathematical function or the difference between the ability of the student and the difficulty of the test item. This function defines the probability of answering the item correctly in such a way that students with lower ability will have a lower probability than students with higher ability of answering the item correctly. Conversely, for any given ability level, students will have a lower probability of answering a difficult item correctly than an easier one. A commonly used model for items that can be scored as being right or wrong (yes/no items) is one that was introduced by Georg Rasch. His model defines the item difficulty as the student ability for which the probability of answering the item correctly is 50 per cent.

The plot in Figure A.14 shows the probability of an item being answered correctly, given a student's ability. The higher a student's ability, the greater the probability of a correct answer. The horizontal axis represents the measure of student ability, while the vertical axis represents the probability or chance of the student succeeding on the item. The chance of success increases as the ability of the student increases. On the right side of the graph, ability increases and becomes progressively greater than item difficulty, resulting in greater probability of success. The chances reduce when the difference between ability and difficulty is negative, as occurs towards the left side of the graph. The horizontal line at 0.5 probability represents the point at which the item difficulty equals the student's ability.

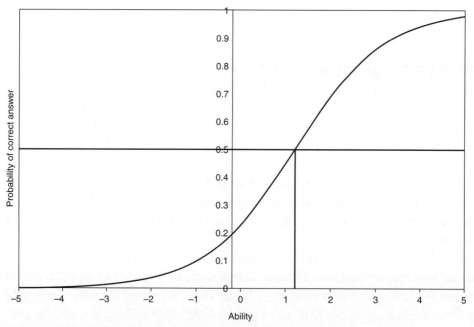

Figure A.14 *Response function for an item showing difficulty = 1.2 (where the probability of a correct answer is 0.5 or 50 per cent)*

From the graph, it can be seen that at the point where student ability equals item difficulty, the slope of the curve is at its steepest. This means that at this point, or close to it, it is possible to distinguish between students with small differences in their abilities. Figure A.15 represents a plot for three simple yes/no (right/wrong) items of different difficulties.

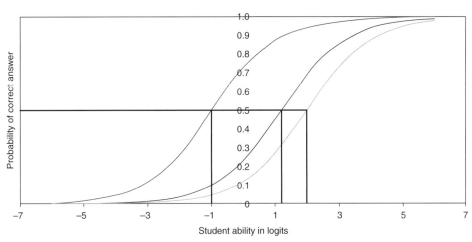

Figure A.15 *Response function for three yes/no items of varying difficulties*

From Figure A.15, it can be seen that the probability of a correct response approaches zero for very low-ability students and approaches one for very high-ability students, irrespective of the item difficulty. A horizontal line at probability of 0.5 on the vertical axis crosses the curves at different points defined by values on the horizontal axis – that is, the student ability. So these are the values of the item difficulty because at these points the item difficulty equals the person ability measures. The further the curve moves to the right the more ability is needed and hence the more difficult the item. In addition, it can be seen that the curves for items with varying difficulties do not cross one another, which means that, at any given ability level, a student has a lower probability of answering a more difficult item correctly. The student with an ability level of 1.2 (as in the previous example) would find the first task easy – represented by the curve in which the student has a 50:50 chance at a logit value on the horizontal axis (–1.0), which suggests that the task was easy relative to the average ability of the group taking the test. But the third graph at the right side in Figure A.14 illustrates an item that our original student would find a little more difficult.

Appendix B
FAQ for PLT

Patrick Griffin

Why does the testing and research focus on literacy, numeracy and problem solving?

The Australian government has asked states to ensure that levels of literacy and numeracy are raised in all groups of students in schools. There is little doubt that these are core and enabling skills for all people, so schools are therefore expected to lift performance in these areas. From an educational point of view, these skill areas are considered to be foundational: it is very difficult for students to learn across the curriculum if they do not have the basic skills in literacy and numeracy. While the skills assessed in the tests are not all of the skills in these areas, the high correlations among the various literacy and numeracy skill sub-domains enable the assessment procedures to focus on these and assume the others. This is, of course, not a law that is applicable to all students, but it is an observation of a typical link between skills in the tested domains and those in other, non-tested domains, given the research evidence in the field.

In the case of students with additional needs, the emphasis is different. The instruments are completed by the teacher, who provides observational data. They emphasise communication and literacy, cognitive and emotional development, and interpersonal skills. For students with additional needs, these are regarded as important enabling skill domains.

An emerging area of great interest is the use of digital tools to support collaboration in problem-solving, creative practices and communication. There are many examples of how computer-based learning environments for collaboration can work to stimulate student learning and the process of inquiry. Collaborative problem-solving skills are considered necessary for success in today's world of work and school. Online collaborative problem-solving tasks offer new measurement opportunities when information on what individuals and teams are doing is synthesised along the cognitive dimension. Students can send documents and files to each other, and in this way work on tasks together. This raises issues regarding interface design features that can support online measurement and ways to evaluate collaborative problem-solving processes in an online context. There are also examples of web-based peer-assessment strategies. Peer assessment has been defined by some as an innovative assessment method, since students themselves are put in the position of evaluators as well as learners. It has been used with success in different fields such as writing, business, science, engineering and medicine.

Why do we recommend online testing and data collection?

Online testing takes considerable work out of the process for the teacher and controls a lot of the data quality-assurance procedures: teachers do not need to administer a paper test; students can receive immediate feedback; errors in data recording are avoided. It also allows targeting of the assessment, which is dealt with elsewhere in this book.

What is meant by outcomes-based assessment, and why is it preferable?

Outcomes-based education and assessment require that individuals are able to show *that* they have learned as well as being able to demonstrate *what* they have learned. A score is not a sufficient metric for an outcomes-based assessment. The output must be a skills description. Outcomes-based assessments focus on demonstrable changes in the learner, and not on transmission of content or a score or code from which we must infer a change in learning. Opponents argue that it is behaviourist in its approach and that, when all the outcomes have been achieved, some intangible aspects of human aesthetics are missing. Their argument is that there are some parts of learning that are not observed or measured in this approach; that assessment reduces education to the level of what can be directly observed and measured; and moreover, that incidental learning – so valued by teachers – is lost, and the assessment of student performance becomes the central issue of education. Our view is that performance assessments are a means through which learning is inferred, and by identifying the cohesive sets of tasks – rather than isolated single tasks – we are able to plan far more efficient development.

What is meant by a developmental progression or continuum?

Any developmental continuum represents two things. The first is the description of the students' development or growth in learning. On a continuum, there are steps or levels through which students progress. The continuum is not a definition of the specific learning progression or pathway of every individual student: it is a description of typical progress. Some students will progress in quite different ways. So the continuum becomes a guide and gives the teacher a general idea of progression. Second, it is a framework to help teachers interpret their observations. The levels on the continuum do not address the relative performance; instead, they describe levels of competence. They provide the teacher with a guide to the ZPD and the point at which the teacher can intervene to improve student learning.

Why are developmental continua used?

The developmental continua or progressions describe the competence levels that can be used to map student performance. The level descriptions allow teachers to design intervention plans and seek advice on interventions targeted at the level of competence of each student. This innovation allows schools to move from performance scores, which can be meaningless, to descriptions of performance in terms of competence levels that are concrete and specific. This makes data more amenable for use in classroom interventions.

Sometimes, the developmental continua are referred to as described scales. These are also known as vertical scales covering a range of levels of development. They are an operational way of using Glaser's definition of criterion referencing, in that they describe stages of increasing competence and make it possible to monitor the growth of individuals, classes and schools, as well as systems. They enable monitoring in absolute terms of competence rather than the relative terms that are available using normative scales such as the 500/100 score system. Their great strength is that they enable interpretation of the 'bands' or 'levels' in terms of instructional intervention. Each level gives the teacher a hint about what should be the point of intervention, or where the student is ready to learn.

What is the underlying theory of developmental assessment?

Developmental assessment is a way of interpreting assessment data. It is not a set of assessment instruments, but a way of using data that instruments yield. It assumes that people grow in ability, sophistication, knowledge and understanding because of opportunities to learn and that assessment can be used to track growth. When using the term 'developmental' in connection with assessment, we are not referring to a cognitive, Piagetian style of development, but to the accumulation of skills, knowledge and attitudes that accrue as a result of exposure to new ideas, new procedures and new opportunities to learn. Adopting a developmental approach to assessment enables an interpretation in terms of the progressive accumulation of knowledge, skills and attitudes from simple to complex, easy to difficult and so on. It assumes that we can interpret this growth or accumulation by observing the changes in indicative behaviours linked to assessment task completion and that people can be ordered in terms of their capacity to respond to increasingly difficult or demanding tasks. It also assumes that the assessment of the person's ability or growth is independent of the set of tasks used. This is one of the most crucial aspects of the approach. For this assumption to hold, the personal attribute assessed (the construct) must be able to be measured by different sets of assessment tasks that independently yield the same conclusion or inference. For example, it should not matter which test of reading comprehension is used: the same conclusion about a student's level of reading comprehension should be reached. This is a property called 'specific objectivity of assessment'.

There are three underlying theories that support a developmental approach to assessment. The first is criterion referencing (Glaser 1963). Glaser proposed the idea that we could infer what a person knows by interpreting the tasks they can perform and emphasised the idea that criterion referencing was the process of monitoring a person's progress through stages of increasing competence. Stages of increasing competence were defined by tasks of increasing difficulty.

The second theory is taken from Vygotsky, who defined the zone of proximal development (ZPD). This is the level of development at which a person is most likely to learn if assistance is provided. It is both a social and cognitive/developmental step; it is the zone between what a student can do and what they cannot do. However, this can be identified only if the student performance is interpreted in a developmental framework.

The third theory is from Rasch (1960, 1980), who showed how it is possible to model mathematically the developmental progression of learning. The theory states that the chances of success can be calculated using measures of ability in persons and difficulty in tasks. The probability of success is a function of the difference between the ability of the person and the difficulty of the task attempted. Rasch showed how to measure both a person's ability and task difficulty using the same metric, and hence how to map both on to the same scale. When the ability of the person is greater than the difficulty of the task, we expect success. When the ability of the person is less than the difficulty of the task, we do not expect success. When the ability of the person is equal to the task difficulty, we expect a 50:50 chance of success.

Because Rasch showed how to measure both a person's ability and task difficulty using the same metric, it is possible to arrange test questions in order of increasing difficulty and persons in order of their ability on the same scale. Then, by identifying the cognitive skill demanded by each item, a developmental progression of skills can be defined to describe the range from the skill that is easiest to demonstrate to the one that is most difficult. Depending on a person's ability, they will be able to demonstrate some of these skills (those below their ability) but not others (those above their ability). Glaser showed that this enabled a process of monitoring a person's progress through stages of increasing competence.

When a student reaches those items where difficulty is equal to their ability, they begin to get some items right and some items wrong. This is Vygotsky's zone of proximal development. The zone is between the skills that can be demonstrated and those that cannot. It is located by arranging test questions in order of difficulty and counting the number of items equal to the person's score, starting with the easiest item. In this way the score on a test becomes a direct pointer to the level of competence that the student has reached. When we examine the items at and about that level of ability, the skills that the student is ready to learn can be identified. The score on a test then becomes a starting point, not an end-point. The stages of increasing competence are identified using groups (clusters) of skills at the same level on the progression and interpreting the underlying 'big idea' that the cluster of skills can represent. These cluster interpretations then become the levels or stages of increasing competence.

The progression provides teachers with a description of a dominant construct that underpins a student's performance on a test. Many people argue that performances are multi-dimensional and multi-faceted, and cannot be represented by a single construct. This may be true, but if it is possible to describe a dominant direction that these skill developments take, we can show teachers how to improve students' learning.

What is meant by a 'developmental' rather than a 'deficit' approach?

By identifying on a continuum the levels reached by each student and identifying the point of intervention reached, we use the descriptions at the levels to identify a set of skills that can be used to scaffold learning. A deficit model examines the items a student has answered incorrectly on an assessment and attempts to fix any problem that the student appears to have. It is often called a 'diagnostic' model and this, in medical terminology, assumes that there is something wrong with the student – something that needs to be fixed. A developmental model takes the approach that every student is developing in a particular growth direction and that if it is possible to locate the point at which the student is developing, and to intervene at that point, it is possible to move each student forward.

Why do we emphasise evidence rather than inference?

We emphasise the idea of evidence rather than inference because it is possible to describe evidence in terms of the behaviours of the students. These are the things that the students do, say, make or write. We can elaborate on each of these four words to devise a range of behaviours that are observable. We emphasise evidence because it is possible to explicitly teach at the level of evidence – that is, we can focus on the behaviours manifested by the students and effect changes in those behaviours, therefore inferring changes in the unobserved or latent characteristics of the student. In other words, we can change what the students do, say, make or write, and infer change in understanding, knowing, thinking and so on.

How does a team encourage challenge without causing offence?

The PLT conversation needs to be shifted away from a focus on what the teacher does and towards a focus on what the student is doing, saying, making and writing. This allows challenge to be discussed in terms of what students are doing. It focuses on evidence. It avoids a focus on inference. If this is not done generally, challenges from team members appear to challenge the authority of the teacher, or even the expertise on display. This can induce a negative response and can be offensive. If the challenge is to seek further evidence of what the students are doing, then the tension can be removed from the conversation.

Why do some students appear to go backwards?

Assessments are fallible. There are several sources of error and not all of them can be controlled, but some can be. The sources of error can be the student, the teacher, the administration, the context or the assessment task itself.

The student

No matter how good the assessment, it is not always possible to fully engage the student to such an extent that they provide their very best performance every time they undertake a test. Sometimes, a student may perform at their best in a baseline assessment at the beginning of the year and under-perform later in the year. On the other hand, some may be totally unengaged by the exercise. Teachers can help students perform at their highest level of capability, but it is difficult for the teacher to overcome the effect on a student who is feeling unwell, who comes from a home where breakfast is not available, whose language is not English, whose family is dysfunctional and distressing to the student, and so on. To some extent these issues can be overcome by the culture of the classroom and the school, but not completely. So a test result must be considered as a measure at one point in time, and this can often be influenced by these factors that operate in the background to the student performance.

The assessment task

Measures of reliability and consistency are taken at an average level over all of the students who take a test. Sometimes tests that look highly reliable at an aggregate level can provide errors at an individual student level because of these background factors and the problems associated with them.

The teacher

Telling the student that the test does not matter, or that the test is critically important, or criticising the test or otherwise expressing a stance on the nature of testing can be counter-productive.

The administration

How the assessment task is administered affects how students have an opportunity to perform. Letting different students do assessments under different conditions will lead to unreliable data and hence uncertain interpretations and doubtful descriptions of competence. This can lead to incorrect interventions.

The context

If the assessment is conducted in severe conditions – too hot, cold, noisy, crowded, messy – or with incorrect equipment, insufficient space, poorly produced assessment materials, this can interfere with the students' performance. All of these issues need to be taken into account, because the gains and losses that students demonstrate in a test performance can be influenced by these factors. The teacher needs to look for anomalies in the data, unusual performances and random patterns of performance, and set a discussion topic for their colleagues. In general, there is a reason why students appear to go backwards in their performance, and there is a reason why some students make spectacular gains. Such results are often attributable to the idiosyncratic influences that each student experiences. However, when the data are aggregated, and many students take the test, it is possible to look at the performance of a whole group of students; it is unlikely that these idiosyncratic issues will be attributable to every student in the class. Thus we can regard class-level results as being more stable than individual student results. It is also likely that school-level results will be more stable than class-level results. The first thing to do when there are anomalies in the data is to try to understand why they occur. This provides a good basis for discussion among the professional learning team members.

Why is teaching to the test not helpful to student performance?

When pressure is exerted on teachers or schools to increase test scores, teachers often respond by teaching to the test. Many people encourage this practice in an attempt to improve test scores. It may increase individual test scores for some students, but it reflects an impoverished and contradictory view of learning.

There is always a temptation, when there is pressure to improve test scores, to focus on the questions that the student answered incorrectly and then teach them how those questions can be answered correctly in future. However, if the test works well, the student should be able to correctly answer the questions for which the difficulty level is lower than the student's ability, while the questions with a difficulty level above the student's ability will probably be answered incorrectly. In between the items that are too difficult and those that are too easy (for that student) there is a range of items that challenge the student. The student will be able to answer some of these questions but not others. These questions are at or about the ability level of the student. If the test is working properly, we can use the score on the test by counting up from the easiest item until the number of items equals the student score. At about this level of difficulty, the student will be getting a mix of right and wrong answers. This is a guide to the student's ZPD. Teachers can use the skills associated with the correctly answered items in this zone to scaffold learning and develop the skills associated with the items in this zone that were answered incorrectly. But trying to teach directly the skills required for the most difficult items on the test would provide the student with a challenge beyond their ability. It could be a waste of time – or worse, could frustrate the student and embed a sense of failure.

The formative purpose of testing is primarily to identify the level of readiness to learn. It is not to demonstrate which student, class or school is the best. By practising and repeatedly rehearsing a test, teachers are cheating themselves and their students of information they can use. For teaching purposes, it is more efficient to use the developmental progression that underpins the test and identify the ZPD as the level at which the student is developing. Teaching at that level will help to consolidate student skills by scaffolding and support the student to move to the next level or stage of competence. This is what is meant by teaching to the construct and not teaching to the test.

Despite a negative view of coaching, students do need to know the strategies to do well on a test. This is called becoming test-wise. It is possible to increase students' skills to a level where they are likely to get more answers correct by being test-wise. This can give them more opportunity to use their knowledge and skills. For this reason, it is better to show the students some test-taking strategies. The score on the test may then better reflect their true ability. However, if teachers improve results by teaching to the test, they should not delude themselves that their students are better readers or better at mathematics. By providing a developmental continuum associated with a test, teachers have access to the underpinning construct.

How does the developmental learning model emphasise *all* student growth and development?

Setting high expectations for all students is an often repeated demand. It is easy to set high expectations for high-performing students. Sometimes, however, it is difficult to set high expectations for low-performing students. Even the expressions 'low-performing' and 'high-performing' have value connotations. Setting standards should be about making sure that every student understands that they are expected to grow and develop. Realistic targets need to be set for every student. Some students will have the capacity to make great leaps, while some will have the capacity to make only small leaps. The size of the leap is not related to the expression 'high expectations'. That expression should mean that every student has an expectation that they will develop by the maximum of which they are capable within a particular time. In other words, it is important to realise the potential of *every* student.

There is a temptation, when teachers are trying to improve school performance, to focus on students at the bottom of the distribution. Teachers spend a great deal of time, effort and resources to improve the performance of students who are struggling. They should continue to do this. However, it is important to concentrate on *all* students, and this is a strength of a developmental approach. A developmental approach does not make any judgements about the level at which a student is operating; it simply begins to identify what a student is ready to learn. This includes students at the top of the continuum as much as those at the bottom of the continuum.

Why do we test at the beginning and end of the year?

Testing is undertaken at the beginning of the year in order to establish a benchmark level of performance for the student. It also enables teachers, at the beginning of the year, to identify the levels for intervention for each student and allows team leaders to bring this information to a team leaders' workshop a few weeks after the first test. At that workshop, the team leaders should be ready to contribute to discussion – similar to that in the professional learning team meetings – on the strategies and resources that would be necessary for groups of students at each level on the progression. A constant of these team leaders' meetings is the diversity and variation in strategies and resources that teams use as intervention for the students. This discussion and reporting among team leaders provide a rich resource for the teachers in schools with PLT. It also establishes an accountability framework for the team leaders. In the end, they must discuss how this data will be used in their teams, and the notes of these discussions will be used later in the year when they discuss progress.

The test towards the end of the year provides a standardised measure of performance in order to document changes in the students. Because the focus is on the measurement of change, the rule for this is, 'If you want to measure change, don't change the measure'. While the teachers may decide to use a more difficult test on the second occasion, if it is still a part of an overall test linked to the developmental continuum then it is still the same measure. The test data from a test late in the school year leave a small window of opportunity to study growth patterns for each individual student. This can be taken into account when framing reports at the school level.

What is the relevance of literacy and numeracy assessment to teachers across the curriculum?

Suppose a readiness report for literacy indicates that a student is on level D. If the student is in Year 2, the implications of this might be reasonably straightforward for primary teachers, but suppose the student is in Year 8. What are the implications for the English teacher, the maths teacher, the science, art, social education, physical education and/or domestic science teacher? Such a level of literacy has serious implications for how the student is taught, and what the student is taught, within those subjects. It is not sensible to assume that whole-class instruction can be followed when some students' reading is at level D but most of the class is at level F. Every subject tends to present information in increasingly sophisticated ways. This occurs particularly in secondary schools where the curriculum is delivered by a range of teachers.

Sentence-level meaning: Interprets meaning (by matching words and phrases, completing a sentence, or matching adjacent words) in a short and simple text by reading on or reading back.

Suppose this is part of a readiness report for a student being discussed by a PLT, and suppose the student is in Year 2. What teaching strategy would you use, given that this is a description of what the student is ready to learn? What strategy would you use if the student were in Year 8? What would a science teacher do? An art teacher? A physical education teacher? How would the team members advise and help each other in identifying strategies to teach this student, given the possible set of backgrounds? Suppose the student is from a low socio-economic background. Suppose they are from a non-English-speaking background, and/or have additional needs. These are the kinds of issues that teachers face all the time, but how can the team help? Clearly the discussion needs to take these issues into account and reach an agreement on the best strategy.

What is meant by peer accountability within the PLT?

Accountability means checking whether a person has discharged their responsibilities. In order to check this, we have to know what those responsibilities were. The PLT discusses each student at each level, and makes decisions about the kinds of appropriate intervention strategies and the materials or resources that might be used to either consolidate the student at that level or move them on to the next level on the continuum. A group decision is made and one of the teachers is charged with the responsibility of implementing those strategies and using the agreed resources. The PLT log is a means of recording these decisions in a brief format. There is no need for long and extensive descriptions, but some record needs to be kept, because one of the questions discussed is how long the attempted strategy needs to be maintained before an effect will be observed. This might take a few weeks or longer. A date is agreed upon so that the teacher can report back to the other members of the PLT about the success, the level of implementation and the relevance of the strategy and/or resources to the learning style and patterns of that particular student or the other students in the target group. This reporting back is an accountability exercise – it is peer accountability. It takes a different view of accountability from the common one in which a teacher is held responsible for average scores of a test. The approach used in a PLT context does not give accountability that meaning at all. It focuses instead on checking that teachers fulfil their responsibilities in using and following the advice of their PLT and acting on the community decision reached between themselves and their peers.

How is the PLT accountable to the school?

In some schools where PLT are used, a new level of accountability is beginning to emerge. When performance and development reviews are undertaken in these schools, the principal interviews and reviews the performance of the team rather than the individuals. This is a powerful method of keeping the teams accountable for their responsibilities of mutual concern, joint decision-making and the progress of student learning under their care.

How frequently should the teams meet and how long should a meeting last?

The number of teachers in a team has a great bearing on the answer to this question. Large teams need to cover a large number of students. If each teacher is charged with the responsibility of bringing the data, work samples and background information on three students to each team meeting, a team of eight, for example, would meet to discuss 24 students. This is not possible in a single meeting, so several meetings would be required to cover this range of students. The number of students that can be discussed in any one meeting may vary from team to team. The length of time it takes to discuss the intervention, the strategy and the resources needed will vary depending upon the teacher's capacity, the control on the meeting agenda, the materials available, the knowledge base of the teachers, the skills base of the teachers and the level of discussion about a student's background and learning style. These are just some of the considerations that need to be taken into account.

The experience of existing schools with PLT would indicate that no meeting should last for more than one hour. We have also learned that teams should initially meet every week. Once the agenda is firm and progress is being made, it may be possible to vary the meeting length and frequency; however, initially schools should plan to give the PLT time and opportunity to meet for one hour each week. It may be that these meetings need to replace other meetings. This is a matter of the priorities of the school.

What does it mean to develop collaborative decision-making?

This is a simple idea, but a complex and difficult thing for many PLT to do. It is made more difficult because the simple sharing of ideas is not enough. Successful PLT need teachers to be able to defend recommendations, materials, strategies and ideas. The defence of these suggestions should be made in terms of what students do, say, make and write. It is easy to share a good idea; it is hard to demonstrate that it is a good idea. Unless the team is convinced that there is evidence of potential success with the recommended strategies, great scepticism should be exercised regarding their success. Collaborative decision-making should be based around the defence of suggestions in terms of the evidence of student change. Only when the team agrees that the evidence is sound should the decision be promulgated.

We can in fact establish some rules of evidence in addition to the *do, say, make* and *write* maxim. Evidence is what we can see, touch or hear. What we need to decide is whether we have *adequate* evidence. Is it *appropriate* to the situation? Is it *accurate*? Is it *accountable*? Is it *achievable*? Finally, is it *authentic* and *current* evidence?

How does a team encourage accountability among its members?

Team logs can help do this. If the team leader maintains a log of the decision-making and the materials and strategies that have been agreed upon, it is a relatively simple matter to use this as a document for accountability at subsequent meetings. Teachers who have not used differentiated instruction, or have not used explicit teaching of specific students, need to be able to defend a change made, and the defence must always be in terms of evidence of student performance. If it produces the desired change, then it is defensible.

What do we mean by the expression 'changing the culture'?

The culture of the school is generally driven by the leadership of the school, and the culture of the PLT is driven in large part by the team leader. The team leader needs to be able to work through the PLT meeting to emphasise the attitudinal shift that is necessary. Teachers need to believe that every student can learn. They need to believe that every student can develop and that it is possible to identify the ZPD. This is supported by a broad repertoire of teaching strategies. Teachers also need a knowledge base of the discipline they are teaching, the pedagogy associated with the discipline, the notion of developmental learning, an understanding of data, an understanding of how assessment and learning are linked through data and a willingness to change. These are important requirements. Sometimes the attitude development is an a priori condition for the successful implementation of the strategy.

What infrastructure is needed in the school?

By and large, the major infrastructure change is the establishment of a timetable for meetings. There may be a need for administrative support in order to fix this change as part of the school schedule, and in order to collect and collate the kinds of information available as a result of the PLT meetings and the team leader meetings outside the school.

Why do we use the expression 'assessment for teaching' and not 'assessment for learning'?

'Assessment for learning' is an attractive expression. It signals that the teacher has the student in mind when undertaking the assessment. It is as if assessment itself will promote learning. It doesn't. The old 'straw man' argument that assessment is damaging to students is often given credibility because teachers claim that assessment promotes learning. The expression 'assessment for learning' promotes that impression. There is an old story used by opponents to testing that it doesn't matter how many times you weigh the pig – it doesn't get any heavier. Similarly, it doesn't matter how many times you assess your students if assessment is what you use for learning, because the students are unlikely to learn much from the assessment. This is why we argue that assessment should be seen as providing information to the teacher to make decisions about intervening with the student in order to promote learning. It is more correct therefore to argue that *assessment is for the teacher and teaching*, because it provides the data and the evidence that the teacher needs in order to make decisions that will promote learning.

How do schools ensure that this process is sustainable over time?

Sustainability is an important concept whenever changes are implemented. At the beginning of each year, team leaders need to re-establish contact with each other. They should be reaffirming and re-establishing the plans for PLT activities for the school year. Structures need to be put in place, such as the beginning-of-year and end-of-year testing programs, and bookings need to be made for use of school computer laboratories or computing facilities. The team leaders need to ensure that all the team members are undertaking professional reading. The system is sustainable if the process is simple, efficient and effective. For that reason, systems and procedures that are technologically inadequate should be replaced by ones that are simple and easy to use.

There is a need for team leaders to revisit the developmental progressions with their team members at the beginning and end of every school year to ensure that the progressions are still current and valid. All members of the teams should be familiar with any updates on the computer network, the school's facilities and timetables. Any new school leaders and leadership teams need to be informed and brought on side with the system. Data discussions need to take place at the beginning of each year, and there must be a complete avoidance of 'watering down' the process. The teams and team leaders need to refresh their approach to collaborative decision-making, to the idea of challenge rather than sharing, and to a focus on evidence rather than inference, and they need to practise these things at the beginning of each year.

It is helpful if schools have contact with other schools that have adopted the same approach to the use of assessment for teaching. Experienced PLT leaders from other schools can be a very useful resource. The PLT leaders in all schools should lead by example in maintaining the action research cycle implemented by the teams. The discussion on professional development should always focus on explicit, focused and targeted teaching using differentiated instruction for different levels of development among the students. These are important requirements for team leader networks and should be maintained in the meeting agendas.

Why is succession planning important?

Leaders will move, retire and leave the system, and new leaders must be ready to step up to the position. Therefore, the importance of a network of experienced leaders is great. There needs to be a maintenance of action research records across schools so that new leaders can access information that will be helpful to them in organising, running and sharing their field team meetings. There needs to be continuous networking of PLT group leaders. They should agree to meet regularly once per term – perhaps in the twilight meeting. Among those team leaders, a leadership group needs to emerge that is responsible for convening the meeting, seeking funding to support it and setting an agenda that will keep the team leaders engaged. Each PLT should have a deputy or a proxy who can attend the team leaders' meetings should the regular leader be unable to attend. This will provide an opportunity for the other team members to learn what happens at the team leaders' meetings, and this in turn can help to support the team leader at school. There should be a folder on the school server that maintains up-to-date information about strategies and materials as well as information from other schools' contacts and lists of experienced people who are willing to share advice. Once it becomes available, this will be an invaluable resource for all teams.

The network of team leaders itself should have an induction plan for new leaders as they come on board. This will lead to the leaders themselves finding a way of developing the skills and attitudes of team leaders as they join and give them assistance in running team leaders' meetings and reinforcing the PLT procedures.

Appendix C
School leaders and assessment

Michael Francis and Patrick Griffin

This appendix has been written specifically for busy school leaders who would like to get an overview of 'assessment for teaching' before tackling the level of detail provided in the book as a whole. It summarises the theoretical basis and the practical application of the program described in the book, spelling out the nature of the support needed and the responsibilities to be exercised if the program is to succeed.

The primary reason for teaching is to facilitate learning. The primary reason for schools to exist is to maximise that learning. The primary role of the school leader is to ensure that such maximisation occurs.

In a study on evidence-based teaching of literacy – the Literacy Assessment Project – conducted by the University of Melbourne in partnership with the Catholic Education Office (Melbourne) over a 10-year period, outstanding early results were observed in some schools. The study was designed to test the effectiveness of using evidence to identify the point on a developmental progression at which students were most ready to learn, so that reading comprehension teaching could be targeted to that point. The purpose of the project was to build teachers' assessment knowledge and skills so they could use assessment data to inform the teaching of literacy. Students were tested at the beginning of the school year to identify their position on a developmental progression, and then taught the necessary skills to move along the progression to the next level. This approach represents a reversal of standard teaching practice in which assessment occurs only after instruction is complete. In the standard approach, assessment is for, or of, learning. In this approach, *assessment is for teaching*.

In the Literacy Assessment Project, a second testing period later in the school year showed that all students could improve. However, the rate of improvement among students at some schools was higher than it was at others. At schools where the greatest gains were made, teaching strategies were shared and discussed by teams of teachers who challenged each other to support their teaching practices with evidence. The teachers in these teams brought a range of observations and experiences to their discussions, but they also ensured that their colleagues did not persist with comfortable or familiar practices that were proving to be ineffective. The view that some students were simply unresponsive to even the best forms of teaching was challenged with evidence that, if teaching is targeted to the level of development demonstrated by students, *all students can learn*.

The purpose of this appendix is to help you as a school leader understand the nature of assessment for teaching, and the benefits that can flow to students, teachers and school leaders from the effective implementation of appropriately supported and differentiated teaching at the point where students are ready to learn. It is also to help you understand your role and your responsibilities in making this happen, and to ensure the sustainability of the program.

Anticipated benefits accruing to teachers and schools using assessment for teaching are:

- improved student learning outcomes
- improved monitoring, analysis and use of assessment data
- greater understanding of student learning needs based on the adoption of a developmental model of learning that focuses on what students can do as a starting point for identifying teaching interventions
- growth in teacher subject, pedagogical and metacognitive knowledge based on increased teacher professional collaboration
- increased evaluation by teachers themselves of their own teaching effectiveness in relation to student achievement over time
- increased levels of teacher trust and empowerment as agents of change
- increased use of the research base and external expertise to provide new perspectives and/or new knowledge.

These goals can be achieved if the procedures outlined in this book, and summarised in this appendix, are implemented. For this to happen, you have a critical role to play. School leaders need to understand what is expected of their teachers in this program, and to help them monitor and support associated changes in teaching practices. Unless changes in teaching practices take place, there can be no expectation of improved performances of the order already being experienced in many schools where the procedures are followed precisely.

It is therefore important – indeed essential – that as a school leader who is considering implementing assessment for teaching, you:

- understand the nature and purpose of the research
- understand the program in which teachers are engaged
- provide the necessary support to teachers
- understand and interpret the results to help formulate supportive policy within your school to assist teachers in improving student learning.

We already know that without the support and engagement of school leaders, the program does not improve student learning as much as in schools where school leadership is fully informed and engaged in the process. Anecdotally, we are able to link lower levels of engagement and support by school leadership to lower performing cohorts of students. Similarly, we are able to link higher performing and higher gain schools to high levels of implementation and procedures supported by engaged school leaders and school leadership teams. We also know that where school leaders enrol teachers and students in the program without consulting them first, they do not perform as well as in schools where teachers volunteer to participate. Schools where teachers are told to participate do not necessarily follow the instructions of the program. This leads to lower levels of performance.

As a school leader, when considering whether or not to introduce 'assessment for teaching' into your school, we encourage you to work with your teachers to determine whether or not they are ready. Just as students have a point of readiness to learn, it is clear that schools and teachers have a point of readiness to participate in this program.

Building readiness to introduce 'assessment for teaching' in a school requires open discussion and consideration of the theory, the evidence, what is involved and what support is needed. Starting without this will condemn the program to failure.

The key elements of 'assessment for teaching', and the ways in which these elements support learning, are as follows.

1 Teaching is guided by what students have learned and what they are ready to learn. In other words, rather than students being 'at, on, above or below expectations' at a particular age – a characteristic of a deficit model – they are described as being at a level of development on a learning progression, regardless of what level their peers may be on. This focuses teaching at the point of individual student need rather than at what is expected of them due to grade level, age, language or socio-economic background.

2 Teachers need to have a common, shared and articulated understanding of the hierarchical nature of learning in their teaching areas. This focuses teachers on the developmental progression or steps that students typically take in learning new skills. It emphasises the need for shared understanding about targeted teaching interventions for each step of the progression.

3 'Every student has a zone of proximal development, and every student can and will learn if teachers can scaffold at and around that zone' (Griffin & Care 2009, p. 58). The zone of proximal development is the zone between the level at which a student can do things without assistance and the level that is beyond their current capacity. Between these two levels is the zone in which the student can succeed with the help of an adult or a more capable peer. Teachers need to develop an understanding of how assessment is used systematically to identify a student's zone of proximal development (ZPD), because that is the point at which the student is most ready to learn, and at which intervention will have the greatest impact (Vygotsky 1986). The existing rhetoric of assessment for learning allows an exemption to the teacher if the students do not learn – it is

the students' fault. If assessment is regarded as an integral part of good teaching, there is no exemption.

4   Teachers work collaboratively in professional learning teams (PLT), not alone. Teachers observe and encourage each other and mutually develop solutions and strategies. Teachers are accountable to each other to ensure that strategies used are evaluated in terms of student outcomes. The collaborative teamwork involves some tension. We encourage teachers to challenge each other by asking what changes would be observable in student outcomes if their colleagues' ideas were implemented.

5   The search for evidence – what students do, say, make and write – is the focus of the work of the PLT. Evidence about what students can do defines the level at which they are operating rather than comparing them with an expected standard. This level is where teaching needs to be directed. Because of this, evidence is examined carefully. This requires a willingness on the part of teachers to engage in professional challenge that also serves to clarify and refine teacher thinking.

6   Evidence is interpreted within a developmental continuum that allows for the identification of a student's ZPD. There are cumulative steps of increasing complexity – for example, in reading comprehension. Using specifically constructed tests that reflect the cumulative steps of increasing complexity in the selected skill, the teacher identifies the point where student understanding becomes inconsistent. This occurs in the student's ZPD, where teaching is to be targeted and learning scaffolded.

7   Teachers – and schools – develop a systematic method of collecting data, a way of interpreting it and systematically making the best use of it. This is facilitated by professional development. This book helps teachers understand how to design and collect valid data, how to record and interpret reports and how to link these to targeted and explicit intervention focused on a level on a developmental progression.

8   A paradigm shift in the teaching culture from deficit to development, in which it is believed all students can and will learn if their ZPD can be identified (Griffin & Care 2009, p. 58), requires changes in teacher language. These are perhaps best expressed in the following principles, which are explained at the end of this appendix in terms of both their meaning and their rationale for use:

- Assessment is for teaching.
- All students can learn.
- Focus on development, not deficit.
- Report skills, not scores.

- Use evidence rather than inference.
- Use more than tests.
- Do, say, make and write.
- Teach to the construct, not the test.
- Target teaching.
- Talk about students, not teachers.
- Identify 'our' students, not 'my' students.
- Challenge rather than share.
- Question practice.
- Collaborate, challenge and check.

The creation of PLT, in which teachers collaboratively examine evidence from their own students and their own practice, supports this change. The use of external expertise to support teacher and PLT professional inquiry, and the acquisition of new knowledge and skills, adds further support.

9 School leaders play a crucial role. They understand the goals, purpose and language of the program and articulate them clearly. They organise the school to ensure that necessary infrastructure and resource support are provided, including dedicated times and locations for regular PLT meetings. They also link financial resource allocation to needs as indicated by evidence, and to strategies that can be linked to improved student educational outcomes.

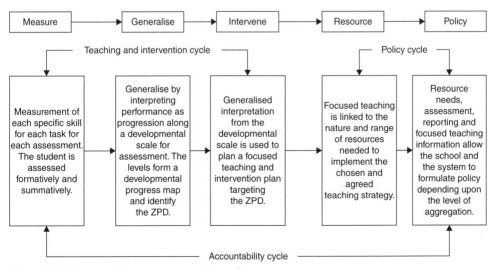

Figure C.1 *Five steps from measurement to policy*

The framework

Griffin's Five Steps from Measurement to Policy provides the framework around which the use of assessment for teaching has been developed. This is shown in Figure C.1. This five-step process (adapted from Griffin 2007) shifts the emphasis of assessment on to targeted intervention, and illustrates how assessment data can be used to inform school policy directly. This is a shift in emphasis from the usual way in which assessment is used: to identify problems that teachers are then expected to fix. Under this process, testing programs stop at the first step – measurement – and report total scores. The appropriate point of intervention is rarely identified, and subsequent teaching tends to focus on what the students *cannot* do (the deficit approach). This results in resources not being matched appropriately and then, at the wider policy level, critics of testing programs charging that testing does not improve learning. This is justified when teachers – mainly because of the unhelpful ways in which assessment information is presented to them – do not know how to use the information to improve their teaching. However, if a developmental progression or criterion-referenced framework is used to its maximum advantage – in a developmental approach based on skills rather than scores – it can and should change

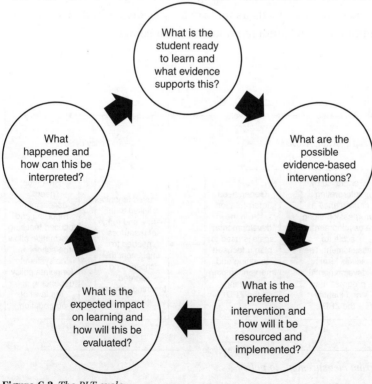

Figure C.2 *The PLT cycle*

teaching and learning. This potential to improve teaching and learning is what the five-step approach represents.

The five-step process leads to a set of questions that aid the practical application of the framework in the classroom. The resulting PLT cycle, shown in Figure C.2, focuses on the practical task of implementing policy in the classroom. It is designed for the implementation of teaching strategies and the assessment of their effectiveness. The cycle renews whenever a review of progress is conducted. The detailed implementation of this cycle is discussed in Chapter 4.

Professional learning teams

When using assessment for teaching, teachers are organised into PLT. Many schools have PLT, but their natures vary considerably. Some PLT are administrative groups, year-level teams or subject departments called by another name and carrying out traditional functions. Others have a generalised professional learning responsibility in their school. The following description of an assessment-for-teaching PLT is of one in which the focus is on student learning outcomes, with continuous teacher professional learning a corollary. The structure and functioning of the PLT are designed explicitly to support these aims.

The PLT typically consists of approximately four to eight members, including a team leader. Each team takes responsibility for a cohort of students, has a specific focus and set of responsibilities, and follows the PLT cycle.

In following the PLT cycle, members of the PLT collaboratively and systematically use evidence – what students do, say, make and write – from testing, combined with evidence from student work, to identify the zone of proximal development for individual students, and to identify groupings of students operating at the same level. Members of the PLT question the evidence assembled to ensure they get an accurate reading of a student's ZPD, on which subsequent teaching interventions will be built, and take joint responsibility for all students covered by the PLT. The PLT uses PLT logs to identify and document learning goals and strategies targeted at student ZPD, and identifies the resources needed to implement those strategies. The PLT creates timelines to evaluate student progress and critically evaluates the effectiveness of strategies and resources used, retaining in a teaching resource bank those strategies that are effective and discarding those that are not. Information from PLT processes feeds directly into school planning and budgeting. Because it establishes and monitors clear learning goals for each student, the PLT knows when the goals are achieved.

The PLT is formally recognised as a major part of the school planning and decision-making structure, and has documented responsibilities. It has support from school leadership and operates in a climate of mutual trust that encourages members to take risks with their learning. The value of the PLT is acknowledged by the fact that it formally meets in school time for a minimum of one hour once per fortnight, and PLT members are allocated an equivalent amount of time to prepare for each meeting. School leaders are required to demonstrate understanding of the role of the PLT and put in place mechanisms to support its operation and development. In this program, school leaders who may be represented on PLT see themselves as learners. They articulate a vision that is focused on student learning outcomes, and actively monitor its implementation. They tangibly support the implementation of new teaching and learning practices linked to improvements in student learning outcomes and ensure achievements are celebrated.

PLT members, and the PLT as a whole, monitor both their own and team development, and take developmentally appropriate steps to build their own knowledge and skills. They consciously work to improve team functioning and effectiveness. PLT members are aware of their own theories of practice, and willingly negotiate new practice when there is clear evidence about how and why it should change.

Implementing the PLT cycle

In working within the framework of Griffin's 'Five Steps from Measurement to Policy', the PLT responds to the questions introduced in the PLT cycle, which manages the practical application of the framework in the classroom.

The first question asks two things:

1 What is the student ready to learn?

2 What is the evidence of this?

To answer these questions, it is necessary to possess some background information about developmental frameworks, and the collection and organisation of assessment data.

Understanding and using assessment data

The first step in using assessment for teaching is to assess evidence of a student's specific capabilities by reference to a developmental framework. The developmental framework includes what is being taught, learned and assessed, and evidence consists of observable actions – what the student can do, say, make or write, thereby demonstrating a level of understanding.

At its most basic, a developmental framework or progression describes a hierarchy of skills, behaviours or knowledge that is either real or hypothesised. If it is real, it has been empirically demonstrated – in other words, there is a significant amount of data that supports the nature and order of the competencies described. There may be exceptions to its universal application, but we can rely on it to be mostly true. If it is hypothesised, it is still a theory. This is not to say that hypothesising is wrong – every empirical framework starts off as a hypothetical one, and it is much better to have a theoretical framework than none at all, because if we had no hypotheses around increasing levels of competency, teaching interventions would be random.

There are, however, numerous examples of empirically established developmental frameworks. Some of these are generic and need to be interpreted or adapted within particular contexts, while others are specifically targeted. Examples of generic developmental frameworks are Bloom's Revised Taxonomy, Biggs' and Collis's Structure of the Observed Learning Outcome (SOLO) (both of which look at cognitive development), Krathwohl's Taxonomy of the Affective Domain (which considers attitudes and behaviours) and Dreyfus's Model of Skill Acquisition (which considers skills or abilities). Examples of specifically targeted frameworks include the Progressions of Literacy, Numeracy and Problem Solving Development that were developed and tested as part of the LAP and ALP projects and that helped inform the development of this book. Teachers can confidently use these progressions to plot what students can do and what they need to do next. Examples of each of these developmental frameworks or progressions can be found in Chapter 2.

The use of developmental frameworks is the antithesis to a deficit approach to assessment and teaching. A deficit approach focuses on describing and then attempting to remediate what a student cannot do. In a developmental approach, the use of developmental frameworks allows teachers to work from where the student is at and what the student can do. The approach allows teachers to critically analyse student performance data to plan, implement and evaluate teaching interventions, and to progressively build increasingly sophisticated understandings of learning and teaching.

If teachers are to adopt this approach, they require more than the mere imparting of new information. If they are going to change their practice, they need to see the value of what they are doing, and to aid them in this, their own progress can be assessed. Their engagement with developmental progressions and evidence-based teaching, which involves the systematic use of data, can be applied not only to the developmental levels of individual students but also to the developmental levels of teachers and PLT. To truly work within a developmental construct, the teacher, the PLT and the school leaders must be able to locate their own development on a relevant developmental framework or progression – one that refers to PLT operations, the challenging of evidence, knowledge of subject matter and so on. Then they can take developmentally appropriate steps to improve their own skills in the light of that information. A developmental progression covering the whole assessment-for-teaching approach is provided at the end of this appendix. Other progressions for teachers and PLT engaging in this approach are provided in Chapters 4 and 5.

Assessment for teaching in a developmental learning framework

If assessment is for teaching and is the starting point for learning, then teaching must *focus on where the student is at*, regardless of an expected standard. It is this point that must be identified for each student. The developmental learning framework used in this book resulted from an amalgamation of the theory and practice of three scholars: Lev Vygotsky, Robert Glaser and Georg Rasch. A detailed description of how the work of these three scholars has been synthesised into the developmental model of learning is included in Chapter 2.

Briefly, Vygotsky argued that the ZPD is the point at which the student is most ready to learn, and where teaching must be focused. Glaser described a theoretical framework of assessment interpretation known as 'criterion-referenced interpretation'. Underlying his concept is the notion of a continuum of knowledge acquisition ranging from no proficiency to high proficiency, where the level of proficiency is indicated by behavioural criteria. When measuring a student's performance, their level of proficiency or competency is located along an increasing continuum of achievement, as indicated by their behaviour. Rasch, using latent trait theory and mathematical modelling, was able to formally measure the location of students' ability and difficulty of test items together on a scale. This provided a mathematical model that could be used within a criterion-referenced framework to link the relative positions of a student and an item on the developmental continuum to an interpretation of what a student is ready to learn.

The combination of these three theories allows assessment results to be interpreted in terms of Glaser's levels of increasing competence and, when interpreted in a Rasch-like manner, to provide an indicator of student ZPD – the point of intervention identified by Vygotsky, where learning can be scaffolded. Thus the combination of the three theories allows teachers' assessment practices to move away from the interpretation of a test score as a piece of summative information about the student's past. Interpretation of the test score becomes the starting point for instruction, indicating where a student's ZPD is located – that is, where they are ready to learn – and focuses attention on the future rather than the past.

The challenge for educators is to identify students' emerging skills and provide the right support at the right time at the right level. Teachers need to be able to identify the ZPD, or the point of readiness to learn, in the domain of learning being mastered. Traditionally, teachers are not trained to use test score data to identify the ZPD for students across particular disciplines. Identifying the ZPD is difficult without developmental continua, and impossible if working with a deficit model.

There are a number of ways in which student ZPD can be identified. The first is through the evidence provided by the use of tests and instruments that have been designed with reference to specific developmental frameworks, and that give a reading on student ZPD. The authors of this book have designed such a series of tests – on reading, numeracy and problem-solving – which can be accessed via the website that accompanies the book. In the program for which these tests were designed, students are tested in reading, numeracy or problem-solving at two points in time each year, initially to establish a performance baseline for each student and thereafter to gauge progress. Once the data are available, it becomes the focus of PLT discussions, in particular those that challenge inferences about student learning. Initially, this is about whether the evidence from the tests confirms teacher knowledge of student performance and placement on a developmental progression and, if not, what other evidence is needed to establish student ZPD accurately. Subsequently, the findings provide the basis for planning teaching interventions targeted at student ZPD. The management of these tests, and the use of the data they provide, are covered in Chapter 3. The authors of this book have also designed a developmental instrument for students with additional needs (SWANs), which performs a similar function. For more detail on this, see Chapter 12.

The second way of getting a reading on student ZPD, especially for areas not covered by tests designed for the purpose, is through the use of Guttman charts. By using a Guttman chart, teachers and PLT can process evidence of student achievement with reference to a developmental framework to identify student ZPDs and common ZPD groups in a learning domain. The information provided by the combination of the theories of Glaser, Rasch and Vygotsky is very important, but such data can be overwhelming if it is not organised in a way that will help PLT manage their teaching effectively. A Guttman chart analysis provides an effective tool to *group* students based on the skills they can demonstrate, and to identify what needs to be taught next to each group of students. Guttman charts are particularly useful when related online testing methodologies are not available in the domain in which teachers are working.

Development and use of Guttman charts

In 1944, Louis Guttman published the steps to produce a *scalogram*, a simple method to gain a picture of qualitative data from questionnaires or tests without the need for an understanding of statistics or time-consuming mathematical analyses. Griffin has built on Guttman's scalogram using the work of Glaser, Rasch and Vygotsky to create a Guttman chart for teachers that allows them to use assessment data and a few basic spreadsheeting skills to get a picture of their class's current learning and future learning needs.

A Guttman chart provides a visual representation of a Guttman analysis, which orders student achievement according to ability and assessment items (questions, observations, survey responses, etc.) according to difficulty. Using this method, students with *similar* skills can be identified and grouped together, and PLT are provided

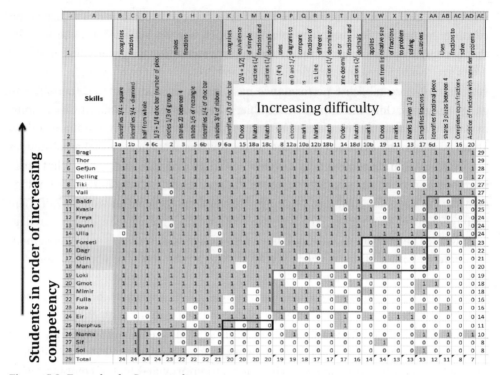

Figure C.3 *Example of a Guttman chart*

with a clear picture of what each group of students is ready to learn. An example of a Guttman chart highlighting ZPD groupings is provided in Figure C.3.

Creation of a Guttman chart provides the PLT with a means of organising data in a meaningful way to facilitate focused discussion and planning for teaching interventions. It gives teachers the chance to generalise from the results on a specific assessment to see student progress on the broader ideas, or construct, underpinning the subject area. Therefore, student progress can be tracked against the construct and teaching interventions can be planned with the aim of developing the student in the underlying construct, not simply remedying deficiencies shown in the skills included in one specific assessment. Again, the findings using a Guttman chart must be subject to challenge by members of the PLT to ensure that accurate readings of student ZPD are made. A detailed discussion of how to create and interpret a Guttman chart is provided in Chapter 10.

Reviewing student progress

Having assembled evidence of student achievement against a developmental framework, student progress is then reviewed to identify the students' ZPD. This is done collaboratively in the PLT meeting. Each member of the PLT takes to the meeting their data on three students (two if it is a large PLT). The students should be at different but agreed levels on a developmental progression. The teacher nominating each student for discussion assembles as much current evidence as possible to identify the student's ZPD. This includes tests and instruments that have been designed with reference to a specific developmental framework and that give a reading on student ZPD, as well as a variety of other assessments, from student reports to work samples and behavioural observations. This discussion should use the language of evidence (what the students do, say, make and write) and infer student knowledge based on the evidence. However, all inferences should be challenged by the team by reference to observable change in student behaviours. The evidence gathered about a student needs to be examined by asking questions such as:

- What can the student do independently?
- What is the student ready to learn?
- What evidence makes this a reasonable assessment of the student's readiness to learn?

The PLT considers each student at the same developmental level before moving to a new level. By the end of the meeting, the PLT should have agreed on the developmental level for each student presented. By following this process, members of the PLT build their understanding of the characteristics of the selected developmental levels, the nature of evidence, the next step for each student and their shared responsibility for student learning ('our students not my students'). As the PLT becomes more skilled in presenting and evaluating evidence, this process can be conducted much more quickly.

Planning evidence-based teaching interventions

PLT decision-making now shifts to the planning of teaching interventions targeted explicitly at student ZPD. This encompasses the second and third questions of the PLT cycle. It involves decisions about what intervention strategy is best for the student in relation to their ZPD – in other words, what they are ready to learn. The PLT takes collective responsibility for determining the teaching intervention for each developmental level, with the classroom teachers implementing the intervention.

Most teachers will find that their classes consist of a range of students at differing levels of development and with differing learning needs and styles. However, this does not mean that the PLT must produce 25 individual learning plans. It is usually found that in any class the majority of students can be grouped into four or five ability groups in relation to the domain being taught. By working together, members of the PLT can find synergies to address the needs of the students in each group.

Once student learning intentions have been identified, it is important for the PLT to work together to devise the teaching strategies, learning activities and associated resource allocation (which includes not just the physical resources to deliver the lesson but also administrative support and any other support that may be needed by the teacher, such as up-skilling in some areas). These should be considered in this order and considered only in the light of their ability to deliver the explicit learning intention. For this reason, a PLT log has been designed to provide a step-by-step guide and to serve as a record of planning decisions made by the PLT. This log is illustrated in Chapter 4, and can be kept in an electronic form on the school server. The PLT should complete the log for a student who is representative of all the students grouped at the designated developmental level, to plan an intervention that can be generalised to that group of students.

The whole PLT needs to be involved in this discussion. Over time, the PLT will build up a bank of successful teaching strategies for students at each developmental level. Because they have been documented using the PLT log, they can be reviewed and discussed. If successful, they can be used as the basis for subsequent learning programs.

The fourth question of the PLT cycle requires the PLT to stipulate expected evidence of student progress. What is it that the student will be able to do, say, make or write that will demonstrate the acquisition of the intended skill? How will acquisition of the skill be checked? This information needs to be included on the PLT log along with a firm date for review of student learning outcomes on completion of the teaching intervention. When such information is explicit, teaching is focused and the effectiveness of the teaching intervention is more easily evaluated.

The fifth question of the PLT cycle is the evaluation question. What were the results? What worked? What did not work? What evidence of student improvement supports your answers to these questions? What are the implications for future teaching?

When the review is complete, the cycle begins again with the PLT considering what the students are now ready to learn.

PLT protocols

Using formal protocols focuses the attention of the PLT to the task at hand. Protocols structure the discussion and give all PLT members a chance to talk and an opportunity to listen. Protocols include adherence to start and finish times, keeping to the agenda (guided by the PLT cycle and the PLT log) and the use of language appropriate for the task.

Language of evidence and language of challenge

In order for the PLT to work successfully, attention needs to be paid by PLT members to the nature and use of language in PLT meetings. Teachers need to draw on a *language of evidence* to make inferences about student development. What a student understands, thinks or believes is not directly observable. We observe students' overt behaviours or actions – that is, what they do, say, make or write. It is from these actions that we infer student achievement or skills, and it is these actions that should be the focus of discussions in the PLT.

Examination of each form of evidence should focus on what a student can do and what the student is ready to learn. The language is important. It reinforces the developmental framework that underpins learning. Discussions that focus on what the student is not able to do will encourage the PLT to operate within a deficit framework. This will lead to talk of 'fixing' gaps in students' learning rather than focusing discussion on moving them forward by scaffolding – direct intervention at adjacent levels of learning by a teacher or a better informed student.

In successful PLT, teachers also need a *language of challenge*. Team members should support their statements about student learning by providing evidence of the things they have observed the student do, say, make or write. PLT members should be encouraged to challenge themselves and each other to ensure any inferences are based on sound evidence. Some examples of the questions that can be asked are:

- If I implement this strategy with my students, what am I likely to see them do? How will it change their observable behaviour – what they do, say, make or write?
- When you say that this strategy was successful with your students, what specific changes did you observe? Would you recommend its use?

It is important to note that the emphasis is to challenge the evidence or inferences rather than criticise or judge. That is, challenge should never be personal. Attention should also be paid to vocal tone and body language. It is important that all members of the team work collaboratively and in support of one another. The team leader acts as a facilitator to establish clear ground rules for participation, and helps to draw out the concerns of all PLT members. This is achieved through establishing a norm of listening, reflecting and challenging, but not criticising.

Elements of effective PLT

Like the individual students for whom they are responsible PLT are 'works in progress', and the current level of success at which a PLT uses developmental continua to inform teaching and learning plans relies on a number of conditions. Experience with PLT across a range of contexts suggests that, ideally, they are made up of between four and eight members, but no more. This permits the support of a team of colleagues while making sure that everybody in the team has an opportunity to contribute to discussion. Successful PLT usually share the following characteristics:

- the engagement and interest of all team members
- a willingness to collaborate and support one another
- acceptance of shared responsibility for all students
- a shift from thinking in terms of 'my class' to 'our students'
- a commitment to the belief that every child can learn
- the practice of challenging rather than merely sharing ideas
- an understanding of the use of student assessment outcomes to inform decision-making, with an emphasis on evidence rather than teacher inference.

Table C.1 *Assessment-for-teaching principles and derived developmental progression*

Level 5 Expert teacher	Approaches student–teacher and teacher–teacher interactions developmentally. Uses a sophisticated evidence-based decision-making approach to professional practice that is common, responsive and transparent. Makes subtle and refined discriminations about student point of readiness to learn and targeted teaching. Takes collective responsibility and holds individuals and teams accountable for student learning.		
Level 4 Proficient teacher	Operates from a developmental paradigm and considers a range of options when targeting teaching and assessment.	Interprets multiple and varied sources of evidence to identify student ZPD based on deep understanding of the hierarchical nature of learning. Collaboratively interrogates evidence to validate conclusions about student learning, clarifying understandings and fostering common practice. Embraces shared accountability.	Formally engages in regular conversations about student learning supported by structures and procedures.
Level 3 Competent teacher	Focuses on underlying skills and adjusts teaching approaches to meet the student's point of readiness to learn in the classroom using a developmental continuum. Uses structures and procedures to support differentiated teaching and assessment.	Routinely collects multiple sources of evidence to identify student achievement, and examines and uses evidence of student learning outcomes in decision-making.	Engages in procedures and routines to support a team approach to professional practice (e.g. joint planning, team teaching and classroom visits). This includes formal discussions between or across year levels or disciplines to investigate student achievement. Acknowledges shared accountability.
Level 2 Advanced beginner teacher	Recognises a range of student learning needs in terms of additional assistance or stimulus, and seeks adjustments to address those needs. Distinguishes between skills and scores.	Distinguishes between evidence and inference about student learning and seeks a range of sources of evidence. Shares instructional activities, strategies and resources based on perceived effectiveness.	Informally compares their students/classes with other teachers, shares aspects of their work and provides feedback about outcomes. Infers shared accountability. Informally discusses individual students in terms of actions they need to take.

Level 1 Novice teacher	Typically teaches to the 'expected' level of performance while recognising that some students need additional assistance.	Focuses on rehearsing responses to a set of defined tasks to maximise scores.	Assesses summatively, usually in the form of tests, with results reported out of a hypothetical perfect score.	Infers learning based on teaching of subject content.	Typically engages in top-down communication and basic information sharing. Avoids contentious issues.	Works and prepares for teaching individually. Addresses teaching as a private activity. 'My class …' Views accountability as personal.	Talks about their own teaching with focus on management, control and content.
Principles	All students can learn Development, not deficit	Teach to the construct, not to the test Skills, not scores	Do, say, make, write Use more than tests	Evidence, not inference	Challenge, not share	Peer accountability – 'our' students, not 'mine'	Talk about students, not teachers
	Developmental learning		Evidence		Collaboration		
Beliefs and values	Knowledge, skills and practices						

These elements are not preconditions, however. As previously pointed out, to truly work within a developmental construct, the teacher and the PLT (and school leaders) also need to be able to locate their own development on a relevant developmental framework or progression. This needs to identify development in terms of PLT operations, challenging evidence, knowledge of subject-matter and so on, and enable teachers to take developmentally appropriate steps to improve their skills in these areas. Successful PLT don't just happen – they are forged by doing their work.

Table C.1 provides a developmental progression, based on Dreyfus's model of skill acquisition, which illustrates how the assessment-for-teaching principles and the developmental progressions come together. It is worth copying and attaching to your office wall. Your teachers will work through the levels of this developmental progression and will have, or build, an understanding of how they come together. The language of the principles will also be part of the discourse of teachers in school.

School leader responsibilities

As a school leader, your role in maximising the potential outcomes of the use of assessment for teaching is significant, as are the potential benefits. School leadership plays an active and central role in:

- providing goals or targets for student learning
- monitoring and collecting evidence of progress
- using this information to stimulate teacher reflection
- putting in place organisational arrangements to support new professional learning and practices, especially time and physical resources
- participating with, motivating and encouraging teachers
- celebrating achievement.

School leaders can have enormous influence on the success or otherwise of the use of assessment for teaching in a school. They can actively support it through the processes outlined above, they can allow the initiative to wither through inattention, or they can kill it outright by assigning it a low priority and denying recognition and necessary support. School leaders may become members of PLT, though it is not a requirement. What *is* necessary is that they build an understanding of the theory, the practice and the potential of the program to focus the work of the school on its core business: improved student learning. At the same time, it is essential that school leaders ensure that the necessary support mechanisms are in place. At a minimum these include:

- symbolic leadership of the program by articulating its purpose, its significance for the school, and the commitments and nature of the support – both immediate and ongoing – that it will be given

- PLT of four to eight participants, and the appointment of a leader for each PLT, preferably as part of the school's formal leadership structure
- provision of formal meeting time during school hours (this includes meeting time adjacent to the school day) of at least one hour per fortnight, and allowance for preparation time
- protection of the work of the PLT, which means that the focus of PLT work is on assessment-for-teaching practices and processes, and the time is not taken up with other responsibilities
- ensuring resources are available to PLT to implement evidence-based teaching (this can relate to flexibility regarding classroom and teacher arrangements, as much as flexibility in subject or department budgets to purchase specific resources)
- monitoring and encouraging the work of PLT
- discussing the work of PLT and the results in school-wide fora.

References

Anderson, IW (ed.), Krathwohl, DR (ed.), Airasian, PW, Cruikshank, KA, Mayer, RE, Pintrich, PR, Raths, J & Wittrock, MC 2001, *A taxonomy for learning, teaching, and assessing: A revision of Bloom's Taxonomy of Educational Objectives*, Longman, New York.

Bagnato, S, Smith-Jones, J, Matesa, M & McKeting-Esterle, E 2006, 'Research foundations for using clinical judgement (informed opinion) for early intervention eligibility determination', *Cornerstones*, vol. 2, no. 3, pp. 1–4.

Biggs, JB & Collis, KF 1982, *Evaluating the quality of learning: The SOLO Taxonomy (Structure of the Observed Learning Outcome)*, Academic Press, New York.

Bloom, BS 1956, *Taxonomy of educational objectives: The classification of educational goals by a committee of college and university examiners*, D McKay, New York.

Bloom, BS, Engelhart, MD, Furst, EJ, Hill, WH & Krathwohl, DR 1956, *Taxonomy of educational objectives: the classification of educational goals. Handbook 1: Cognitive domain*, Longman, New York.

Burbules, NC 1993, 'Savage inequalities: An interview with Jonathan Kozol', *Education Theory*, vol. 43, no. 1, pp. 55–70.

Care, E, Griffin, P, Hutchinson, D & Zhang, Z forthcoming, 'Large-scale testing and its contribution to learning', in C Wyatt-Smith, V Klenowski & P Colbert (eds), *The enabling power of assessment*, Springer, Dordrecht.

Coles-Janess, B & Griffin, P 2009, 'Mapping transitions in interpersonal learning for students with additional needs', *Australasian Journal of Special Education*, vol. 33, no. 2, pp. 141–50.

Csikzentmihalyi, M 1990, *Flow: The psychology of optimal experience*, Harper and Row, New York.

Department of Education and Early Childhood Development (DEECD) 2009, *Pathways to re-engagement through flexible learning options: A policy direction for consultation*, Victorian Government, Melbourne.

——2012, *Student attitudes to school survey*, DEECD, Melbourne.

Dewey, J 1938, *Experience and education*, Collier Macmillan, New York.

Dreyfus, HL & Dreyfus, SE 2004, 'From Socrates to expert systems: The limits and dangers of calculative rationality', viewed 12 September 2013, <http://socrates.berkeley.edu/~hdreyfus/html/paper_socrates.html>.

Dreyfus, SE 2004, 'The five-stage model of adult skill acquisition', *Bulletin of Science, Technology & Society*, vol. 24, no. 3, pp. 177–81.

Dreyfus, SE & Dreyfus, HL 1980, *A five-stage model of the mental activities involved in directed skill acquisition*, University of California, Berkeley, CA.

DuFour, R, Eaker, R & Many, T 2010, *Learning by doing: A handbook for professional learning communities at work*, 2nd ed., Solution Tree Press, Bloomington, IN.

Fowler-Finn, T 2013, *Leading instructional rounds in education: A facilitator's guide*, Harvard Education Press, Cambridge, MA.

Frost, K & Ridsdale, R 2012a, 'Curriculum teams' curriculum', adapted from the Wellington Network, Warragul Regional College, Warragul, Vic.

——2012b, *Formative assessment strategies booklet*, Warragul Regional College, Warragul, Vic.

Fullan, M, Cuttress, C & Kilcher, A 2005, 'Eight forces for leaders of change', *Journal of Staff Development*, vol. 26, no. 4, pp. 54–64.

Gentile, C 1992, *Exploring new methods for collecting students' school-based writing: NAEP's 1990 portfolio study*, National Centre for Education Statistics, Washington, DC.

Glaser, R 1963, 'Instructional technology and the measurement of learning outcomes: Some questions', *American Psychologist*, vol. 18, pp. 519–21.

——1981, 'The future of testing: A research agenda for cognitive psychology and psychometrics', *American Psychologist*, vol. 36, pp. 923–36.

Griffin, P 1970, 'Multilevel non-graded mathematics', *Vinculum*, vol. 7, no. 4, pp. 109–27.

——2001, 'Performance assessment of higher order thinking', paper presented at the annual conference of the American Education Research Association, Seattle, WA, 10 April.

——2007, 'The comfort of competence and the uncertainty of assessment', *Studies in Educational Evaluation*, no. 33, pp. 87–99.

——2009, 'Teachers' use of assessment data', in C Wyatt-Smith & JJ Cummings (eds), *Educational assessment in the 21st century*, Springer, Dordrecht, pp. 183–208.

Griffin, P & Care, E 2009, 'Assessment is for teaching', *Independence*, vol. 34, no. 2, pp. 56–9.

——2012, 'Pathways of educational leadership: Monitoring and developing skill levels among educational leaders in Australia', in L Volante (ed.), *Challenges in school leadership in the 21st century*, Springer, Dordrecht, pp. 95–120.

Griffin, P, Care, E, Francis, M, Hutchinson, D & Pavlovic, M 2012, 'The influence of teaching strategies on student achievement in higher order skills', paper presented at the ACER Research Conference 2012, Sydney.

Griffin, P, Care, E & McGaw, B 2012, 'The changing role of education and schools', in P Griffin, B McGaw & E Care (eds), *Assessment and teaching of 21st century skills*, Springer, Dordrecht, pp. 1–15.

Griffin, P, McGaw, B & Care, E (eds) 2012, *Assessment and teaching of 21st century skills*, Springer, Dordrecht.

Griffin, P, Murray, L, Care, E, Thomas, A & Perri, P 2010, 'Developmental assessment: Lifting literacy through professional learning teams', *Assessment in Education: Principles, Policy & Practice*, vol. 17, no. 4, pp. 383–97.

Griffin, P, Woods, K & Awwal, N 2012, *Abilities based learning and education support for students with additional needs: 2009–2011*, Assessment Research Centre, University of Melbourne, Melbourne.

Guttman, L 1950, 'The basis for scalogram analysis', in SA Stouffer et al. (eds), *Measurement and prediction*, Princeton University Press, Princeton, NJ, n. p.

Halverson, R, Grigg, J, Prichett, R & Thomas, C 2005, *The new instructional leadership: Creating data-driven instructional systems in schools*, WCER Working Paper No. 2005–9, Wisconsin Center for Education Research, Madison, WI.

Hattie, J, 2009, *Visible learning: A synthesis of over 800 meta-analyses relating to achievement*, Routledge, London.

Hesse, F, Buder, J, Care, E, Griffin, P & Sassenberg, K 2012, 'A framework for teachable collaborative problem solving skills', viewed 20 July 2013, <http://ATC21s.org>.

Juratowich, R [Warragul Regional College Principal] 2009, Interview with author.

Krathwohl, DR 2002, 'A revision of Bloom's Taxonomy: An overview', *Theory into Practice*, vol. 41, no. 4, pp. 212–18.

Krathwohl, DR, Anderson, LW & Bloom, BS 2001, *A taxonomy for learning, teaching, and assessing: A revision of Bloom's Taxonomy of educational objectives*, Longman, New York.

Krathwohl, DR, Bloom, BS & Masia, BB 1964, *Taxonomy of educational objectives. Handbook II: The affective domain*, Longman, New York.

——1971, *Taxonomy of educational objectives: The classification of educational goals. Handbook II: Affective domain*, Longman, New York.

Kubiszyn, T & Borich, G 2009, *Educational testing and measurement: Classroom application and practice*, Wiley Jossey-Bass, Hoboken, NJ.

Lamprianou, I & Athanasou, JA 2009, *A teacher's guide to educational assessment*, rev. ed., Sense, Rotterdam.

Leithwood, KA 1992, 'The move toward transformational leadership', *Educational Leadership*, vol. 49, no. 5, pp. 8–12.

McCloskey, G 1990, 'Selecting and using the Early Childhood Rating Scales', *Topics in Early Childhood Special Education*, vol. 10, no. 3, pp. 39–64.

McTighe, J & Wiggins, G 2004, *Understanding by design: Professional development workbook*, Association for Supervision & Curriculum Development, Alexandria, VA.

Miller, R 2011, *Vygotsky in perspective*, Cambridge University Press, Harvard, MA.

Payne, DA 2003, *Applied educational assessment*, Wadsworth Thomson Learning, Belmont, CA.

Platt, A & Tripp, C 2008, 'Communities that undermine learning', *Leadership*, September, pp. 18–22.

Rasch, G 1960, *Probabilistic models for some intelligence and attainment tests*, Neilson & Lydiche, Copenhagen.

——1980, *Some probabilistic models for the measurement of attainment and intelligence*, MESA Press, Chicago.

Roberts, E & Griffin, P 2009, 'Profiling transitions in emotional development for students with additional learning needs', *Australasian Journal of Special Education*, vol. 33, no. 2, pp. 151–60.

Santiago P, Donaldson, G, Herman J and Shewbridge C 2011, *OECD Review on Evaluation and Assessment Frameworks for Improving School Outcomes*, OECD, Sydney.

Scardamalia, M, Bransford, J, Kozma, B & Quellmalz, E 2010, 'New assessments and environments for knowledge building', in P Griffin, B McGaw & E Care (eds), *Assessment and teaching of 21st century skills*, Springer, Dordrecht, pp. 231–300.

Sergiovanni, TJ 1992, *Moral leadership: Getting to the heart of school improvement*, Jossey-Bass, San Francisco.

——2006, *The principalship: A reflective perspective*, 5th ed., Pearson Education, Boston.

Shulman, L 1987, 'Knowledge and teaching: Foundations of the new reform', *Harvard Educational Review*, vol. 15, no. 2, pp. 1–22.

Thorndike, EL 1920, 'A constant error in psychological ratings', *Journal of Applied Psychology*, vol. 4, no. 1, pp. 25–9.

Thurstone, LL 1927, 'A law of comparative judgement', *Psychological Review*, vol. 34, pp. 278–86.

Tomlinson, C 2008, 'The goals of differentiation', *Educational Leadership*, vol. 66, no. 3, pp. 26–31.

UNESCO 1994, *The Salamanca Statement and Framework for Action on Special Needs Education*, adopted by the World Conference on Special Needs Education: Access and Equity, Salamanca, Spain, 7–10 June.

United Nations, Department of Public Information 2006, Convention on the Rights of Persons with Disabilities, viewed 25 September 2012, <http://www.un.org/disabilities/convention/conventionfull.shtml>.

Universities Admission Centre 2012, *All about your ATAR*, viewed 12 September 2013, <http://www.uac.edu.au/documents/atar/All-About-Your-ATAR.pdf>.

US Department of Education 2012, *Individuals with Disabilities Education Act* (IDEA), viewed 25 September 2012, <http://idea.ed.gov>.

Victorian Department of Education and Early Childhood Development (DEECD) 2012, 'Abilities Based Learning and Education Support' (ABLES), viewed 26 September 2012, <http://www.education.vic.gov.au/healthwellbeing/wellbeing/ables.htm>.

Vygotsky, LS 1978, *Mind in society: The development of higher psychological processes*, eds M Cole, V John-Steiner, S Scribner & E Souberman, Harvard University Press, Cambridge, MA.

——1986, *Thought and language*, MIT Press, Boston.

——1993 [1929], *The collected works of LS Vygotsky, Volume 2: The fundamentals of defectology (abnormal psychology and learning disabilities)*, trans. RW Rieber & AS Carton, Plenum Press, New York.

——1997, *Educational psychology*, trans. R Silverman, Taylor and Francis, Boca Raton, FL.

Warnock, M 1978, *The Warnock Report: Special educational needs. Report of the Committee of Enquiry into the Education of Handicapped Children and Young People*, Her Majesty's Stationery Office, London.

Wilhelm, J, Baker, T & Dube, J 2001, *Strategic reading*, Heinemann, Portsmouth, NH.

Wiliam, D 2012, 'Designing feedback as part of a system', *Educational Leadership*, vol. 70, no. 1, pp. 30–4.

Wilson, M 2005, *Constructing measures: An item response modeling approach*, Lawrence Erlbaum, Mahwah, NJ.

Wilson, M & Draney, W 1999, *Developing maps for student progress in the BEAR Assessment System*, University of California Press, Berkeley, CA.

Wood, D, Bruner, J & Ross, G 1976, 'The role of tutoring in problem solving', *Journal of Child Psychology and Psychiatry*, vol. 17, no. 2, pp. 89–100.

Woods, K 2010, 'The design and validation of measures of communication and literacy to support the instruction of students with learning disabilities', PhD thesis, Melbourne Graduate School of Education, University of Melbourne.

Woods, K & Griffin, P 2013, 'Judgement-based performance measures of literacy for students with additional needs: Seeing students through the eyes of experienced special education teachers', *Assessment in Education: Principles, Policy & Practice*, vol. 20, no. 3, pp. 325–48.

Index